Wandering and Return in
Finnegans Wake

Wandering and Return in *Finnegans Wake*

AN INTEGRATIVE APPROACH TO JOYCE'S FICTIONS

Kimberly J. Devlin

PRINCETON UNIVERSITY PRESS

PRINCETON, NEW JERSEY

PROPERTY OF
CLACKAMAS COMMUNITY COLLEGE
LIBRARY
WITHDRAWN

Copyright © 1991 by Princeton University Press
Published by Princeton University Press, 41 William Street,
Princeton, New Jersey 08540
In the United Kingdom: Princeton University Press, Oxford

Library of Congress Cataloging-in-Publication Data

Devlin, Kimberly J.
Wandering and return in Finnegans Wake : an integrative
approach to Joyce's fictions / Kimberly J. Devlin.
p.   cm.
Includes bibliographical references and index.
1. Joyce, James, 1882–1941. Finnegans wake. 2. Travel
in literature. 3. Return in literature. I. Title.
PR6019.O9F578   1991   823'.912—dc20   90-47136

ISBN 0-691-06886-0 (alk. paper)

This book has been composed in Adobe Sabon

Princeton University Press books are printed
on acid-free paper and meet the guidelines for
permanence and durability of the Committee on
Production Guidelines for Book Longevity
of the Council on Library Resources

Printed in the United States of America by Princeton University Press,
Princeton, New Jersey

1   3   5   7   9   10   8   6   4   2

To Bill

---

with thanks and love

CONTENTS

PREFACE

THE MAIN premise of this study is that *Finnegans Wake* is an uncanny text, in the sense of its being at once strange and familiar. The strangeness of the *Wake* would be debated by very few of its readers: newcomers to the text, such as my students, inevitably sense its literary otherness immediately; even its scholars usually acknowledge an awareness of its resistance to comprehension and totalizing critical analysis. If intellectual uncertainty is important in the production of the feeling of uncanniness, as Freud initially speculated—"the uncanny would always be that in which one does not know where one is, as it were"[1]—then *Finnegans Wake* is surely an uncanny work, the ultimate in alien and disorienting textual territory. What reader has not heard himself addressed in the words of the textual exegete in 1.5, where the *Wake* self-reflexively announces itself as a space in which one easily loses one's bearings: "You is feeling like you lost in the bush, boy? You says: It is a puling sample jungle of woods. You most shouts out: Bethicket me for a stump of a beech if I have the poultriest notions what the farest he all means" (*FW* 112). But without denying the text's insistent strangeness and its concomitant ability to frustrate the reader's quest for "what the farest [Joyce] all means," this study aims to show that, like the uncanny phenomena discussed by Freud, the *Wake* is also residually enlaced with the familiar. If the *Heimliche* in *unheimlich* sensations is that which was once thought or believed, the psychic fictions of the self's earlier ontological phases, repressed and forgotten, then the *Heimliche* in the *unheimlich* text of the *Wake* is that which was once written, the literary fictions of Joyce's earlier artistic phases, ostensibly finished and put aside.

My title refers, on one level, to the relationship between *Finnegans Wake* and the earlier works. The weird Wakean dreamworld is a departure from Joyce's prior "waking" fictions, but also, more importantly I think, a reexamination of many of their concerns from simply a different perspective—that of the unconscious mind: the *Wake* turns the trajectory of Joyce's literary career into both a wandering and a return. My premise involves the Freudian notion of psychological return: obsessions, scenarios, and images from these earlier texts resurface in Joyce's final dreambook but in uncanny forms, transformed and yet discernible, in the same way that impressions from waking life reappear in dream thoughts. Whether or not Joyce worked these returns of the waking fictions into his final dreambook with a deliberate and systematic effort is difficult to say and perhaps a moot point. If Freud is correct about what Lacan calls

"L'Instance de la lettre dans l'inconscient" (initially translated as "The Insistence of the Letter in the Unconscious"),[2] then it is safe to assume that Joyce's earlier works were with him, at some level, when he composed the *Wake*. Although some returns are so specific that they are clearly intentional, others perhaps manifested themselves spontaneously in the process of composition, through involuntary association, much like the uncanny psychic affects described by Freud.

My title also plays on a central Homeric trope, which I use in different ways throughout this study, here to describe a strategy for reading Joyce's final oeuvre. In *The Odyssey*, of course, the return is to the homeland, the familiar kingdom, the wandering is the confrontation with the foreign, the unfamiliar, the terrors of the world beyond the home. For the reader, *Finnegans Wake* demands a similar sort of Odyssean wandering through the strange, in the form of the alien text of dream; but because it contains what I call "returns" of the earlier works, the reader is impelled to return to this more homely fictional terrain and read the strange through it. I use the earlier fictions, in other words, as an entry to the *Wake*, usually starting each section with a discussion of some aspect of them in order to illuminate features of the dreamtext. But ultimately my integrative methodology establishes a symbiotic interpretive relationship between the *Wake* and the fictions that preceded it: they help us to understand the dense and convoluted narrative of the night, but it—paradoxically—often sheds light on Joyce's narratives of waking reality. In my experience of reading it, *Finnegans Wake* clarifies rather than obscures Joyce's central imaginative and intellectual concerns. My methodology does not pretend to be definitive or exhaustive, to account for every detail of Joyce's most cryptic oeuvre; but I do hope it encourages other admirers of the earlier fictions to wander into the dreamworld and rediscover these familiar texts in their fascinating uncanny forms.

Like Odysseus, Joyce was a relentless wanderer, perhaps the twentieth century's most vagrant of authors. His male protagonists invariably share this predilection for roving: if the perambulations of Stephen and Bloom take us on an external odyssey through the labyrinth of Dublin, the perambulations of HCE, the sleeping Wakean "scatterling" (an archaic word for a vagrant), take us on an internal odyssey through the labyrinth of dream ("Well, he was wandering, you bet, whatever was his matter, in his mind too" [FW 508]). As I explain in my opening chapter, Joyce represents all three of these characters preeminently as wanderers in the word, in language itself, and turns their psyches into sites of relentless textual return. Although it lays out premises central to later sections, the first chapter is the one part of my study aimed primarily at newcomers to the *Wake* who may be finding themselves "lost in the bush." Through references to both "Circe" and Freudian theory, I give an overview of the principles of unconscious thinking at work in the *Wake*, an introduction to the dreamtext's logic, with the hope that such a discussion will help disoriented readers find their bearings. This introductory section closes with some specific preliminary examples of what I mean by "returns" of the earlier works in the *Wake* as initial demonstrations of the dream's uncanniness.

Freud maintains that dreams record the return of repressed wishes, that they deviously encode in their discursive structures interdicted desires. Joyce, I argue, believes this Freudian hypothesis, and in constructing his literary version of a dreamtext, he creates an elaborate transcript of desire: the language of the *Wake* is threaded in complex ways with countless psychic wishes, as well as oppositional anxieties. But the way in which language insistently records the return of desire, betraying forbidden impulses (sexual ones in particular), interests Joyce long before the writing of the *Wake*. My second chapter traces throughout his works the inscription of moral wanderings—errancy or "deviance"—in discursive structures of all varieties (dreams, rituals, gestures, letters, everyday speech). Joyce's admirers have often vehemently defended him against accusations of pornography; yet if pornography is not his genre per se, it is nonetheless a genuine concern within the fictions themselves. His works frequently explore the pornographical impulse—the need to write desire, to transform it into text—as well as pornographical pleasure, arousal from textual artifacts. His fictions ultimately represent the inseparability of the textual and the sexual: desire permeates language, appropriating it for libidinal ends, and language permeates desire, turning it into a scripted construct, a construct contingent upon the sign.

Chapter 3 focuses on the quest for identity in the *Wake*, a quest thwarted by the dream's representation of the self as multiple representations. Joyce's nightworld suggests that selfhood is in essence protean inscription, a process of perpetual figuration and refiguration. Enmeshed in discourse, Joycean wanderers know the self only *as* discourse, as textuality subjected to endless revision. In its examination of the inconclusive quest for selfhood, this chapter treats the dream as a variation on a specific type of uncanny text—the ghost story: the *Wake* generates tales that turn the dreamer's present self into an elusive phantasm but that conjure up simultaneously representations of his former selves—textual ghosts of sorts that freely roam the night. Wandering out of identity in dream allows for the uncanny return of multiple earlier phases of being. Freud argues that dreams always contain a regressive trajectory, that one dimension of them explores prior ways of thinking and feeling; many of the anxieties and desires plumbed in the *Wake* are connected to the roles of father and husband, yet they also betray the preoccupations of the younger self, whose predominant familial roles are son and sibling. Fo-

cusing on the returned son within the dreamer, the second part of this
chapter traces Joyce's revisionary treatment of what Freud calls the "family romance"—the psychic longing for highborn progenitors. The dream
reinscribes the wanderings of not only Odysseus, but also Telemachus,
the archetypal son in search of a renowned father.

The final dreamtext records a recollective return of past phases of
being and an anticipatory wandering into a future state of nonbeing—
death itself. As a funereal fiction, *Finnegans Wake* contains returns of
Joyce's two earlier explorations of death rituals—"The Sisters" in *Dubliners* and the "Hades" episode of *Ulysses*—but these rituals are revisited
from the elided perspective: the previously unrepresented vantage of the
dying man who ends up as the corpse. My fourth chapter examines the
difficulties of thinking death even from the perspective of dying: death is
invariably subjected in dream to wishful anthropomorphisms that im-
pose the contours of life and the concerns of the living onto a radically
"other" state. If death is literally unimaginable, a necrocentric perspective
a paradox in terms, dying, Joyce implies, is less elusive, a part of living
and being, but in reverse as it were. Dying is envisioned as physical dispossession and psychical dissolution, as a process of un-becoming. Discursively it is figured as a loss of one's significance, in every sense of the
word—one's name, one's identity, one's importance. The second part of
chapter 4 examines Joyce's experimentations with linguistic and narrative forms in the *Wake* that constitute an effort to inscribe dying as the
disappearance of inscription itself, as a collapse of the differences that
make language and definable being possible, as a movement from significance into nonsignificance.

Cultural significance—in its Lacanian sense of both meaning and importance—is at the heart of my discussion of mediated selfhood in chapter 5. In this section I focus on the pivotal role the signifying gaze of
the other plays within human consciousness throughout Joyce's fictions.
The self's enthrallment to the other's eye is dramatized most vividly in the
Wake, where the dreaming subject conceives of himself pervasively as
object, scrutinized by a gaze alternately flattering and critical, either be-
stowing significance or taking it away. I discuss the ontological indeterminacy examined in chapter 3 as a consequence of the indeterminacies of
intersubjective self-perception, as a function of the elusive nature of what
the other's eye sees. The power of the gaze to decenter and destabilize the
self expresses itself formally in the *Wake*'s odd, controversial narrative
structure: I argue that the dreamtext unravels largely from the vantage of
the internalized gaze, its innovative form constituting an attempt to represent the other within the self—a presence often elided by the waking
mind. In its pervasive uncanniness, structural as well as thematic, Joyce's

final oeuvre inscribes the dream return of a psychic obsession that surfaces initially in his earlier explorations of the self-conscious subject.

Chapter 5 closes with a preliminary exploration of the sexual dynamics of intersubjectivity, an issue that provides the focus for the chapter that follows. I examine, in particular, Joyce's recurrent depiction of men looking at or imagining a female I/eye. If recent studies and conference sessions are any indication, Joyce's attitude toward "matters feminine" (U 346/284) will remain a provocative ongoing debate for some time to come. But what I aim at in chapter 6 is not so much an assessment of Joyce's own (male) conceptions of the female, but rather an analysis of his look at male vision and male envisioning in themselves. I try to trace, in other words, his self-reflexive representation of male representations of the sexual other. Joyce's works frequently explore the en-gendered power structures imposed on intersubjective perceptual relations in waking reality: in the realm of viewing, male characters assume the position of the watching subject or the voyeur, forcing women into the position of the watched object or the exhibitionist; in the realm of writing, men conceptualize themselves as the determiners of meaning or the creators, turning women into the bearers of meaning or the created. These androcentric perceptual paradigms, at work in the conscious thoughts of Joycean males, elide female subjectivity, negating its presence and its power. But in the unconscious fantasies of both "Circe" and *Finnegans Wake*, I argue, the sexual dynamics of intersubjectivity often return in inverted form, as women assume the place of the viewing or writing subject, reassigning men to the role of the viewed or written object. This inversion functions to expose the way men are unconsciously determined by the sexual other: they frequently derive their sense of self-worth and desirability from the female gaze. An integrative methodology is crucial here, for Joyce's nightworlds inscribe subversive alternatives to the waking status quo. In their contrasting representations of male vision and envisioning, Joyce's works offer a critique of androcentric perceptual patterns.

My final chapter examines the most sustained male imagining of the female voice in the *Wake*, ALP's famous monologue at the end of the dream. A particularly overdetermined site of returns, this speech is a palimpsestic fantasy, created from three superimposed temporal perspectives available from the waking fictions: it records a series of ambivalent feelings toward the feminine from the vantage of a son (like Stephen Dedalus), of a husband (like Leopold Bloom), and of a father (like Mr. Hill from the early short story "Eveline"). In the final pages of the dream, Joyce returns us to three familial crises from his earlier works but asks us to look at them as they might have been dreamed by the male figures involved. The imagined voice of the ALP (who is at once mother, wife, and daughter) is structured around a dialectic of male wishes and fears: on the one hand, the dreamer appropriates the female as the idealized object of his desires; on the other, he acknowledges her resistance to androcentric wishes and—in the *Wake*'s abrupt indeterminate ending—her elusive escape from the dreaming imagination itself.

The endings of Joyce's fictions are famous for their open-ended quality; I hope this study demonstrates that he not only avoided closure but regarded it as impossible. Joyce scholars have often noted his explicit interest in Vico's theory of the perpetual return of prior ages. I suggest that the *Wake* records his implicit interest in the psychic counterpart to historical repetition: the insistent internal return of earlier narratives, the compulsion to reinscribe the already inscripted, a compulsion modulated by indestructible anxieties and desires. Stories never end for Joyce, but only rest, waiting to be retold consciously by the waking subject or reconstructed unconsciously by the dreaming one. It is these dream revisions, of course, that fascinated Joyce during the last phase of his artistic career. He admired them, I suspect, because unconscious rewritings of prior texts—more so than conscious ones—are agents of occluded insights and repressed truths. For all their obscurity, Joyce's final dream tales have a clarifying function in their insistence on mentioning what their waking counterparts forgot to tell.

ACKNOWLEDGMENTS

I WAS assisted in the writing and revising of this book by three fellowships that allowed leave-time from teaching: the Alice Freeman Palmer Fellowship, granted by Wellesley College; a Rackham Predoctoral Fellowship, granted by the University of Michigan; and a Junior Faculty Development Award, granted by the Regents of the University of California. The Committee on Research at the University of California, Riverside, provided research assistance, a much-needed computer, and funds for countless other expenses. I thank them all for their financial support of my project.

I would also like to thank several individuals for the interest they have shown in my work and the inspiration they have provided in their own. William Steinhoff's enthusiasm for Joyce sparked mine in his graduate proseminar at the University of Michigan, and his thoughts about *A Portrait of the Artist* and *Ulysses* have influenced my approach to these works. Ira Konigsberg's graduate courses on critical theory awakened an interest in language and semiotics that has helped to enrich my appreciation of Joyce. I am indebted to the late John Hannay for getting me started on this project, for patiently reading various tentative early drafts, and for discussing ideas with me along the way. His encouragement and friendship sustained me during graduate school as they continue to do today. I also owe enormous thanks to Margot Norris, who directed this project as a dissertation. Her course on *Finnegans Wake* at the University of Michigan inspired me to pursue research on Joyce's final oeuvre, and her intellectual concerns have left a decided mark on my own. She has proven to be not only a generous mentor, but also a wonderful friend.

Many other Joyceans have read this book (or sections of it) over the past few years. For their assorted comments, queries, and outright corrections of errors, I would like to thank, in particular, Berni Benstock, Shari Benstock, Shelly Brivic, Vince Cheng, Garry Leonard, Patrick McCarthy, and Thomas Staley. I am also very much indebted to Roland McHugh for his *Annotations to "Finnegans Wake."* As a nonpolyglot, I found this reference work indispensable to my understanding of the *Wake*; I would like to acknowledge it here as the source for the majority of glosses on foreign words and phrases throughout this book.

For listening to ideas, for interest in the progress of my work, for friendly advice and support, I would like to thank Ruth apRoberts, Rise Axelrod, Steve Axelrod, Ed Baker, Ed Eigner, Carole Fabricant, John Ganim, George Haggerty, Stephanie Hammer, Ralph Hanna, Eric Jager, Harriet Linkin, Peter Mileur, Alice Wexler, Deborah Willis, and Claudia

Yukman. I am also grateful to Christina Root, whose personal warmth and sense of humor have enlivened me during many years of friendship.

Parts of this book have appeared previously as articles or essays. Chapter 5 was first published in *PMLA* 104 (1989): 882–93, and is reprinted by permission of the copyright owner, The Modern Language Association of America. A section of chapter 6 appeared as "The Female Eye: Joyce's Voyeuristic Narcissists" in *New Alliances in Joyce Studies*, ed. Bonnie Kime Scott (University of Delaware Press, 1988). A shorter version of chapter 7 was first published as "ALP's Final Monologue in *Finnegans Wake*: The Dialectical Logic of Joyce's Dream Text" in *Coping with Joyce: Essays from the Copenhagen Symposium*, ed. Morris Beja and Shari Benstock (Ohio State University Press, 1989). I thank both presses for their permission to use this material here. I would like to thank Robert E. Brown, my editor at Princeton University Press, for his interest in my manuscript and his expeditious handling of it. I also appreciate the efforts of Nina Morgan, my graduate research assistant, for her help in preparing the manuscript for publication and for the hours spent in the library on my behalf.

I have been blessed with a family that is both affectionate and indulgent. I appreciate their financial and moral support, as well as their unflagging interest in a project on the most arcane classic of modern literature. Special thanks to my parents, Jerell and Hugh Devlin, my grandparents, Jewell and Walter Lundell, and my in-laws, Nena and William Dahling. My most deeply felt thanks must be reserved for my husband, Bill Dahling, Jr., whose enthusiasm, encouragement, and faith have been unconditional from the start.

ABBREVIATIONS

In REFERRING to Joyce's works, I use the following editions and abbreviations. In parenthetical citations to *Ulysses*, the first page number refers to the earlier edition, the second to the more recent one. When there are discrepancies between the two editions, I quote the 1986 text. All ellipses and brackets within quoted material are mine, unless otherwise indicated.

CW   *The Critical Writings of James Joyce*. Edited by Ellsworth Mason and Richard Ellmann. New York: Viking, 1959.

D   *Dubliners*. New York: Penguin, 1985.

E   *Exiles*. New York: Penguin, 1983.

FW   *Finnegans Wake*. New York: Penguin, 1984.

Letters   *Letters of James Joyce*. Vol. 1, edited by Stuart Gilbert. New York: Viking, 1957. Vols. 2 and 3, edited by Richard Ellmann. New York: Viking, 1966.

P   *A Portrait of the Artist as a Young Man*. New York: Viking, 1968.

SH   *Stephen Hero*. New York: New Directions, 1963.

U   *Ulysses*. New York: Random House, 1961 and 1986.

Wandering and Return in
Finnegans Wake

Chapter 1

INTRODUCTION:
TEXTUAL WANDERING AND RETURN

IN *ULYSSES* Joyce stresses the impact of language upon the individual mind with an explicitness unprecedented in western literature. Representing Dublin in 1904 as a complex network of textuality, he shows his characters in the process of ingesting the standard dosage of print—newspapers, textbooks, letters, fliers, advertisements, novels—and makes their streams of consciousness appropriately dense in allusions to cultural artifacts of all varieties—spoken texts, written texts, visual texts. Bloom's thoughts, for instance, are interwoven with endless snippets from various books, school lectures, political speeches, operas, pantomimes, and popular songs. Given the multifarious fabric of his mind and his elaborate visions of the East, first-time readers of *Ulysses* may be surprised to discover in "Eumaeus" that Bloom, in contrast to his Homeric precursor, "by a trick of fate . . . had consistently remained a landlubber except you call going to Holyhead [seventy miles away on the coast of Wales] which was his longest" (*U* 626/512). Bloom's wanderings among the foreign have taken place only within textuality, in the act of reading about it, seeing visions of it in popular theater, or hearing accounts of it from those who have had a wider scope of physical travels. After his fantasy of the East in "Lotus Eaters," which includes the figure of Turko the Terrible from the pantos, he hints at the textual mediations inherent in his mental meanderings: "Probably not a bit like it really. Kind of stuff you read: in the track of the sun" (*U* 57/47). If *The Odyssey* is an epic of an oral culture, an epic in which rhetorical performance and storytelling play a central role, then *Ulysses* is an epic of an oral *and* literate culture, an epic in which the presence of the scripted sign (be it written or visual) is felt as strongly as that of the spoken one.

Joyce's interest in the self wandering in the word is anticipated in *A Portrait of the Artist as a Young Man* and even in *Stephen Hero*, the remnant of its earlier draft. We get a glimpse of Dublin as a modern textual city when Stephen, in the course of his wanderings through the slums, "read all the street-ballads which were stuck in the dusty windows of the Liberties. He read all the racing names and prices scrawled in blue pencil outside the dingy tobaccoshops, the windows of which were adorned with scarlet police journals. He examined all the book-stalls which offered old directories and volumes of sermons and unheard-of treatises" (*SH* 145). In both versions of the novel, Stephen immerses himself in the written word, in the texts of Dumas, Byron, Aristotle, Aquinas, Dante, Machiavelli, Shakespeare, and Ibsen (to name but a few). As he walks to school in the final chapter of *Portrait*, the plays of Hauptmann, the prose of Newman, the dark humor of Guido Cavalcanti, and a song by Ben Jonson come to mind when he passes various associative landmarks. But *Portrait*, in particular, stresses as strongly the internal impact of more immediate discourse, the psychic insistence of voices expressing cultural expectations of compliance and conformity:

> While his mind had been pursuing its intangible phantoms and turning in irresolution from such pursuit he had heard about him the constant voices of his father and of his masters, urging him to be a gentleman above all things and urging him to be a good catholic above all things. These voices had now come to be hollowsounding in his ears. When the gymnasium had been opened he had heard another voice urging him to be strong and manly and healthy and when the movement towards national revival had begun to be felt in the college yet another voice had bidden him to be true to his country and help to raise up her fallen language and tradition. In the profane world, as he foresaw, a worldly voice would bid him raise up his father's fallen state by his labours and, meanwhile, the voice of his school comrades urged him to be a decent fellow, to shield others from blame or to beg them off and to do his best to get free days for the school. And it was the din of all these hollowsounding voices that made him halt irresolutely in the pursuit of phantoms. He gave them ear only for a time but he was happy only when he was far from them, beyond their call, alone or in the company of phantasmal comrades. (*P* 83–84)

Portrait dramatizes these cultural exhortations that beg Stephen's allegiance to class, church, country, family and friends, through the linguistic appeals of figures throughout the novel. Far from being "hollowsounding," easily dismissed for "phantasmal comrades," these voices beckon Stephen repeatedly and often have an undeniable psychic affect. *Portrait* closes with Stephen's well-known resolution to fly by the nets that shackle the individual, to disengage himself through exile from the allegiances he sees as constraining bonds that interfere with his artistic freedom. Yet in their final conversation, Cranly suggests to Stephen that a complete rejection of the cultural voices that have made a bid for the individual's loyalties may well be a logical impossibility, stressing their residual permeation of even the mind resistant to their call: "It is a curious thing . . . how your mind is supersaturated with the religion in which you say you disbelieve" (*P* 240).

Although the style of *Portrait* shifts from chapter to chapter to reflect the evolving consciousness of the artist and his changing textual authorities and allegiances, it is not until *Ulysses* that Joyce fully integrates content and narrative method, by making the power of language over the self both a thematic and formal issue. In fashioning Stephen's discourse, both internal and spoken, Joyce creates a linguistic hodgepodge that incorporates phrases from the cultural texts the young intellectual deliberately appropriates, the material befitting his consciousness, as well as those voices he would rather reject. The words of representative shacklers and betrayers—of the Jesuits, various family members, Davin, Kevin Egan, Mulligan, and Haines—return incessantly in Stephen's psyche throughout June 16 and into the early morning of the next day, when he hears in the sound of chiming bells the words from the prayer for the dying, the words presumably spoken by the pious at his mother's death. Through Joyce's technical representation of Stephen's consciousness in earlier parts of the novel, we get a sense of the individual as a site of internalized discourse, the texture of which is determined by forces stronger than conscious wishes or volition. Stephen's quest for artistic freedom and autonomy is compromised by the ontological condition of the cultural self, enmeshed in the language of the other.

In a letter to Valery Larbaud, the French translator of *Ulysses*, Joyce explained that it was not necessary to punctuate the internal monologues with quotation marks because the reader "will know early in the book that S.D.'s mind is full like everyone else's of borrowed words" (*Letters* 1:263).[1] The instruction is echoed in *Finnegans Wake*, when the commentator on the letter in 1.5 explains that the reader should not infer "from the nonpresence of inverted commas (sometimes called quotation marks) on any page that its author was always constitutionally incapable of misappropriating the spoken words of others" (*FW* 108). The comment also applies to the *Wake* as a whole, for Joyce has turned his dreamer's mind into a repository of textual detritus so vast and eclectic that his specific identity and the facts of his life remain hopelessly obscured. Even more so than Stephen's or Bloom's, his mind is "supersaturated" with the gleanings of the cultures that have preceded him, gleanings available only through language. The "ancient legacy of the past" has been transmitted to the dreamer "type by tope, letter from litter, word at ward" (*FW* 614–15). Sheldon Brivic has written that in the *Wake* Joyce "emphasizes the role of language as the medium men use to record and organize the dreams that make up reality, as Vico and Lacan's Freud do"; but he also implies, unnecessarily I think, that the artist adhered to the Jungian notion of the collective unconscious.[2] The richly allusive fabric of the *Wake* may simply suggest that the dreamer, like anyone else, has been shaped by textual internalizations, and hence is not only a father but also a son, a psychic repository of cultural inheritances.

The "borrowed words" in the *Wake* are woven into voices—several of them distinct and identifiable—that resound throughout the dream.

Rather than possessing any exterior autonomy, these voices have much the same status as the hallucinations in "Circe": seemingly external, but surely internal because tinged by the dreamer's personal desires and fears. As I will argue more extensively in a later chapter, the *Wake* unfolds, by and large, from the vantage point of the internalized other and is dominated discursively by its collective speech. The voices in the *Wake* are the dream version of the words of others that run through our minds, that we hear in our own trains of thought: the streams of consciousness in *Ulysses*, of course, provide ample precedent for this phenomenon, but in Joyce's final dreamtext these words predominate, emphasizing even more clearly the subject's determination by the other. The subjective consistency of the various speech acts in the dream has led several critics to assume, quite logically I think, that HCE is the dreamer: he is identified as such *not* because he is the main speaking subject—his speeches form only a small portion of the dreamtext—but because he is the main discursive subject of the *Wake*'s various utterances. The psychic register of the voices is widely variable: some flatter the subject, uttering the language of desire, while others are overtly hostile and slanderous. The speech of the other in dream distinctly compromises the self's integrity, as moral being and autonomous individual.

An increasingly explicit portrayer of a consumer culture, Joyce makes the ultimate consumer the human psyche, relentlessly ingesting the word. His method of intertextual characterization suggests that, to some extent, people are what they eat—in the sense of their mental rather than physical diet.[3] As the guide to the verbal "middenhide hoard" in the *Wake* makes clear, language is food for thought, the mind's material sustenance, as well as its currency, the medium of human exchange: "Here (please to stoop) are selveran cued peteet peas of quite a pecuniar interest inaslittle as they are the pellets that make the tomtummy's pay roll" (*FW* 19). During a homework lesson aptly glossed as "THE INFLUENCE OF THE COLLECTIVE TRADITION UPON THE INDIVIDUAL," the young students of 2.2 sit down to digest a "stew of the evening, booksyful stew" (*FW* 268). In "Nestor," similarly, Stephen recalls the students at the library in Paris as "fed and feeding brains about me" (*U* 25/21), while at lunch hour Bloom reminds himself more colloquially, "Never know whose thoughts you're chewing" (*U* 171/140). In "Aeolus" when Bloom hears the men in the newspaper office mocking Dan Dawson's inflated rhetoric, he thinks to himself, "All very fine to jeer at it now in cold print but it goes down like hot cake that stuff" (*U* 126/104); later he will think of this language as "flapdoodle to feed fools on" (*U* 161/132). In Joyce's fictions the acquisition of ideas and information is repeatedly equated with ingestion, the physical substance of the diet being language itself.

Because the artistic representation of the mind is dependent on access to its material sustenance, the abode of the artist Shem in 1.7 is well stocked with rubbish which is at once gustatory and linguistic: "rindless raisins," "curried notes," "painful digests," "once current puns, quashed quotatoes, messes of mottage," "stale shestnuts," "toothsome pickings, cans of Swiss condensed bilk," "borrowed plumes"—in short, "alphybettyformed verbage" (*FW* 183). The young artist's precocious fascination with language in *Portrait* ("Words which he did not understand he said over and over to himself till he had learned them by heart" [*P* 62]) and the older intellectual's garner of words in *Stephen Hero*, collected in the name of "an idealising, a more veritably human tradition" (*SH* 26), are comically exposed in the Wakean portrait of the artist as forms of infantile avarice and gluttony, as a lingering presocial desire for the property of others and a regressive oral voracity: "All the time [Shem] kept on treasuring with condign satisfaction each and every crumb of trektalk [*trek*: appetite in Dutch], covetous of his neighbour's word" (*FW* 172). Anxious to participate in language, the child steals or consumes it. If he later regrets the self-alienating appropriation, he will eventually learn to exploit it, turning the borrowed words of others into the very fabric of art.[4]

• • •

The most fundamental of Freud's contributions to our understanding of unconscious life lies in his insistence that dreams, far from being strange and alien constructs, are forged from this language "digested" during the day, that they are the uncanny textual return of familiar words and images inscribed in memory. He repeatedly demonstrates how dreams are created from the communal and individual archives of man, combining remembered bits of history, science, folklore, literature, and myth, with scraps of more personal recollection, images and phrases from the subject's individualized past. Interweaving psychic records both public and private, the hallucinatory texts of the unconscious in "Circe" have a very similar fabric. As Joyce's interest in the unconscious becomes increasingly prominent in his fictions, his conception of both the texture of its byproducts and the logic of its mechanisms becomes, in many respects, explicitly Freudian.[5] The Freudian elements inherent in many of the technical features of the Circean hallucinations provide a convenient introduction and entry point to the more complicated logic of the Wakean dream.

Freud's most radical discovery revealed that the transformation of digested waking impressions into dream thoughts involves processes that are not senseless or incoherent but rather perfectly intelligible albeit purposely ingenious. In *The Interpretation of Dreams* he emphasizes that the unconscious should be conceived of, not as a psychic locus, but rather as a dynamic "system" or "agency" that produces meaning through discernible laws of structuration,[6] that "makes sense," in other words, according to its own particular logic. Summarizing Freud's insight, Jacques Lacan writes, "at the level of the unconscious there is something at all points homologous with what occurs at the level of the subject—this thing speaks and functions in a way quite as elaborate as at the level of the conscious, which thus loses what seemed to be its privilege."[7] Joyce's conception of the unconscious in "Circe" is similar to Freud's: although the action of the episode takes place in Dublin's red light district, the locus of the unconscious fantasies remains indeterminate. The unconscious is felt not so much as a psychic region but rather as a structuring mechanism that reshuffles the components of waking perceptions in complex but logical ways. As Hugh Kenner writes, "we have the impression, as we read the Circe episode, that we have encountered all its ingredients before, only in a different arrangement."[8]

In *Ulysses* waking perceptions and recollections are metonymic rather than holistic: events, people, and things are recorded and recalled in impressionistic fragments rather than complete images. In the unconscious phantasms of "Circe" these metonymic scraps return, having been rearranged and reassembled, the individual visions and speeches being condensations of details from various associatively connected sources, like the overdetermined dreamtexts analyzed by Freud. Hence Mrs. Yelverton Barry (see *U* 465/379–80) is a composite of disparate impressions, many of them related to Molly: the time she alludes to—half past four on a Thursday—is Bloom's estimation of when his wife's affair was consummated; she mentions a novel by Paul de Kock, the author Molly has requested; her accusation against Bloom—of having been voyeuristically watched by him in a theater—is based on an experience Molly has had; and her attire resembles in part the outfit Molly wore on the occasion (see *U* 284/233). The well-dressed accusatory specter is probably motivated, in addition, by Bloom's voyeuristic interest in the society lady in "Lotus Eaters" and by the secret correspondence he starts opening shortly before he notices her, for Mrs. Yelverton Barry also accuses him of having written her a letter signed with an alias. Although a few of the metonymies that form this fantasy have links to other women, most of them suggest that it functions, on one level, like a Freudian screen memory, behind which lies the familiar figure of Bloom's own wife.

Far from being a random riot of images, the temporal ordering of the various specters also has a distinct logic to it, a logic governed by psychic association. In the opening sequence of figures, for example, the appearance of Bloom's chiding mother is followed by that of his chiding wife, toward whom he often acts submissive and filial.[9] His disquieting hallucination of his inevitable confrontation with his adulterous spouse is conveniently cut short: the reality of the brothel zone momentarily intrudes when a Bawd enters advertising fresh maidenhead, precipitating a vision of *Bridie* Kelly, a girl Bloom has had some sort of erotic encounter with as a youth—as such, she is associatively linked to both the Bawd's cry and the hallucination of Molly, a subsequent sexual partner and his actual *bride*. One of Joyce's many batlike females (see *U* 441/361), Bridie evokes the phantasm of Gerty MacDowell, another youthful temptress, over whose exhibitionist display a bat has quietly fluttered. The recollection of two nubile females naturally leads to thoughts of a third, Mrs. Breen, née Josie Powell, whom Bloom has had a flirtation with in his bachelor days. When she inquires about the contents of Bloom's package (a crubeen and a trotter), Richie Goulding and Pat the waiter suddenly appear, linked to the question by Bloom's implicit memory of his dinner at the Ormond bar. Richie enters fantasically adorned with ladies' hats (*U* 446/365), dressed as Bloom saw him returning one morning from an all-night rampage (see *U* 88/73). Bloom's subsequent conversation with Josie Breen centers on an unattractive hat she bought upon the advice of another woman. Like the technique governing the formation of Freudian dreams, that of "Circe" plays heavily on substitutions and associations. The parade of phantasms has a private idiosyncratic continuity to it, a continuity created by perceived similarities between one figure and the next or by metonymical links, by contiguous images attached to them.

Some of the associative links binding the temporal sequence of "Circe" remain more obscure. We may wonder, for instance, why the two accusatory watchmen loom forth when Bloom stops to feed the protean dog, at the moment of a seemingly charitable act. The subsequent appearance of the gulls is logical enough, as Bloom has thrown morsels to them earlier in the day, as is the vision of the besotted Bob Doran feeding Garryowen. The ensuing apparition of Signor Maffei, the cruel animal trainer from *Ruby: the Pride of the Ring*, marks an associative reversal. Bloom himself has a humanitarian attitude toward animals, as he futilely tries to convince the watch, earlier thinking perceptively about the sadism that lies behind the gay facade of a circus. What in Bloom's gesture, then, summons forth these menacing apparitions who order him to "commit no nuisance"? Before he actually feeds the dog, "*he unrolls one parcel and goes to dump the crubeen softly but holds back and feels the trotter*" (*U* 453/370). If the cuts of meat are at all phallus-shaped, Bloom may fear that the imagined watchmen suspect him of masturbating, or even worse: they subsequently inform him they are working for the "Prevention of Cruelty to Animals" (*U* 454/371), perhaps in an indirect accusation of sodomy.[10] But Bloom's puzzling paranoia in the face of offering food to a dog may also have been triggered by a fleeting and careless thought of his from earlier in the day: speculating about how people figure out whether or not a food is poisonous, he remembers the adage, "Try it on the dog first" (*U* 174/143). This possible psychic impetus behind the paranoiac hallucination suggests the way in which the unconscious mind often treats the thought as the deed, idle speculation as performative intent. The Circean vision anticipates the Wakean dream, where velleities are frequently turned into vividly dramatized enactments.

"In unconscious thinking," Freud writes, "every train of thought is yoked with its contradictory opposite";[11] in "Circe," similarly, many of the hallucinations, as Florry says, "go by contraries" (U 571/466), expressing psychic ambivalences, interrelated fears and desires. The initial vision of Molly, dominant and seductive in Turkish garb, is later reversed when Bloom haughtily rejects her in favor of the princess Selene ("*The former morganatic spouse of Bloom is hastily removed in the Black Maria*" [U 483/394]). Bloom's visions of himself as persecuted, slandered, and abased are countered by his dreams of public acclaim and adulation. Stephen's guilt-ridden vision of his pious mother is inverted in the grotesque and sacrilegious spectacle of the black mass. Freud's postulate provides the psychological correlative to Bruno's principle of contraries—so central to the *Wake*—that states that " 'every power in nature must evolve an opposite in order to realize itself.' "[12]

Finnegans Wake is a literary descendant of "Circe" in its technical use of restructuration, condensed and overdetermined images, associative and substitutive logic, and dialectical reversals; but its most Freudian feature is its distinctly materialist representation of the human mind. The legacy of the fall in the *Wake* is a palpable physical chaos, a fragmented and scattered human form that often turns into a rubbish heap. As an early description of it makes clear, however, the rubbish heap also functions as an internal metaphor for the multifarious resources the unconscious taps in order to construct the dream itself: "Countlessness of livestories have netherfallen by this plage, flick as flowflakes, litters from aloft, like a waast wizzard all of whirlworlds. Now are all tombed to the mound, isges to isges, erde from erde" (FW 17). An archaeological site of sorts, a tomb of the past, the dump contains crumbled buildings ("livestories") fallen near a beach ("plage") that tell the story of previous civilizations, supplying inscriptions of their history; but the dump is also *Finnegans Wake* itself, the dreamtext that recounts the "countlessness of livestories" fallen onto the page of HCE's mind, providing traces of his human past. Mapping Joyce's interest in the major digs and discoveries at the turn of the century, Jackson Cope has suggested that the *Wake* resembles an archaeological mound, that archaeology is its "art."[13] In the dream, indeed, mound, mind, and man become one, united in the image of the "middenhide hoard" (FW 19).

Both the rubbish heap and the dreamer's psyche are reservoirs of textual detritus from a conglomeration of sources. The "middenhide hoard" contains "objects" that are at once pieces of junk and food, letters of the

Greek and Hebrew alphabets, and proper names: "What a mnice old mness it all mnakes! A middenhide hoard of objects! Olives, beets, kimmells, dollies, alfrids, beatties, cormacks and daltons" (*FW* 19). By conflating litter and letters here, Joyce emphasizes simultaneously the linguistic nature of all material, its status as sign, and the materiality of language, its status as physical substance. The hoard is retrieved not only through an archaeological dig, an external search for the relics of the past, but also through memory, internal recall, as the *mn-* prefixes indicate. The mound contains "ruins," traces of the past, while the mind contains "runes," inscriptions of text ("But the world, mind, is, was and will be writing its own wrunes for ever, man, on all matters that fall under the ban of our infrarational senses" [*FW* 19–20]). Joyce's conception of the psyche's material resources as a repository of archaeological rubble allows him to collapse the distinction between litter and letter, to combine the concept of accretive matter with that of inscription. It is articulated informally in a letter to Harriet Shaw Weaver, written several years before the *Wake* was even started: "My head is full of pebbles and rubbish and broken matches and lots of glass picked up 'most everywhere' " (*Letters* 1:167). A self-reflexive image of the inventory of the dreamer's "house of thoughtsam" reinforces the connection between mound and mind:

> and, an you could peep inside the cerebralised saucepan of this eer illwinded goodfornobody, you would see in his house of thoughtsam . . . what a jetsam litterage of convolvuli of times lost or strayed, or lands derelict and of tongues laggin too, longa yamsayore, not only that but, search lighting, beached, bashed and beaushelled *à la Mer* pharahead into faturity, your own convolvulis pickninnig capman would real to jazztfancy the novo takin place of what stale words whilom were woven with and fitted fairly featly for. . . . (*FW* 292)

A version of the rubbish heap, the image here is of beach strewn with flotsam, jetsam, lagan, and derelict, with an accumulated wreckage of thoughts ("thoughtsam"), litter and literature ("jetsam litterage"), history ("times lost"), past civilizations ("lands derelict"), and multiple languages ("tongues laggin"). It recalls both the "plage" inscribed with "livestories" and the littered shoreline rife with "signatures" that Stephen walks along in "Proteus": "These heavy sands are language tide and wind have silted here. And these, the stoneheaps of dead builders. . . . Sands and stones. Heavy of the past" (*U* 44/37).

When it returns in dream, this verbal kelter of "stale words" has been transformed by the unconscious, replaced with the "novo" in a process seen everywhere in the text. The discourse of the *Wake* is notoriously protean, the litterish letters, as material substance, being subject to psychic flux and erasure. Like the pieces of litter in the dump, words and phrases resurface in the dream having melted into others, so that "Persse O'Reilly" (*FW* 44), one of the names of the fallen father, will return later as "*Prszss Orel Orel*" (*FW* 105), "Persic-Uraliens" (*FW* 162), "P.R.C.R.L.L. Royloy" (*FW* 378), "Persee and Rahli" (*FW* 497), "Parasol Irelly" (*FW* 525), "appeers as our oily" (*FW* 570), or "Purses Relle" (*FW* 580), the first inscription reduced to a mere trace after it has been fused with countless others. The prosaic discourses of a laundrywoman or weatherman merge with the reverential rhythms of the litany to form irreverently secularized exclamations: "Lord help you, Maria, full of grease, the load is with me!" (*FW* 214); "Hail many fell of greats! Horey morey smother of fog!" (*FW* 502). The process of linguistic melding is often combined with a kinetic scrambling of the individual figures, letters turning into a sort of psychic movable type ("The movibles are scrawling in motions, marching, all of them ago, in pitpat and zingzang" [*FW* 20]). The date on the letter found in the dump, for instance, may be "31 Jan. 1132 A.D." (*FW* 420) or "31 Jun. 13, 12. P.D." (*FW* 421), the latter a slightly erased and reshuffled variant of the first. Letters are the litter that memory accumulates and the unconscious plays with, the physical detritus that is "variously catalogued, regularly regrouped" (*FW* 129).

If in "Circe" the unconscious is felt as a transforming mechanism, in the *Wake* it is explicitly described as such. In one of the work's numerous self-reflexive moments, the agency creating the dreamtext is represented as "our wholemole millwheeling vicociclometer . . . autokinatonetically preprovided with a clappercoupling smeltingworks exprogressive process . . . [that] receives through a portal vein the dialytically separated elements of precedent decomposition for the verypetpurpose of subsequent recombination" (*FW* 614). Under the self-generating (or autokinetic) energy of the unconscious, language is put through a "smeltingworks," forever decomposed and recomposed. Broken down into bits that are then fused or "coupled" into new elements, the words in the *Wake* are subjected to a process somewhat similar to the stewing of the relics in the midden: "A bone, a pebble, a ramskin; chip them, chap them, cut them up allways; leave them to terracook in the muttheringpot" (*FW* 20). Generating in the process an expansive and multilayered vocabulary, the workings of the unconscious prove the prisonhouse of language to be a fairly spacious confine.

The language of the dream resembles the rich, multivalent language generated by the Freudian unconscious, where signifiers are often created from several others, which are in turn links in complex associative chains. If in "Circe" the images and speeches are semiotic hybrids created from numerous sources, in the *Wake* this condensation takes place at the level of the word itself. Characterized by an overdetermination and a chaotic mutability, the discourse of the *Wake* renders problematic conventional notions of referentiality: words and phrases are always suspended between possible meanings, eliminating stable and unequivocal sense. But the careful work of Roland McHugh begins to suggest what other critics have long suspected—that the dream's complicated and compacted discourse is highly logical. In *The "Finnegans Wake" Experience*, McHugh's reading of a passage from 2.3 accounts for almost every letter in the explicated text and produces in the process a wonderfully coherent dualistic dream image,[14] reminiscent of a picture produced from a double negative, like the superimposed faces in Freud's dream of his friend R. and his Uncle Josef.[15] The *Wake*, in other words, is suspended between a playful recreation with and an intelligible re-creation of the language that provides its base. The work is characterized by a linguistic freeplay, but a freeplay that often has a rationale to it, so that the dream becomes a "chaosmos" (*FW* 118), a paradoxically chaotic order, an antic yet patterned cosmos. The textual flotsam and jetsam from which the dream is forged may be unabashedly unoriginal, but it is relentlessly transfigured so as to effect a linguistic liberation. Writing his final dreamtext, Joyce realized that freedom lies not in a flight from the voices that shape the self, but in the imaginative transmogrification of them that takes place in the sleeping mind.

The logic of the *Wake* has long been recognized as being rooted in elaborate puns, verbal coincidences and contiguities. As Joyce may have learned from Freud, the crucial difference between unconscious and conscious thinking lies in the former's sensitivity to the material base of language:

> Because the unconscious treats words like objects, it is alive to their sounds, their literal and archaic meanings, and their uses in every known context. Words alone, therefore, can generate images and scenarios in dreams. . . . The auditory contingency of *letter* and *litter* may have prompted the merger of ALP as scavenger with ALP as author the Letter, in the image of the hen scratching the Letter/litter from the dump.[16]

The klang association continues in the vision of ALP as a *little* woman or, in her youthful manifestation, as Alice *Liddell*, and in the dominant natural image of the female as the sea, in Greek, *thalatta* (cf. "*Thalatta! Thalatta!* She is our great sweet mother" [*U* 5/5] with "The letter! The litter!" [*FW* 93]). The French word for the sea—*la mer*— explains why the female is represented, idealistically, as the Virgin *Mary* and, in less flattering form, as a *mare* who with age turns into a *nag*—not only in her physical attributes but also in her discourse: "And who eight the last of the goosebellies that was mowlding from measlest years and who leff that there and who put that here and who let the kilkenny stale the chump" (*FW* 142). In the approximate homonyms and synonyms for any given word lie the proliferative configurations of dream figures and images.

Verbal coincidences and contiguities often animate entire chapters, influencing their form or producing bifurcations in the narrative. In 2.1 the double meaning of the word *play* gives the children's game a theatrical framework,[17] while in 2.2 the students' math lesson is also a study of the secrets of sexual reproduction, with the twins learning to *multiply* in both senses of the word. The innocuous hypothesis that HCE works as an *earwigger*, advanced at the opening of 1.2, produces a chain of malicious gossip perpetuated by *eavesdroppers* and *busybodies*, the archaic sense of the word *earwigs*. Like the earwig insect, the scandalous talk pierces the ear or, in French, *perce l'oreille* ("a slightly varied version of Crookedribs confidentials . . . hushly pierce the rubiend aurellum of one Philly Thurnston" [*FW* 38]), so that the rann fashioned from the gossip is logically entitled the Ballad of Persse O'Reilly, the song being about not a known individual but rather a person who is only a whispered rumor. The conceptual key to 3.1 lies in the word *deliverance*, with its suggestion of an act of salvation (Jesus carrying the cross) or the running of an errand (Shaun delivering the letter to save HCE).[18] The word in its archaic sense can also describe a rhetorical performance, which helps to explain why the chapter takes the shape of a speech or a sermon, complete with its thoroughly mundane moral exemplum, the fable of the Ondt and the Gracehoper. Shaun becomes a "postal cleric" (*FW* 485), a bearer of epistles in every sense of the phrase, like the letter-carrying Father Conmee of "Wandering Rocks." Chapter 3.3 similarly activates both the secular and religious resonances of language, in this case the word *deposition*, a giving of legal testimony or the removal of Christ's body from the cross for burial, the thirteenth station of the *via crucis*: the four old men interrogate the supine Shaun, who has been transferred between 3.2 and 3.3 from an upright position ("bigmouthed poesther, propped up, restant, against a butterblond warden of the peace" [*FW* 429]) to a horizontal one ("heartsoul dormant mid shadowed landshape" [*FW* 474]).

The linguistic logic of the *Wake* helps to explain the connection between the two versions of the sin in the park that appear in 1.2 and then undergo countless transformations throughout the rest of the dream. Toward the beginning of the chapter, HCE is described watching a play (*FW* 32) and shortly afterward appears as a watchguard ("posted at Mallon's at the instance of watch warriors of the vigilance committee" [*FW* 34]). But then in an interesting twist, we hear the account of the sin in which he is accused by the spying sons, "the shomers" (*shŏmer*: watchman in Hebrew), of having "behaved with ongentilmensky immodus" in the pres-

ence of the urinating girls (*FW* 34). Next follows the story of his encounter with the pipe-smoking cad, who asks him the time because his watch
is slow, whereupon HCE draws his own watch (his "waterbury") out of
his pocket (*FW* 35). As in the Circean hallucinations, the two scenes are
linked by a metonymic association, here in the form of the word *watch*,
which suggests to the unconscious alternately voyeurism and time. The
verbal coincidence connecting these scenes is reinforced, moreover, by a
psychological association: the encounter with cad is riddled with oedipal
anxiety, a simple allusion to time triggering a series of defensive gestures
on the part of the father, including thoughts of shooting the impertinent
questioner; containing similar elements of intergenerational strife, the
scene that precedes it reflects the father's fear of the sons' voyeurism, of
their learning of his sexual secrets in order to defeat and replace him. Both
are connected to the primal scene in 2.2 where the sons' watching of the
sex act signifies their fall into sexual knowledge and foreshadows the
father's attendant decline, his overthrow in 2.3 by the new generation
time has brought forth.

In *Joyce's Book of the Dark*, John Bishop suggests that *Finnegans
Wake* "not simply resists visualization, but actively encourages its reader
not to visualize much in its pages"; he later adds, however, that visual
dreams do sporadically fill the dark interior of the sleeping mind "with
spectral outpourings of vision and color."[19] I would argue that the *Wake*
is pervaded throughout by an elaborate visual dimension governed by an
imaginative visual logic, the effects of which can be most clearly felt in the
work's ongoing ocular puns. Joyce, like Freud, conceives the unconscious
mind as being sensitive to optical as well as auditory contingencies, to
images whose contours resemble each other in some way. Hence the
fallen father will appear as an overgrown baby, a massive whale, a mountain, a volcano, a burial mound, a mausoleum, a museum of artifacts, an
archaeological site, the rubble of fallen walls or monuments, the debris on
a battlefield, or a pile of rubbish or offal, although linguistic connections
reinforce the string of images (mountain/mound, mausoleum/museum,
rubble/rubbish, baby/Babylon/Babel: "an overgrown babeling" [*FW* 6],
whale/wall/offal: "offwall" [*FW* 3]). In many images, in fact, auditory
and optical similarities work symbiotically, so that the phrase "with lar-
rons o'toolers clittering up and tombles a'buckets clottering down" (*FW*
5) will return later as "with lines of litters slittering up and louds of latters
slettering down" (*FW* 114), the vision of the protean contours of the city
transforming itself into the protean text of the letter: the two phrases are
linked not only by their verbal resonances, but also by a visual nexus, by
the fact that the letter here has assumed its recurrent guise as a map of the
landscape, as geographical textuality with its wild nonlinear print
("These ruled barriers along which the traced words, run, march, halt,

walk, stumble at doubtful points, stumble up again in comparative safety" [*FW* 114]).

The "Circe" episode provides precedence for visual contiguities shaping unconscious thoughts, when Bloom's bar of lemon soap turns into the sun or when the wallpaper in the brothel (*"The walls are tapestried with a paper of yewfronds and clear glades"* [*U* 502/410]) contributes to his hallucinatory recollection of the yew trees from his high school trip to Poulaphouca. Joyce also seems to have been familiar with the optical transformation in the "French Nurse's Dream" that appears on the last page of *The Interpretation of Dreams*.[20] In this pictorially represented dreamtext, the tiny micturating child produces a steadily growing stream of urine that flows into the street and turns into a full-blown river, down which a series of increasingly large boats sail. In the *Wake*, similarly, a urinating child (albeit female rather than male) becomes an imagistic variant of the fluvial dream woman, who is sailed upon by river vessels of all varieties. The opening of the ALP chapter (*FW* 196) reproduces the rough triangular configuration seen in three of the frames of the Freudian dreamtext and crowns the verbal delta with an "O" that suggests the source of the river; the letter also visually reduplicates the "puncture" (*FW* 299) the young male students locate in their female text in 2.2, the vaginal aperture they confuse with both the urinary and rectal ones.

In its visual dimension, the *Wake* can clearly be seen as a compromise text, like the dreams dissected by Freud, a text driven by conflicting impulses: the id's need to speak its unlawful desires and the counterforce of the superego (the law of the father internalized) that censors the id's communiqués. Setting up a mode of thought connected and yet counter to waking processes of ideation, the logic of the unconscious becomes devious, willfully circuitous. Guilty or disturbing recollections, for instance, return hidden behind more psychically neutral ones, which become the equivalent to Freudian screen memories, like the dream in the case history of the Wolf Man (actually entitled "From the History of an Infantile Neurosis"). Thus in the *Wake*, male voyeurism, exhibitionism, and sexual arousal lurk—not very subtly—behind the recurrent images of men wielding telescopes, flashlights, swords, and other weapons:

> This is the Willingdone branlish his same marmorial tallowscoop Sophy-Key-Po for his royal divorsion on the rinnaway jinnies. (*FW* 9)

> Chuffy was a nangel then and his soard fleshed light like likening. (*FW* 222)

> He knows for he's seen it in black and white through his eyetrompit trained upon jenny's and all that sort of thing (*FW* 247)

> With guerillaman aspear aspoor to prink the pranks of primkissies (*FW* 340)

Jaun, after those few prelimbs made out through his eroscope the apparition of his fond sister Izzy (*FW* 431)

The dame dowager's duffgerent to present wappon, blade drawn to the full and about wheel without to be seen of them. The infant Isabella from her coign to do obeisance toward the duffgerent, as first furtherer with drawn brand. (*FW* 566)

These are obvious versions of the dreamer's sin, polymorphous and indeterminate in its configurations, but other screen memories are more cunning. The account in which HCE spies on and/or exposes himself to the urinating girls is reduced to an image of Noah watching the rainstorm through a telescope, peering out of his ark to see if the flood is over yet (see *FW* 178), of a man fishing with a rod in a stream (see *FW* 76), or of young boys venturing out to watch the river Liffey or to row on it, the male exhibitionist becoming adolescent "exhibitioners": "If tomorrow keeps fine who'll come tripping to sightsee? . . . The Belvedarean exhibitioners. In their cruisery caps and oarsclub colours" (*FW* 205). These imagistic condensations can be seen as visual palimpsests that inscribe the innocuous and unobjectionable onto the partially erased text of taboo desires; they are the optical equivalent of the dream's double talk, which produces multiple levels of meaning often at hypocritical variance with one another. In the *Wake* the law of the father is not so much totally overturned, but rather outwitted by the cunning counter law of the unconscious.

Reading the *Wake* demands simultaneous attention to several textual dimensions: a vertical axis along which one finds multiple meanings and images in isolated words or phrases; a horizontal axis along which one finds threads of narrative; and a recursive axis along which one finds earlier parts of the dream returning in altered form. Michael Begnal suggests that the recursive dimension of the *Wake* is rooted in textual linearity and yet contributes to the vertical density of the dream:

We arrive at *Wake* meaning through a process of accrual, so that each new element or piece of plot makes sense only as it reminds us of what has gone before and as it restates a basic crux or situation. The repetition of theme or incident [along the horizontal axis] necessitates the building of vertical towers of information which require immediate reference back to their analogues.[21]

Exactly how much "plot" can be found along the horizontal axis has been the source of critical disagreement. While stressing the obstacles to narrative found in the techniques of digression, interpolation, and recurring leitmotiv, Begnal maintains nonetheless that "*Finnegans Wake* does have a plot, it does tell a story, if only a reader can bring new critical perspectives to bear upon the text."[22] Bishop, on the other hand, argues that "if one operates on the premise that *Finnegans Wake* reconstructs the night, the first preconception to abandon wholesale is that it ought to read anything at all like narrative or make sense as a continuous linear narrative whole."[23] Neither critic is absolutely wrong, for at points linear narrative does disappear in the *Wake* (as Begnal himself argues for certain parts of the text), and yet at others clear dramas and stories emerge. The *Wake* lacks "*a* plot"—multiplicity is one of its governing principles—but it does contain what Begnal more accurately describes as "a series of incidents or miniplots."[24] The logic of the dreamtext hinges upon several textual axes that often compete with one another for our attention; while a reader may choose to concentrate on one dimension over others, none of them should be categorically dismissed or ignored.

One limitation to both Bishop's and Begnal's different approaches to the *Wake* can be found in their shared elisions of the dream's affective import. Bishop argues that Joyce's "book of the dark" is embedded with representations that refer back to the somnolent body, that spring from somatic sources. In reading the *Wake*, he claims, "one [has] to become familiar with a set of representational mannerisms peculiar to the working of the night, one of which has to do with the latent omnipresence of the sleeper's body beneath *all* the manifest appearances of his dream" (emphasis added).[25] This thesis is convincing (if overstated), but it ignores the psychological sources of the *Wake*, the intangible wishes and anxieties the unconscious labors to articulate in dream representation. Many of the somatic images that Bishop traces throughout the text—particularly the ones of physical inertia, deafness, and blindness—are *not*, from my perspective at least, psychically neutral. The reference to a "benighted irismaimed" (*FW* 489), for instance, which Bishop plausibly connects to the closed and darkened eyes of the sleeper, also clearly describes the dream figure whose vision is threatened with blindness as a frightening punishment—just as Stephen's is in the opening section of *Portrait*—for a frequently voyeuristic transgression ("*Thsight near left me eyes when I seen her put thounce otay ithpot*" [*FW* 262]). The somatic images in the dream, in other words, are often infused with psychic fears or desires. In contrast to Bishop, Begnal focuses on the dream's narrative structure, but when he does discuss its content he likewise neutralizes its affective dimension: he dismisses oedipal anxiety in the *Wake* as a sustained critical delusion ("To be realistic for a moment, fathers and mothers are not generally overthrown by sons and daughters, no matter how often this critical chestnut has been used to describe the *Wake*") and whitewashes the work's disturbing polymorphous sexual perversity ("There is indeed a great deal of sexual innuendo throughout the narrative, but the only sexual activity which is described takes place between adults".[26]

Like the Circean hallucinations, the *Wake* is an essentially kinetic text, impelled by what Stephen calls the "kinetic emotions," desire and loathing, longing and fear (*P* 205). Thus "the obscurity of *Finnegans Wake*" that Bishop rightly celebrates as "its essence and glory"[27] is a function of not only the literal physical darkness of sleep but also the figurative psychic darkness of dreams. Messages from the unconscious are often formally obfuscated because their content is either profoundly disturbing or embarrassingly egotistical. By looking at some of the oppositions found along the horizontal axis of the dreamtext, one can see the wishes and anxieties, the dialectics of kinetic emotion, that govern Wakean representation.

Clive Hart has argued that everything in the *Wake* exists in dialectical versions, that duality is "perhaps the most important of all [its] basic structural concepts"[28]—"there being two sights for ever a picture" (*FW* 11). Threatening images of devious betrayal on the part of the opposite sex, for instance, are inevitably inverted in optimistic ones of loyal devotion. Hence in a well-known passage from 1.8, ALP dutifully brings the ailing and exhausted HCE a lavish breakfast in bed: "And an odd time she'd cook him up *blooms* of fisk and lay to his heartsfoot her meddery eygs, yayis, and staynish beacons on toasc and a cupenhave so weeshywashy of Greenland's tay or a dzoupgan of Kaffue mokau an sable" (*FW* 199, emphasis added). John Henry Raleigh has argued that this passage can be read as a continuation of *Ulysses* and provides proof that Molly did indeed serve Bloom breakfast on June 17, 1904.[29] But given the inverted version of this image in 1.1, where the husband *becomes* the breakfast, where HCE is *served as* both fish and eggs by ALP (see *FW* 7 and 12), one cannot take either of the contradictory scenarios as proof of any external state of (fictional) affairs. The connected oppositional imagoes make sense rather as a psychic expression of an egotistical male desire for a subservient woman countered by an uneasy fear of a more treacherous spouse.

In the *Wake*, as in "Circe," many of the dialectical images revolve around power struggles between the sexes, with visions of enslavement or entrapment countered by ones of domination. The roving male sailor must be "Cawcaught. Coocaged" (*FW* 329), the domestic ALP's "young-free yoke stilling his wandercursus" (*FW* 318); but at other points it is the elusive, fluvious ALP who must be captured and confined by her husband: "He harboured her when feme sole, her zoravarn lhorde and givnergenral, and led her in antient consort ruhm and bound her durant coverture so as she could not steal from him" (*FW* 243). The contrasting images suggest that HCE, like Bloom, has a mixed but not unusual reaction to wedlock, feeling anxiety at the thought of surrendering his own freedom, yet also a desire to have some control over the woman he loves. The fear of her "steal[ing] from him" recalls, in addition, the implicit psychic impetus behind Bloom's sexist jurisdiction over the family coffer, which Molly records in her monologue ("I could often have written out a fine cheque for myself and write his name on it for a couple of pounds a few times he forgot to lock it up" [*U* 780/642]). Analogous vehicles for expressing the need to govern and subdue a possibly errant spouse are religious conversion ("It is the circumconversioning of antelithual paganelles by a huggerknut cramwell energuman" [*FW* 512]) and educational discipline ("with fairskin book and ruling rod, . . . her chastener ever I did learn my little ana countrymouse in alphabeater cameltemper" [*FW* 552–53]), although these visions are elsewhere inverted, leaving it ambiguous as to which party must be brought under the yoke of civilization's structures. Once again, these images will be familiar to the readers of Joyce's earlier works: they recall both Bloom's use of higher learning in his attempts to divert a restless Molly and Stephen's thoughts in *Stephen Hero* of his mother's analogous tactics for domesticating an unruly Simon: "His mother, in fact, had so far evangelised herself that she undertook the duties of missioner to the heathen; that is to say, she offered some of [Ibsen's] plays to her husband to read" (*SH* 87).

·   ·   ·

I hope these last few examples begin to hint at the way the earlier works return in the dream in uncanny guises, transformed and yet recognizable. The "countlessness of livestories" that have fallen onto the page of the dreaming mind include the stories that Joyce himself scripted. Begnal has noted that Wakean voices often explicitly remind us to remember, impelling us to look backward in the narrative in order to make sense of what we are reading;[30] the recurrent appeals to memory, I would add, also implicitly direct us to our recollections of the prior fictions. As many critics have long noted, the identity of the Wakean dreamer remains deliberately indeterminate; but Joyce gives us clues how to read the dream of this elusive being through references to the situations—both psychic and physical—of his earlier characters. Zack Bowen has suggested that in *Ulysses* the protagonists often "share common identities and experiences, so [that] themes become interchangeable, intertwined, and hence consubstantial." This "communality of existence" that becomes "the narrative pattern of [*Ulysses*]"[31] also governs the logic and structure of the *Wake*. It helps to conceptualize the dreamer, I think, as a composite figure—a "Here Comes Everybody" (*FW* 32)—who incorporates into his multiplicitous self Joyce's two most famous heroes, Leopold Bloom and Stephen

Dedalus, as well as some more peripheral characters (such as Simon Dedalus, for instance). If in Bloom and Stephen we find the return, after a fashion, of Odysseus and Telemachus—as well as numerous other parallel figures from the past (Shakespeare, Moses, Christ, Daedalus, Icarus, Hamlet, Lucifer, etc. . .)—then in HCE we find the return of Bloom and Stephen, pulling in their wake an even richer panoply of analogical types. To demonstrate the way the psyches of earlier Joycean males seem to contribute to the dream's complex overdetermined visions, I would like to look first at the dream woman ALP once more; then at a particular scene, the Butt and Taff skit in 2.3; next at some of the figurations of the dream father HCE; and finally at 2.4, also known as the Tristan and Iseult chapter.[32]

The verbal contiguity that renders ALP as *mère* and *mer*, is a return, of course, of Mulligan's description of the sea as "our great sweet mother" (*U* 5/5). His further metaphorization of the *mère/mer* as a bed ("Make room in the bed" [*U* 22/19]), which Stephen recalls in "Proteus," also resurfaces in the dream when ALP becomes the "allaphbed" (*FW* 18). The visual logic behind the images of the central Wakean female can be explained most clearly by looking back at other impressions and memories from the "Proteus" section and tracing their unmistakable returns in the dreamtext: in her dialectical role as burier and retriever of physical detritus, ALP is an amalgam of the actual women who cross Stephen's ken on Sandymount strand as well as their associative figurations in his psyche. Like the putative midwives whom he imagines are going down to the water's edge to hide "a misbirth with a trailing navel cord" (*U* 37–38/ 32), the dream mother is visualized secreting the dead in the sea or simply subsuming it into her own watery presence ("hiding the crumbends of his enormousness in the areyou lookingfor Pearlfar sea" [*FW* 102]); in reverse she appears as the vagrant female cockle picker, garnering from the sea and shoreline materials for sustenance ("she'll loan a vesta and hire some peat and sarch the shores her cockles to heat and she'll do all a turfwoman can to piff the business on" [*FW* 12]). The perceptual linking of these antithetical women may have its source in Stephen's momentary confusion of the midwives and the gypsies when he first sees the latter from a distance ("From farther away, walking shoreward across from the crested tide, figures, two. The two maries. They have tucked it safe mong the bulrushes. Peekaboo. I see you. No, the dog. He is running back to them. Who?" [*U* 45/37]). Watching the gypsy woman with her "spoils slung at her back" at closer range, Stephen associates her with the moondrawn bay carrying its load of flotsam and jetsam, which he imaginatively transforms into her womb, an internal "winedark sea," the primal "allaphbed," which reminds him in turn of his often pregnant mother. The various images melt into one another in his mind: "She trudges, schlepps, trains, drags, trascines her load. A tide westering, moondrawn, in her wake. Tides, myriadislanded, within her, blood not mine, *oinopa ponton*, a winedark sea. Behold the handmaid of the moon. In sleep the wet sign calls her hour, bids her rise. Bridebed, childbed, bed of death, ghostcandled" (*U* 47–48/40). ALP is the byproduct of a similar though even more extended transformation of analogous visions. The sea dragging along assorted litter and the turfwoman's sack full of hoardings become the mother's prolific womb carrying its litter of 111 children; Pandora's box filled with its chaotic progeny; the sack of a female Santa Claus stuffed with litter for her litter, gewgaws for her children; her mailbag filled with letters; or her head stuffed with 111 pieces of gossip, the verbal litter she passes on to her priest. The litter and gossip the mother hoards are often represented as keepsakes, mementoes of the past ("poor souvenir as per ricorder and all for sore aringarung" [*FW* 210]), similar to those saved by May Dedalus, nostalgic for better days: "Her secrets: old featherfans, tasselled dancecards, powdered with musk, a gaud of amber beads in her locked drawer. A birdcage hung in the sunny window of her house when she was a girl" (*U* 9–10/8). In dream the mother's marital oppression is vividly visualized, when the violent conquest of the female is represented as an act of putting the girl in the birdcage itself: "he raped her home, Sabrine asthore, in a parakeet's cage, by dredgerous lands and devious delts" (*FW* 197).

Several of Stephen's earlier perceptions from *Portrait* find their way into the Butt and Taff skit. Although this dream scene pulls into it impressions from throughout the novel, it uses most clearly details from chapter 1, such as the name of Stephen's first school—"we were all under that manner barracksers on Kong Gores Wood together" (*FW* 348)—the episode being narrated, on one level, from the perspective of students. Toward the opening of the scene, Taff crawls out of a cesspool ("*porumptly helping himself out by the cesspull*" [*FW* 338]), perhaps the Wakean return of Stephen climbing out of the square ditch, its vaguely cloacal overtones in his recollections (see *P* 10–11) rendered explicit in the dreamtext. Dramatizing the revolt of youth against an authority figure, the skit makes sense as what Stephen or the other boys at Clongowes would dream in response to being unfairly punished by the masters for the mysterious transgression committed by the older students. Turning the confrontation into a full-scale military coup, the Wakean episode literalizes the suggestion made when the boys realize that even the innocent will be feeling the fathers' wrath: "Let us get up a rebellion, Fleming said. Will we?" (*P* 44). When Butt hesitates in his revolt, he reminds himself of the oppressive taboos that the father establishes: the phrase "think of that when you smugs to bagot" (*FW* 345) conflates the forbidden smugging attributed to the errant schoolmates with the similarly prohibited smoking of tobacco, surreptitiously indulged in by adolescent students in *Portrait*'s second chapter. The historical encrustations in the Butt and Taff skit, denser than in most other parts of the dream, may be rooted in Stephen's sense of his filial challenge to Father Dolan's reign of terror as having solid precedent in earlier eras ("He would go up and tell the rector that he had been wrongly punished. A thing like that had been done before by somebody in history, by some great person whose head was in the books of history" [P 53]). The schoolroom designations that divide the boys figuratively into the Yorks and the Lancasters, in dream divide father and sons into actual warring political factions, the students fighting, generally, for liberation from patriarchal tyranny and, more specifically, for an unsupervised recess period: "Hulp, hulp, huzzars! Raise ras tryracy! Freetime's free! Up Lancesters! Anathem!" (FW 348).

The second scene at Clongowes in the opening chapter of *Portrait* marks the incipience of Stephen's realization that father figures are often flawed. His ambivalent vision of fathers as still awesome and yet capable of error permeates the sons' representation of HCE at this particular point: they are initially impressed by his elaborate uniform and medals but come to recognize him as an errant mortal. A specific detail from a later scene in which Stephen recognizes even more clearly the limitations of his religious patriarchs returns in Butt and Taff's discussion of the father's apparel: "Come alleyou jupes of Wymmingtown that graze the calves of Man!" (FW 339). With its explicit mention of men dressed in conventionally female attire, this reference to the director's conversation with Stephen about "*les jupes*" worn in some clerical orders clarifies the director's evasive ellipsis, adumbrating the word he hesitates to speak—presumably "effeminate" or "feminine": "The capuchin dress, he thought, was rather too . . ." (P 154, Joyce's ellipsis). The director's casual discussion of clerical attire, which Stephen senses is "disingenuous" (P 155), functions as a test of sorts: he presumably wants to gauge Stephen's response to the idea of men in skirts in order to make sure his interest in a religious vocation is not motivated by homosexual or transvestite impulses. In the Butt and Taff section of the *Wake*, I would argue, this scene is scandalously reinterpreted: the son figures' ultimate anal impalement of the father, a version of their rape of him, suggests that the test aimed at preventing homosexuality in the clerical orders is reassessed in dream as a sexual overture, as a hint at homosexual desires that the sons' aggressively fulfill. In the *Wake* the patriarch's flaws are located not in any mere intellectual limitations, as they are in *Portrait* (see P 156), but rather in his moral errancy, his repressed and unacknowledged interest in the sexually taboo.

The father in the Butt and Taff section (and elsewhere in the dream) is a composite figure created in part from a number of patriarchs represented in *Portrait* and *Ulysses*. The sons' description of HCE's impressive attire that turns the heads of female admirers, for instance—"Obriania's beromst! From Karrs and Polikoff's, the men's confessioners. . . . Mousoumeselles buckwoulds look. Tenter and likelings" (*FW* 339)—resonates of Simon's description of Stephen's grandfather: "He was the handsomest man in Cork at that time, by God he was! The women used to stand to look after him in the street" (*P* 92). HCE's martial contours in 2.3 recall Stephen's dream at Clongowes of his father as a marshal. As *"the jesuneral of the russuates"* (*FW* 349), the dream pater becomes Jesus, the general of the Jesuits and of the Russians—perhaps the csar whose petition for universal peace Stephen refuses to sign in *Portrait*'s final chapter, dismissing him with the statement "Keep your icon. If we must have a Jesus, let us have a legitimate Jesus" (*P* 198). In his recurrent guise of the assassinated Russian General, Bobrikoff or "bobbycop" (*FW* 338) in particular, HCE is the dream return of the Russian governor-general of Finland shot on June 16, 1904,[33] whom Stephen is jokingly accused of killing in the "Aeolus" chapter (*U* 134/111). In his threatening guises, "old Dolldy Icon" (*FW* 339) contains unmistakable semiotic residues of earlier paternal figures, overthrown or repudiated for their oppressiveness.

The defeated and fallen father is represented in dream as a gigantic mound or stranded whale covered with tiny creatures—"Men like to ants or emmets wondern upon a groot hwide Whallfisk which lay in a Runnel. Blubby wares upat Ublanium" (*FW* 13). This image can be read as a visual condensation of two separate visions from *Portrait* and *Ulysses*: Stephen's thoughts of "a plain of peace whereon antlike men laboured in brotherhood, their dead sleeping under quiet mounds" (*P* 126) and his somewhat similar historical recollection in "Proteus" of a "school of turlehide whales stranded in hot noon," crawled upon and hacked up by "a horde of jerkined dwarfs," a starving Dublin populace (*U* 45/38). Many of Bloom's thoughts and perceptions also contribute to the dream father's contours, HCE taking shape as Sinbad the sailor, Van der Decken of *The Flying Dutchman*, the duke of Wellington, Turko the Terrible, and a humpbacked Norwegian captain. The three most prominent inanimate configurations of the males in the dream can be linked to Bloom's metempsychotic transformations into features of the landscape. In "Calypso" he recalls that he also exists as a range of mountains ("Inishturk. Inishark. Inishboffin. At their joggerfry. Mine. Slieve Bloom" [*U* 58/48]), and in "Nausicaa" he identifies with both a tree and a stone, the dominant dream images for the sons Shem and Shaun ("Like to be that rock she sat on" [*U* 376/308]; "Bat probably. Thinks I'm a tree, so blind. . . . Metempsychosis" [*U* 377/309]).

The Tristan and Iseult chapter of the *Wake* allows us to see most clearly the way Joyce combines the perceptual experiences of his earlier figures to create a dreamtext of overdetermined returns with multiple possible origins. Norris has pointed out that 2.4 contains several references to the trip to Cork in *Portrait*, particularly in the recurrent conjunction of "colleges" and "auctions," two of this section's prominent motifs. She notes, however, that in the *Wake* we find an interesting shift in perspective on the earlier familiar scene: "the 'Tristan' chapter encourages us to revisit Cork from Simon's point of view, and to drink with him (uncontaminated by his son's emotional aridity) the bittersweet cup of kindness and memory."[34] 2.4 is indeed rich in details from Simon's sentimental journey: fond reminiscences about youth and achievements (cf. "Thanks be to God we lived so long and did so much good" [*P* 95] and "all the good or they did in their time" [*FW* 397]); regretful sighings over the vanished feast of prosperous days ("the barmaisigheds" [*FW* 387]) in the company of barmaids and fellow tipplers; nostalgic laments over lost friends, those "scattered and dead revellers" (*P* 91) literally dispersed and destroyed in 2.4 in a series of disastrous shipwrecks (such as that of "the Flemish armada, all scattered, and all officially drowned" [*FW* 388]). As the past floods into the present in the meandering recollections of the four old men, however, the dead in a sense return, if only discursively: the voice of uncle Charles, another deceased member of Simon's past, speaks in 2.4 lamenting death itself (cf. "Too bad! Too bad! said uncle Charles" [*P* 32] and "Ah, now, it was too bad, too bad and stout entirely, all the missoccurs" [*FW* 391]).

The old men who narrate 2.4 continually confuse past and present, after the fashion of the nostalgic Simon, wishfully denying the passage of time ("For the most part they spoke at crosspurposes when a name was mentioned, the waiter having in mind the present holder and Mr Dedalus his father or perhaps his grandfather" [*P* 89]). Simon's rhetoric during the Cork trip is full of self-serving denials, repressions, and distortions, many of which are exposed and corrected when this journey of return returns in the *Wake*. Simon, for instance, represents his young friends from the medical college as "gentlemen," "fine decent fellows" (*P* 91); in 2.4 the college resurfaces as "the grandest gynecollege" (*FW* 389), its students' interest in medicine impelled by a decidedly prurient curiosity ("when they were all four collegians on the nod . . . peep of tim boys and piping tom boys, raising hell while the sin was shining" [*FW* 385]). In a playful transformation of an earlier detail, the *anatomy theater* revisited by Simon returns in dream as a commercial *theater* where men watch the sentimental plays of Dion Boucicault in order to indulge a voyeuristic interest in the *anatomy* of the female lead ("a strapping modern old an-

cient Irish prisscess, so and so hands high, such and such paddock weight
. . . nothing under her hat but red hair and solid ivory" [*FW* 396]). The
opening song in 2.4 provides a blatant mockery of Simon's pathetic brag-
gadocio about his ability to compete with and beat his son athletically,
and baldly exposes the sexual insecurities implicitly impelling such pro-
fessions of virility ("*Hohohoho, moulty Mark! / You're the rummest old
roaster ever flopped out of a Noah's ark / And you think you're cock of
the wark. / Fowls, up! Tristy's the spry young spark / That'll tread her and
wed her and bed her and red her*" [*FW* 383]). At the most ironic moment
in Cork, Simon complacently denies Stephen's interest in girls, the bur-
geoning adolescent sexuality made patent to the reader ("He's not that
way built, said Mr Dedalus. Leave him alone" [*P* 94]): Simon is unconsciously threatened, of course, by the prospect of filial maturity and his
own attendant paternal decline. In the vivid picture of the son's sexual
prowess in 2.4—the recurrent image of Tristan seducing Iseult—the aging
father's defensive repression is effectively unsealed, the denied thought
finding graphic expression in the dream.

The songs woven into the reminiscences of the old men—the strains of
Auld Lang Syne ("The Good Old Times"), Tommy Moore's melodies,
and other sentimental tunes that evoke the lost past—may be the dream
returns of the music in the Cork episode: Simon's singing, his remembrance of a friend's *come-all-yous*, the brass instruments heard playing in
the street, and the sound of a piano, floating out of an open window (*P*
88–90). But the conjunction of music and shipwrecks also clearly evokes
the myth of the Sirens and returns us to the corresponding section of
Ulysses, another chapter that thematically intertwines drinking, nostal-
gia, and songs resonant of loss ("Thou lost one. All songs on that theme"
[*U* 277/228]). The old men of 2.4 are rendered as a musical ensemble
("The Lambeg drum, the Lombog reed, the Lumbag fiferer, the Limibig
brazenaze" [*FW* 398]), and like the patrons of the Ormond bar, they
console themselves with drink ("And stiller the mermen ply their keg"
[*FW* 399]). Interestingly, the number of sentimental reminiscers vacillates
between three and four ("the three jolly topers, with their mouths water-
ing, all the four, the old connubial men of the sea" [*FW* 386]), as if they
are the dream reincarnation of the trio of lovelorn men from "Sirens"—
the aging widower Simon Dedalus, the bachelor Ben Dollard, and the
lapsed priest Father Cowley—that becomes a quartet if one adds Bloom,
the imminent cuckold. While the narrators of 2.4 recall the past through
song, the spry young Tristan—as in Joseph Bédier's rendering of the
myth[35]—serenades Iseult off in the woods, warbling his birdsong to
please her: "she murmurously, after she let a cough, gave her firm order,
if he wouldn't please mind, for a sings to one hope a dozen of the best
favourite lyrical national *blooms* in Luvillicit, though not too much, re-

flecting on the situation, drinking in draughts of purest air serene and revelling in the great outdoors" (*FW* 385, emphasis added). Given the clear reference to his name in this passage, this vision can be read as the disguised dream return of the thought Bloom represses in the "Sirens" chapter: his younger rival singing to his younger wife with the hope of gaining "luvillicit," after having consumed the aphrodisiac oysters that Bloom thinks about with anxiety earlier in the day ("cuddling and kiddling her, after an oyster supper" [*FW* 385]). In 2.4, as in *Ulysses*, the young lover uses music to seduce the woman, while the older men use it to seduce themselves. Indeed, the sentimental narrators are in a position similar to Bloom's in the Ormond bar. While jaunty Boylan rides off to a musical tryst with a sexual climax, Bloom must be content with just the music, music that subliminally reminds him of his imminent cuckolding while also providing a psychic escape ("Wish they'd sing more. Keep my mind off" [*U* 280/230]). The maudlin songs of 2.4 are similarly ambiguous, reminding the four men of their lost youth and sexual vigor, while offering simultaneously a surrogate pleasure.

I find in 2.4, however, references to yet another scene from the earlier fictions: a specific vision at the end of *Portrait* of "incestuous love," imagined by Stephen as a brother and sister embracing amid "wet silent trees" near a "shieldlike witnessing lake"; the male in the fantasy turns out to be Davin, the champion of nationalist causes also known for his athletic interests (*P* 228). This strange erotic vision is preceded by Stephen's thoughts about the birds overhead as symbolic portents and is followed by Emma Clery's explicit social snub of him (see *P* 232). After this snub, Stephen wonders if some sort of flirtation exists between Emma and Cranly, but he also reveals, in a moment of intense sexual bitterness, that he resents and envies Davin even more ("Well then, let her go and be damned to her. She could love some clean athlete who washed himself every morning to the waist and had black hair on his chest. Let her" [*P* 234]): Davin is the friend whose innocence and physical robustness Stephen thinks hold a distinct sexual appeal. I would argue that this narrative sequence, with that bizarre sexual fantasy in the middle of it, contributes to the general contours and specific details of 2.4. Hovering birds identified as "auspices" (*FW* 384), for instance, circle above the lovemaking of Tristan and Iseult, which takes place alternately in the woods and on a body of water (cf. the trees and the lake in Stephen's vision). The scandal of the dream vision ("a seatuition so shocking and scandalous" [*FW* 385]) lies in its sexual betrayal and in its incest, for the couple is also Arrah-na-Pogue and her brother, to whom she delivers a letter through a kiss that in 2.4 becomes luridly sexual. The brother figure resembles Davin in his Irish nationalism ("the hero, of Gaelic champion" [*FW* 384]) and in his physical prowess, an earlier description of this young athletic male clearly echoing Stephen's resentful thought: "the foodbrawler . . . with hiss blackleaded chest" (*FW* 144). Even Emma's surname slips into 2.4, if only under the guise of "O'Clery" (*FW* 385), the common surname of three of the four masters.

This chapter of the *Wake*, in other words, combines scenes from fictions that Joyce read (Boucicault's *Arrah-na-Pogue* and Bédier's version of *Tristan and Iseult*, to cite the most prominent) with analogical scenes from fictions that he wrote. Details from Simon's trip to Cork, Bloom's dinner at the Ormond bar, and Stephen's vision at the end of *Portrait* are superimposed on account of their shared psychic import, all three experiences being enmeshed with anxieties about loss and sexual usurpation. The overdetermined dream vision of dispossession becomes, paradoxically, a site of repossession as well: a repossession of the dreamer's past which manifests itself as moments from the lives of familiar Joycean characters, lives intermixed—in dream as in waking reality—with ineluctable mythic parallels.

Artistic creativity for Joyce is re-creativity, and finally a doubled re-creativity: if his earlier works record transmutations of cultural myths, his final oeuvre reforges his own personal transcripts of that inheritance. Literature becomes a site of revision, supplementation, and elaboration— initially, of the fictions constructed by others and, ultimately, of the fictions constructed by the self. On a practical level, Joyce's re-creativity directs us, in our interpretive quests, not only outward to helpful source books, lists of annotations, dictionaries, and encyclopedias, but also inward to the web of interconnections the writer weaves between his disparate texts. This re-creativity also suggests that art is, in some ways, inherently obsessive, an inevitable reinscription of particular psychic concerns. Stephen's theory of Shakespeare in "Scylla and Charybdis" makes it clear that Joyce was by no means ignorant of the compulsive mechanisms propelling and influencing representation. Yet Joyce acknowledges—both in and through Stephen's exegesis (which indirectly articulates all of Stephen's *own* concerns)—the unconscious force of those mechanisms: composing his final dreamtext, Joyce probably surrendered, to some extent, to their ineluctable insistence. The *Wake* is a literary palimpsest whose multiple layers of cryptic inscription can often be deciphered as Joyce's own earlier writing. In his final work, he puts that writing to sleep, as it were, only to record its relentless return.

Chapter 2

TEXTUAL DESIRE: LANGUAGE AND
THE RETURN OF THE TABOO

IN JOYCE'S fictions, the voice of the father operates as the vehicle of law, while providing simultaneously the inadvertent evidence of its failure. The moral errancy inscribed in Stephen's literal wanderings into the brothel district ("He had wandered into a maze of narrow and dirty streets" [*P* 100]) is checked by the voice of Father Arnall, preaching hellfire and eternal damnation; yet the voice of the father in this section is also compromised in several ways. Father Arnall employs grotesque, sensory language to lead the young boys to spiritual purity and salvation; in his efforts to make the boys repent and transcend physical desires, he generates rhetoric curiously permeated with the physical itself. He asks his listeners to imagine "millions upon millions of fetid carcasses massed together in the reeking darkness, a huge and rotting human fungus," describing hell in graphic detail as "a strait and dark and foulsmelling prison," as "a vast reeking sewer" (*P* 119–20). Elaborated on a conscious level for rhetorical effect, the sermon betrays a veiled obsession with the nether regions it purports to condemn. If Father Dolan flogs the students with his pandybat as a means of reifying the law, Father Arnall flogs them with words, assaulting them with images that are revealingly dirty, scatological, and sadistic in their evocation of physical torture.

On the one hand, language provides the medium through which the law of the father is internalized and reinforced, but on the other, it always holds the capacity to reveal guilt, to expose the profane impulses and interests that betray man's fallen state. Father Purdon of "Grace," for instance, reveals his worldliness not only through his misreading of the gospel but also through his mercantile metaphors. The priest that listens to Stephen's confession in *Portrait* uses a similarly suspect figure of speech: "As long as you commit that sin, my poor child, you will never be worth one farthing to God" (*P* 144). Interdicted thoughts and impulses expressing themselves both in unexpected verbal intrusions and in verbal gaps, the discourse of the dreamworld is riddled with Freudian slips or lapses—linguistic falls as it were—and with hesitancies that are just as telling, like Bloom's stammering and truncated confession to the imperious Bello of "Circe": "I rererepugnosed in rerererepugnant . . ." (*U* 538/ 439, Joyce's ellipsis). Wakean discourse is fallen in every sense of the word: errant and sinuous in its syntactical structures; fractured and shattered in its lexical forms; unstable and guilt-ridden in its meanings. The dream's patriarch is branded a "scutterer of guld" (*FW* 340)—a stuttering utterer of guilt and a scattering utterer of gold (in a monetary context, an "utterer" is a passer of counterfeit currency). The appellation condenses the the guilty verbality and the mercantile mentality seen in Father Purdon and Stephen's confessor. Throughout the Joycean universe, the fallen nature of various paternal authorities is revealed preeminently in the act of speech.

The ambiguity of the patriarchal voice, at once authoritative and subversive, returns in its clearest form in the recurrent Wakean thunderwords. Interpreted as a divine interdiction, the thunder that interrupted the random copulating of the primitives in Viconian mythology scared them into the caves and subsequent domesticity, creating the earliest form of social order. The thunder reverberates in the dream as the sound of a door slamming shut on the male wanderer, similarly domesticated and confined; but it is also the din of the father's guilty crash to earth, his loud nervous cough, and his embarrassing flatulent or defecatory emission—the signifiers, in short, of his mortal, errant state.

Guilty impulses also speak through the language of behavior, through the signifying displacements inherent in compulsive acts and gestures. In his essay on "Obsessive Acts and Religious Practices," Freud elaborates the connection between personal and communal "ceremonials," both being "religiously" performed and characterized by prohibitions and acts of penance. But obsessive acts and religious rituals constitute compromise gestures, Freud argues, because they involve behavioral displacements, substitute acts and objects that compensate for the prohibited instinct, that allow it to find an alternative means of expression: "they always reproduce something of the identical pleasure they were designed to prevent; they serve the repressed impulse no less than the repressing element."[1] Several details in *Portrait* suggest that Joyce was thoroughly familiar with unconscious displacements, particularly as they manifested themselves in religious rites. James Naremore has pointed out that, as part of the routine of supererogatory piety described at the beginning of chapter 4, Stephen "fingers a set of rosary beads in his pocket, in surrogate masturbation."[2] The young penitent replaces sexual releases with verbal ones, in the form of exclamatory prayers and litanies: "Then, almost at the instant of that touch, almost at the verge of sinful consent, he found himself standing far away from the flood upon a dry shore, saved by a sudden act of the will or *a sudden ejaculation*" (*P* 152, emphasis added). Whether or not he learned it from Freud, Joyce fully understood the way the id appropriates language—be it verbal or behavioral—for its own ends: structures that serve *homo significans* also serve *homo libidi-*

nosus. Cultural discourse functions as the medium of desire, as the vehicle that unwittingly speaks and betrays the culturally tabooed.

Confession is the religious ritual that interested Joyce most as a sanctioned substitution for interdicted impulses. The perverse confessor returns in his fictions with an obsessive regularity: in *Portrait* Stephen is attracted to the priesthood so that he can hear the shameful confessions of women and girls; in *Ulysses* Molly senses the gratuitous curiosity in the priest's interest in the exact nature and extent of her transgression; and in *Finnegans Wake* Shaun admits that his duties as a confessor have left him "well voiced in love's arsenal" (*FW* 438) so that he is able to describe prohibited sexual activities with remarkably accurate detail. As described by the Wakean female penitents, confession is a striptease of sorts, the act of hearing it the auditory equivalent of voyeurism ("Now promisus as at our requisted you will remain ignorant of all what you hear and, though if whilst disrobing to the edge of risk . . . draw a veil till we next time!" [*FW* 238]). Joyce probes the submerged guilty motives of the confessee through Bloom's thoughts on the ritual in "Lotus Eaters": "Confession. Everyone wants to. Then I will tell you all. Penance. Punish me, please. Great weapon in their hands. More than doctor or solicitor. Woman dying to. And I schschschschschsch. And did you chachachachacha? And why did you? Look down at her ring to find an excuse. . . . Then out she comes. Repentance skindeep" (*U* 83/68). In this anatomy of the rite, the penitent is motivated not by any genuine shame or contrition, but by complementary needs for self-exposure and punishment.

Rather than driving interdicted desires underground, civilization provides surreptitious outlets for them within its own structures. The ritual of confession allows for the verbal return of tendencies that are at once sadistic and masochistic as well as voyeuristic and exhibitionist. This economic combination of illicit impulses emerges in Joyce's early story of "An Encounter," where the strange old man plays the role of priest and penitent simultaneously, prying into the young boys' intimacies while openly confessing his own prurience ("He began to speak to us about girls, saying what nice soft hair they had and how soft their hands were and how all girls were not so good as they seemed to be if one only knew" [*D* 26]). After he presumably masturbates, he turns into the sadistic, chastising priest whose verbal flagellations, however, are directed in part at himself, in a gesture of self-punitive masochism that the scared boy does not recognize as such: the unruly youth who "ought to be whipped and well whipped" (*D* 27) is, on one level, a screen image of the transgressive elder. Joyce describes this bizarre ritual in terms of psychological compulsion, the man giving the youth "the impression that he was repeating something which he had learned by heart or that, magnetised by some words of his own speech, his mind was slowly circling round and round in the same orbit" (*D* 26). The man's ceremonial is performed religiously in both senses of the word—as an obsessive reenactment of an inculcated Catholic rite. In the putative service of censuring desire, the Church insists that desire be spoken, re-presented, reexpressed, in an ecclesiastically sanctioned version of the repetition compulsion. As Joyce knew from firsthand experience (and as his infamous letters to Nora suggest), the most ironic effect of Catholicism can be found in its inadvertent promulgation of pornology—the obsessive articulation of taboo, the textualization of the sexual.

The Shaun figure in Book 3 of the *Wake* functions as Joyce's most thoroughgoing exposé of the guilty cleric, whose behavior forms a series of thinly disguised sublimations, incessantly betraying the desires they replace and only inadequately conceal. As a dream figure who incorporates characteristics of several earlier Joycean priests (and their surrogates), he also provides another example of the return of the waking fictions in the dreamtext. I find in Shaun residues of Father Moran, the priest who attends the Irish league classes with Emma and Stephen: Father Moran's "neat head of curly black hair" (*SH* 65), for instance, resurfaces in Shaun's "frizzy hair and . . . golliwog curls" (*FW* 430) that his female penitents enjoy mussing. In *Stephen Hero* Father Moran is represented as a singer of sentimental songs who "was for many reasons a great favourite with the ladies" (*SH* 65). In the *Wake* the unspecified reasons for the popularity of the singing priest are clarified, when Shaun's vocal performances turn into a barely disguised erotic exhibition for his female audience. The "kinantic" (or kinetic) soup he imbibes to prepare for his performance and the masturbatory pose he strikes as his voice swells to an operatic climax mark the priest's singing as a sexually charged act: "his voixehumanar swelled to great, clenching his manlies, so highly strong was he, man, and gradually quite warming to her (there must have been a power of kinantics in that buel of gruel he gobed at bedgo)" (*FW* 441). Joyce represents clerical interests in all varieties of the arts as by-products of repressed sexuality, as substitute physical pleasures masked as aesthetic ones. As Bloom thinks in the "Lotus Eaters" chapter where sensory indulgence is explored at length, "Those old popes keen on music, on art and statues and pictures of all kinds" (*U* 82/67).

Father Moran's seemingly intellectual pursuit of Irish history and language has a similarly suspect erotic impetus, his desire to read Irish legends emerging in the dream as a disguised interest in red Irish leggings: the nightworld hints that he attends those league classes because they provide an opportunity for voyeuristic observation of the opposite sex. The priest's dutiful guidance of his female confessees is reduced to a pleasurable discussion of proper attire that permits an exploration—both verbal and visual—of various intimate female zones: "he next went on (finefeelingfit!) to drop a few stray remarks anent their personal appearances and the contrary tastes displayed in their tight kittycasques and their smart frickyfrockies, asking coy one after sloy one had she read Irish legginds and gently reproving one that the ham of her hom could be seen below her hem and whispering another aside, as lavariant, that the hook of her hum was open a bittock at her back to have a sideeye to that" (FW 431). "Dressed like an earl in just the correct wear" (FW 404), Shaun applies his fastidious fashion standards to himself—as the elaborate catalogue of his apparel suggests—to produce an air of stylishness that bespeaks an unconscious desire to impress the female other. He is reminiscent of the immaculately attired young priest in the second chapter of *Portrait*, who reminds Stephen of his father's saying—"you could always tell a jesuit by the style of his clothes" (P 84). Shaun's desires are further revealed in the provocative odors he emits ("smilingly smelling . . . the nice perfumios that came cunvy peeling off him") that cause the young girls to buzz around him like a swarm of bees ("on their best beehiviour . . . they were girls all rushing sowarmly for the post as buzzy as sie could bie" [FW 430]). He becomes the dream incarnation of the clerics Bloom thinks about in "Nausicaa": "Mansmell, I mean. Must be connected with that because priests that are supposed to be are different. Women buzz round it like flies round treacle. Railed off the altar get on to it at any cost. The tree of forbidden priest" (U 375/307). Because of his celibacy, Shaun emits a similarly enticing "mansmell" that differentiates him from sexually active men by recording his repressed and unsatisfied eroticism in the silent semiotics of scent.

Given Shaun's occasional confusion of the female with food—"Goodbye, swisstart, goodbye!" (FW 454)—his compulsive gluttony can be interpreted as a displaced sexual voracity, a substitutive oral pleasure, one form of appetite subsuming another and becoming excessive in the process of compensation. Traces of Cranly also return in this clerical gourmand whose arguments are repeatedly infected by his obsession with food: in *Stephen Hero* Stephen characterizes his friend's "method in argument" as a reduction of "all things to their food values" (SH 208), and in *Portrait* he envisions him as "a guilty priest" who hears confessions but lacks the power of absolution (P 178), presumably because of his compromising sexual interests, in Emma Clery in particular. Shaun not only hears confessions but also feels a compulsive need to confess himself, his unlawful tendencies explicitly demanding discursive form: "And I will confess to have, yes. . . . Thrubedore I did! Inditty I did" (FW 411). But like the old man's in "An Encounter," Shaun's discourse of confessional intimacy and self-exposure is mixed with its opposite, the language of chastisement. In his speech clear echoes of Father Arnall's hellfire sermon return—"Words taken in triumph, my sweet assistance, from the suffer-

ant pen of our jocosus inkerman militant of the reed behind the ear" (*FW*
433, cf. *P* 108))—to render transparent the perverse impulses unconsciously compelling religious exhortations. When the priest's audience
turns female in 3.2, his sadistic discourse becomes explicitly sexual: "I'll
be all over you myselx horizontally . . . or I'll smack your fruitflavoured
jujube lips well for you. . . . I'll just draw my prancer and give you one
splitpuck in the crupper, you understand, that will bring the poppy blush
of shame to your peony hindmost till you yelp papapardon" (*FW* 444–
45). Although he sometimes emerges—particularly in 3.2—as the religious conman, the conscious fraud, Shaun at other points exhibits a will-
ful deafness to the hypocritical nature of his words. After he condemns
the language of Shem as "the fuellest filth" (*FW* 419), his listeners are
forced to ask him, "have you not . . . used up slanguage tun times as
words as the penmarks used out in sinscript with such hesitancy by your
cerebrated brother . . . ?" (*FW* 421). In Joyce's exposé, the irony of the
guilty priest lies in the gap between praxis and knowledge. Appropriately
aligned with the eye rather than the ear, Shaun is the confessor who cannot hear the revealing confessions inherent in the semiotics of his own
rhetorical performance.

·   ·   ·

Although Shaun can be read as a version of the priest figures that serve as
Stephen's rivals, he is also linked to Stephen himself, particularly in his
guilty confessional language. Highlighting confession as a central motif in
Portrait, John Hannay describes it as a sort of kinetic art, "designed precisely to create a sense of loathing for one's sins and a desire for spiritual
purity," but an art often driven by unrecognized erotic motives.[3] The suspect impetus behind Stephen's recurrent desire for confession becomes
clearest when it expresses itself as an urge to write pornological letters,
intended not for a forgiving priest, of course, but for an innocent and
unsuspecting girl: at a moment of supposed contrition he recalls "the foul
long letters he had written in the joy of guilty confession and carried
secretly for days and days only to throw them under cover of night among
the grass in the corner of a field or beneath some hingeless door or in
some niche in the hedges where a girl might come upon them as she
walked by and read them secretly" (*P* 116). The desired aim of this
"guilty confession" is not the forgiveness anticipated by the remorseful
penitent, but rather the shock anticipated by the flasher, the verbal exhibitionist. The pornological impulses behind Stephen's illicit written confessions cast a perverse shadow on the motives behind his sanctioned oral
ones. Through the language used to describe the confession at the end of
chapter 3, Joyce labels the act as merely another version of Stephen's
earlier articulations of the dirty word ("The last sins oozed forth, slug-

gish, filthy" [P 144]). Reduplicating his compulsion to write his sins, Stephen's compulsion to speak them becomes a questionable gesture of penitence: it supports Freud's contention that obsessive ceremonials often "fall more and more under the sway of the instinct and approach nearer and nearer to the activity which was originally prohibited."[4]

Regardless of how dreamy the construct, most of the young artist's literary productions in *Portrait* are driven by sexual impulses, are marked as expressions and confessions of erotic longing. As such, they anticipate many of the private correspondences to self and others that circulate in *Ulysses* through the larger network of textuality in both past and present: Martha and Bloom's correspondence; Boylan's note to Molly; the suggestive letters Bloom once wrote to his future wife; the fake missives Molly has sent herself just to get something in the mail; Gerty MacDowell's "lovely confession album . . . to write her thoughts in" (*U* 364/298). An innocent formality on the surface, even Milly's thank-you note circuitously announces her interest in Bannon and, even more obliquely, hints at a girlish crush on Boylan ("Tell him silly Milly sends my best respects" [*U* 66/54]). Much of the personal writing in *Ulysses* is impelled by desire: as Roland Barthes points out, "the fulfilled lover has no need to write, to transmit, to reproduce. . . . In the lover's realm, there is . . . nothing but signs, a frenzied activity of language: to institute, on each furtive occasion, the system (the paradigm) of demand and response."[5] Inscriptions of longing, letters are documents both compromising and compromised—they often speak and bespeak desire evasively, indirectly, just as rituals and obsessive gestures do. In Joyce's works, it is only in the nightworlds that their dangerous and revealing status is fully recognized. Hence much of the evidence brought against the beleaguered Bloom during his Circean trial is guilty textuality: scandalous letters presented by various women, written overtures he has made, even if only in his imagination.

In "Ithaca" Bloom adds his fourth letter from Martha to her previous ones, which he keeps in a locked drawer containing all sorts of mementoes, including some compromising obscene pictures. This accumulated detritus anticipates the Wakean rubbish heap, as Kenner's description of it implies: "the catalogue of objects . . . would have much to tell Holmes and tells us quite as much. . . . It is like an archaeologist's midden-hoard, and we may remember how characteristic of the nineteenth century was skill at reading mute evidence."[6] But whereas this "midden-hoard" in *Ulysses* simply contains numerous letters, the one in the *Wake* becomes numerous letters through an ingenious imagistic transformation (see *FW* 11). The dreamer envisions the remains of his fallen self as a text that relentlessly changes its contours, strewing the *Wake* with "a letters" (*FW* 278)—a singular missive in plural versions.

The guilt-ridden nightletter that returns throughout the dream is textually fragmented, parts of it having supposedly rotted away while buried in the earth, although its gaps may not be literal: the deletions may simply be the work of the dream censor, of conveniently partial recall. Shari Benstock argues that the letter's missing content is desire repressed, desire present *in absentia*, its course consequently circuitous, the text falling prey to purloinings, transferences, delays, and misplacements.[7] The taboo status of the letter is also betrayed in the ambivalent treatment of it, a treatment that becomes a revealing statement in itself. In 1.5 in particular, the transcript is intellectualized, subjected to elaborate formal exegesis, perhaps to divert psychic attention away from its content; it is also fondled as an erotic object, punctured with a series of phallic instruments, melted, and flushed—only to resurface later in the dream. "It is not a hear or say of some anomorous letter" (*FW* 112), we are assured, yet this disclaimer may well be defensive. The letter does often sound amorous or anomalous or *anomos* (lawless in Greek), and hence—not surprisingly—anonymous, its "anomorous" author remaining indeterminate. "Secret satieties and onanymous letters" (*FW* 435) returns us to Bloom's correspondence with Martha, whose most recent missive he considers masturbating over in the bath. One of the footnotes in 2.2 suggests that it has been deliberately shredded, like the envelope to this earlier text of desire that Bloom guiltily tears up in "Lotus Eaters": "Something happened that time I was asleep, torn letters or was there snow?" (*FW* 307).

The difficulties involved in interpreting the Wakean letter stem not only from narrative lack, the gaps in the document, but also from narrative excess, its numerous versions. Commenting upon its final appearance in Book 4, Bernard Benstock writes, "The last version of the letter . . . is the longest and most fully developed (and one can even suspect that it contains *more* than it actually should)."[8] As the parenthetical comment suggests, the linguistic excess of the final version may render the reader suspicious, creating obfuscations and uncertainties as successfully as any straightforward elisions: suspended between narrative surfeit and paucity, the letter becomes paradigmatic of the dream as a whole. In its attempt to conceal guilty truths from the dreamer, the censor works alternately with scissors and pen, through informational omission and overload.

The textual evidence against the father is slippery, constantly shifting its contours. If over the course of the dream the letter's message varies in both length and content, over the course of 1.5 its form becomes protean, appearing alternately as an archaeological artifact ("a genuine relique of ancient Irish pleasant pottery"), a decayed photo negative ("Heated residence in the heart of the orangeflavoured mudmound had partly obliterated the negative to start with" [*FW* 111]), and a map serving a "geodetic" purpose. The letter's teastain and "acquired accretions of terricious matter" (FW 114) hint that it is also a piece of soiled toilet paper, the evidence of the father's urination and defecation, the proof of his subjection to mortal, bodily functions: as such, it is a version of the desecrated piece of sod that precipitates the shooting of the Russian General, "that sob of tunf [he grabs] for to claimhis, for to wollpimsolff" (FW 353). In this capacity, the Wakean letter can be read as the dream return of the soiled scrap of Titbits Philip Beaufoy confronts Bloom with in "Circe," that earlier verbal artifact put to practical use. Because low-quality literary efforts are often labeled as a figurative sort of "shit," later in the dream the image of the letter undergoes a further transformation, assuming its lowest guise: "he downadowns his pantoloogions and made a piece of first perpersonal puetry that staystale remains to be. Cleaned" (FW 509). In an imagistic inversion, the artifact is not soiled by the father but rather becomes the excremental discharge itself, the "pleasant pottery" taking shape as "perpersonal puetry."

The proliferation of textual evidence in the Wake gives the dream a decidedly paranoiac atmosphere, guilty language not simply betraying the father but also actively turned against him by his imagined detractors. The weapon that slays the patriarch is not the mistletoe that brings down the mythic Balder but rather "mistletropes" (FW 9), the aggressive and compromising language of the other. HCE is threatened by private documents and public media, the ancient punitive flood from the Bible turning into a modern downpour of scandalous textuality—"the rann that flooded the routes" (FW 580). The dream explores the dangers of living in a textual society, the slanderous potential of language in the hands (or mouths) of others making HCE uneasily suspect that "all rogues lean to rhyme" (FW 96). In Joyce's contrasting arenas of waking and night life, textual dissemination has very different functions. By the light of day, the newspapers form the city's lifeblood, either vital or attentuated, its "circulation" (to use the pun Joyce exploits in "Aeolus"), its network of communal information and misinformation that sways public opinion and determines what people come to believe as fact; in the nightworlds of "Circe" and Finnegans Wake, the newspapers pose an acute psychological threat. During Bloom's humiliating public trial, a man enters heralding the recent printing of the "Messenger of the Sacred Heart and Evening Telegraph with Saint Patrick's Day supplement. Containing the new addresses of all the cuckolds in Dublin" (U 469/383). In the Wake, immediately after the "lipoleums" have routed "Willingdone" in the opening assault on the father, carrier pigeons fly directly to the newspaper offices while other birds crow the news from on high: "Our pigeons pair are flewn for northcliffs [Northcliffe: an Irish newspaper magnate]. The three of crows have flapped it southenly, kraaking of de baccle to the kvarters of that sky" (*FW* 10–11). The washerwoman later gossip that the story has indeed hit the press—"It was put in the newses what he did, nicies and priers, the King fierceas Humphrey, with illysus distilling, exploits and all" (*FW* 196)—the physical skirmish between sons and father now transformed into a legal battle between father and king, a higher patriarchal authority. The news of the dreamer's mishap proceeds to circulate through a range of cultural media, in a fashion quite typical of the modern world. As Bernard Benstock notes, "The story of Earwicker's fall makes history and literature. It is broadcast, televised, filmed, bruited about; and every source of communication conspires against the publican in spreading the news."[9] Accordingly, the gun that threatens to shoot the father turns into a journalist's camera ("His snapper was shot in the Rumjar Journaral" [*FW* 341]) or the "*spraygun*" that bombards a television screen with electrons to produce the visual image (*FW* 349), so that HCE becomes "the most broadcussed man in Corrack-on-Sharon" (*FW* 526). These visions bespeak irrational unconscious fears of finding oneself on the front page or the nightly news in a variety of compromising positions.

Actual crimes and unconscious interdicted impulses are similar insofar as both leave in their wake traces of transgression: physical evidence (the fingerprint, the thread of clothing, the stray hair) and neurotic symptoms (inexplicable pains, nervous coughs, aphasias, amnesias). In *Finnegans Wake* the distinction collapses, the dreamer's fear of concrete evidence—his vision of himself as compromising litter and letters—constituting the major symptom of his guilt. In increasingly explicit forms, Joyce represents the way signs of all varieties—verbal, behavioral, material—inadvertently betray the self and its secrets ("You have your cup of scalding Souchong, your taper's waxen drop, your cat's paw, the clove or coffinnail you chewed or champed as you worded [the letter], your lark in clear air. So why, pray, sign anything as long as every word, letter, penstroke, paperspace is a perfect signature of its own?" [*FW* 115]). The letter may remain unsigned, but it is marked as an evidentiary advertisement of polymorphous wishes and fears—a representation in miniature of the dreamtext itself. Traditional signatures are rendered superfluous in the *Wake*, copious alternative forms of inscription always speaking in their place.

•   •   •

Joyce's fictions document the indestructible nature of desire, its relentless and insistent linguistic return. But if desire has the power to transform and distort language, language in turn has a decided influence on desire. The forms and objects of desire in Joyce's works often have a distinctly textual imprint, his characters imitating fictional models in their behavior or appropriating them for erotic fantasy.[10] The daydreams of the adolescent Stephen are shaped by nineteenth-century romance novels and the mariolatrous textuality of the church; the desires of Gerty MacDowell—his female counterpart to some extent—are determined by an odd confluence of Catholicism, sentimental fiction, and fashion magazines. Molly Bloom arranges the adulterous liaison she may well have encountered in the novels of Paul de Kock, while her husband identifies with the self-flagellated hero of Sacher-Masoch's *Venus in Furs*. The Wakean dreamer borrows myths of desire from the entire storehouse of literature and recorded history as prototypes for a spectrum of interdicted sexual impulses.

As much as Joyce's characters are manipulated by textuality, they also in turn manipulate it, language providing for them a secret source of erotic pleasure. In a culture marked by elaborate sexual prohibitions, desire is never repressed but only displaced; if it cannot be enacted, it is invariably scripted. For the four impotent old men in the Wakean dream, writing about desire provides an alternative to performing desire—in preparation they sharpen up "their penisills" (*FW* 566). Language serves as the medium that speaks and betrays desire, and as the medium that arouses it. Bloom satisfies his masochistic streak not with whips and chains but with words, schooling Martha in verbal cruelty through his unusual correspondence. Her most recent missive is only hesitatingly sadistic, but for Bloom stimulating nonetheless. Joyce's works suggest that in a society where language both mediates and delimits desire, language easily becomes the object of desire through a simple displacement, people locating erotic potential in textuality itself and employing it for seductive ends. Many of his characters read for pleasure, in every sense of the word.

In his aesthetic theory in *Portrait*, Stephen acknowledges a connection between reading and desire, although he stigmatizes it as a negative one. He maintains in his opening hypothesis that an improper piece of art can be distinguished from a genuinely aesthetic one based on the effect it has on the audience:

> You see I use the word *arrest*. I mean that the tragic emotion is static. Or rather the dramatic emotion is. The feelings excited by improper art are kinetic, desire or loathing. Desire urges us to possess, to go to something; loathing urges us to abandon, to go from something. These are kinetic emotions. The arts which excite them, pornographical or didactic, are therefore improper arts. The esthetic emotion (I use the general term) is therefore static. The mind is arrested and raised above desire and loathing. (*P* 205)

Like the Aristotelian premise it attempts to elaborate, Stephen's assumes that audience response is predictable and homogeneous. When Lynch cites as counterevidence his autographing of the backside of the

Venus of Praxiteles, Stephen dismisses it as simple perversity ("—I speak of normal natures" [P 205]). Lynch persists in countering Stephen's academic theory with wry remarks that comically critique the young aesthete's carefully affected intellectual pose ("—That's a lovely one, said Lynch, laughing again. That has the true scholastic stink" [P 214]). This mockery not only deflates the seriousness of the dialogue but also subverts Stephen's facile assumptions about the relationship between text and audience, the dry, abstract, and emotionless statements of the aesthete incongruously eliciting laughter, cynical commentary, and bawdy double-entendres. When Lynch asks for a definition of beauty, Stephen revealingly decides to discuss female beauty: "—Let us take woman, said Stephen. / —Let us take her! said Lynch fervently" (P 208). Exploiting the slippery, equivocal nature of language, the kinetic Lynch can reinterpret the most mechanical academic formula as an erotic resolution. In the process he highlights the intellectual's inadvertent betrayal of his continuing preoccupation with the opposite sex, exposing the irony of the randomly selected example. Lynch's comic reaction to Stephen's aesthetic theory is of a piece with his reaction to an aesthetic object, a classical statue. Both suggest the impossibility of predicating in advance the impact a text will have on its audience, the response it will provoke. Stephen's first supposition, in short, is undermined by the logical corollary to the intentional fallacy: a reader's potential response to a text cannot be anticipated any more surely than the author's original intent can be recuperated. Lynch as interlocutor provides a sly critique, in dramatic form, of the validity of Stephen's classical premises.

Given the potentially idiosyncratic nature of reader response, no text can be neatly labeled as "didactic" or "pornographical," or be guaranteed a safe place outside the realm of the improper arts, assured of an aesthetic reading rather than a kinetic one. Any text can excite desire, relatively innocuous or aesthetic ones as readily as those that seem more clearly pornographical, and Joyce shows this through his representation of the reading process within his fictions. Classical statues, sentimental songs and plays, reform novels, dry textbooks, asexual Victorian romances, Renaissance epics, the Bible itself—all these are as capable of eliciting kinetic affects as is a book like *Sweets of Sin*. The older artist exposes the truth that the young one ignores: that a reader can find kinetic potential in almost any text, regardless of the apparent intentions of the author.

Stephen implies that his friend's reaction to the Venus of Praxiteles is abnormal, perverse, but within the context of Joyce's fictions it is not unusual in the least. Bloom thinks of the naked statuary goddesses in the National Museum as visually attractive objects for voyeuristic men such as himself ("They don't care what man looks. All to see" [U 176/144]), and Molly's response to a statue of a male nude is even more graphically kinetic:

> that lovely little statue he bought I could look at him all day long curly head and his shoulders his finger up for you to listen theres real beauty and poetry for you I often felt I wanted to kiss him all over also his lovely young cock there so simple I wouldnt mind taking him in my mouth if nobody was looking as if it was asking you to suck it so clean and white he looks with his boyish face. . . . (*U* 775–76/638)

Joyce populates his works with characters who respond to texts sexually, who are attracted to art that makes an erotic impact. In fact, in Joyce's fictions, textuality is the major source of arousal, his characters responding, more often than not, to language rather than any immediate contact. In a questionable dissociation of the "animal" and "mental" worlds, Stephen claims that "the desire and loathing excited by improper esthetic means are really unesthetic emotions not only because they are kinetic in character but also because *they are not more than physical*. Our flesh shrinks from what it dreads and responds to the stimulus of what it desires *by a purely reflex action of the nervous system*" (*P* 206, emphasis added). But in the context of Joyce's fictions this argument is reductive, for the various kinetic responses to nude statues do entail a process of intellectual association: not at all illogically, Lynch, Bloom, and Molly mentally link marmoreal statues with warm, human flesh, recuperating the sexual origin of the cold artistic image. Joyce's characters can respond with desire to the most abstract, bland, or seemingly aesthetic of texts because of language's evocative, associative potential, because of its power to call forth what is not immediately present. Language becomes the site where the intellectual and erotic converge.

The evocative force of textual artifacts—artistic or otherwise—invalidates Stephen's classical assumptions of "*integritas*" and "stasis," the inviolable wholeness of the object and the perceptual arrest of the subject. The text's associative potential prevents it from being "luminously apprehended as selfbounded and selfcontained upon the immeasurable background of space or time which is not it" (*P* 212). Correlatively, the mind's activation of this potential makes "static" apprehension a logical impossibility. Within Joyce's fictions, "static" responses to texts, both visual and verbal, are as conspicuously absent as kinetic ones are abundant. Rather than culminating in any sort of mental arrest, reading inevitably leads to psychic activity, much of it directed by unconscious forces. Indeed, the role the unconscious plays in perceptual activity is precisely what Stephen's theory elides. As Freud repeatedly demonstrates, the mind is forever accumulating impressions and entangling them in unconscious and complex associative chains that in turn influence later thoughts. As

Stephen and Bloom read the text of Dublin on June 16, 1904, the paths their musings take are affected not only by what they see and hear but also by the contingent ideas and recollections these perceptions awaken from the reservoir of memory, their psychic lives being inherently dynamic. In *Finnegans Wake*, the associative nature of thought comes even more clearly to the fore, the dreamtext at points traveling madly down trails of similar sounding signifiers, unable to arrest the linguistic play of the unconscious mind: "Ten men, ton men, pen men, pun men, wont to rise a ladder. And den men, dun men, fen men, fun men, hen men, hun men wend to raze a leader" (*FW* 278). Rather then containing themselves in a complete, harmonious, and radiant presence, unconscious thoughts are hopelessly proliferative, with one piece of textuality relentlessly generating more: the letter in 1.5 spawns elaborate academic exegesis, the homework lesson in 2.2 is supplemented by complicated marginalia and footnotes, and the account of the father's sin in Phoenix Park in 1.2 produces a wild network of gossip, which in its turn produces a ballad.

In contrast to the image of the cold classicist that appears in chapter 5, the portraits of the younger artist emphasize his vulnerability to the kinetic potentialities of language. Despite its scientific connotations and context, the word *Foetus* has the power to evoke an image of prurient engravers, afflicted, the adolescent Stephen assumes, by the same "brutish" malady that plagues him. It awakens repressed sexual desires through its unconscious associations: "His recent monstrous reveries came thronging into his memory. They too had sprung up before him, suddenly and furiously, *out of mere words*" (*P* 90, emphasis added). Later when the director mentions "*les jupes*," a tiny flame kindles on Stephen's cheek, his recent piety being no protection against "*the names* of articles of dress worn by women or of certain soft and delicate stuffs used in their making [which] brought always to his mind a delicate and sinful perfume" (*P* 155, emphasis added). Stephen's repressive defenses against kinetic thoughts and yearnings often crumble under the impact of evocative words.

The earliest inchoate longings mentioned in the novel are kindled in Stephen, not by an actual person, but by a fictional text, a linguistic construct in the form of the heroine of *The Count of Monte Cristo* ("He returned to Mercedes and, as he brooded upon her image, a strange unrest crept into his blood" [*P* 64]). In the second chapter of *Portrait*, as Stephen's desires become stronger and more apparently erotic, this "strange unrest" undergoes a discernible transformation, becoming first a "stream of gloomy tenderness" (*P* 77) and finally "a cold and cruel loveless lust" (*P* 96). His private reveries also slowly change, his mind ultimately figures as a "den of monstrous images" (*P* 90). Initially, however, Stephen identifies with Edmond Dantès and imagines himself refusing the fruit offered by the adored Mercedes, haughtily resisting the mythic bait of the primal fall. In his second fantasy initiated by thoughts of the romance heroine, he significantly revises the scenario: Stephen envisions some sort of dreamy sexual consummation in which his "weakness and timidity and inexperience" magically evaporate (*P* 65). This consummation is glaringly absent from *The Count of Monte Cristo*—much, perhaps, to the disappointment of some readers, Stephen Dedalus apparently included. Edmond Dantès and the doomed Mercedes are eventually reconciled as friends, but never united as lovers. Stephen supplements the romance text, creating in his imagination the sexual scenario the novel evades.

When Stephen goes through his phase of obsessive piety, his textual desire simply undergoes a displacement, the young penitent finding secret pleasure in the more sensual passages of the Bible itself. His favorite religious book evokes "a faded world of fervent love" and interweaves the communicant's prayers with imagery from the canticles (The Song of Solomon). As Stephen reads it, "an inaudible voice seemed to caress the soul . . . and the soul seemed to answer with the same inaudible voice, surrendering herself: *Inter ubera mea commorabitur*" (*P* 152). The Latin phrase means "he shall lie betwixt my breasts" and supposedly provides a figure for the Church's love of Christ.[11] Stephen may well be seduced, however, by the "caress" of the literal sense, feeling his soul "surrendering" to the book, whose unconscious appeal is not difficult to understand.

Rooted in a notion of "static" apprehension that denies the force of the unconscious, the aesthetic theory of the budding classicist sounds suspiciously like a series of abstract intellectual formulas that have little to do with "the reality of experience" Stephen ultimately resolves to confront. Naremore has aptly described it as "an elaborate defense mechanism, a withdrawal from reality. . . . [Stephen] wanders the ugly, commercialized streets of the city, meditating on art in order to ward off reality";[12] I would add that the unaesthetic reality that Stephen tries to bar from consciousness is inner as well as outer. In chapter 2 he attempts "to build a breakwater of order and elegance against the sordid tide of life without him and to dam up . . . the powerful recurrence of the tides within him" (*P* 98); in chapter 5 he is still fighting against both of these "sordid" currents. Stephen's theory is a repressive response to his own decidedly kinetic responses to linguistic constructs, his assumption of aesthetic "stasis" betraying his desire to freeze the evocative force of the text, to dam up the associative currents of his own thoughts.

I suspect, in other words, that Stephen's theory is included in *Portrait* not to tell us anything profound about aesthetics but rather to tell us something about the aesthete. The "Proteus" section of *Ulysses* demonstrates even more clearly that elaborate intellectual speculations are often defensive retreats from libidinal impulses—impulses that can never be absolutely extruded, however, from abstruse mental theorizing. Stephen's recurrent contemplation of visual transparency and opacity, for instance ("Diaphane, adiaphane" [*U* 37/31]), emerges as a sort of intellectual screen for thoughts about ocular frustration and satisfaction. The sexual residue behind the highbrow speculations is made clear when the thought of "the ineluctable modality of the ineluctable visuality" leads to a recollection of the "virgin at Hodges Figgis' window" and—more specifically—to a visualization of what lies beyond the veil of her immediately visible form: "Bet she wears those curse of God stays suspenders and yellow stockings, darned with lumpy wool" (*U* 49/40). Indeed, voyeuristic curiosity informs Stephen's musings and perceptions throughout the chapter: when he sites the gypsy couple, he immediately focuses on the woman's pinned-up "skirties," a selective vision anticipated in his earlier memory of a blasphemous prayer for ocular indulgence ("You prayed to the devil in Serpentine avenue that the fubsy widow in front might lift her clothes still more from the wet street" [*U* 40/34]). Stephen emerges as the kinetic reader par excellence in his repeated sexualization of nature's "signatures"—in his interpretation of the sea as a womb, for instance, or in his transformation of the writhing weeds into exhibitionistic women "hising up their petticoats" (*U* 49/41). In "Proteus" we discover that Stephen's recent reading material is, figuratively speaking, female clothing: "Rich booty you brought back; *Le Tutu*, five tattered numbers of *Pantalon Blanc et Culotte Rouge*" (U 42/35). Stephen's speculations on the strand foreshadow the "Nausicaa" episode, where Bloom, in the same vicinity, will perform parallel kinetic readings of female semiotics (clothing in particular) and indulge voyeuristic desires in less disguised forms.

"Nausicaa" reexplores the erotic potential of religious and romance textuality represented earlier in *Portrait*: hymns from the Benediction service provide the seductive background music for sexual arousal and the sentimental dreams from romance literature lead kinetically to erotic fantasy. Gerty's musings about "that poem that appealed to her so deeply[,] . . . *Art thou real, my ideal?*" culminate in reveries with clear sexual undertones: "If she saw that magic lure in his eyes there would be no holding back for her. Love laughs at locksmiths. She would make the great sacrifice. Her every effort would be to share his thoughts" (*U* 364/298). Realizing the inappropriate turn her fantasy has taken, Gerty guiltily switches her thoughts here from sexual to emotional intimacy, as "from everything in the least indelicate her finebred nature instinctively recoiled" (*U* 364/298–99). She transforms her illicit daydream of sexual freedom into a more acceptable one of platonic love, reassuring herself that "they would be just good friends like a big brother and sister without all that other" (*U* 364/299). Her daydream then concludes with the contradictory resolution, "Come what might she would be wild, untrammelled, free" (*U* 365/299). Nurtured on romance like young Stephen Dedalus, Gerty has read "that book *The Lamplighter* by Miss Cummins"

(*U* 363/298) and attempts unsuccessfully to model herself after its exemplary and asexual heroine, Gertrude Flint.[13] Rather than inspiring purity, romance fiction only stimulates Gerty's latent eroticism, producing dreamy yearnings with decided sexual reverberations. While Bloom masturbates physically, she masturbates mentally, spinning fantasies with concupiscent undercurrents.

Popular nineteenth-century novels with didactic ends, both *The Lamplighter* and *The Count of Monte Cristo* make their moral messages palatable by using as their medium tales of adventure and romance. Not surprisingly, their fictive representations of love and desire elide the force of physical attraction, sexual gestures being limited to affectionate gazes, kissed hands, and occasional embraces. In Cummins's novel, the rare moments of more intense passion are followed by inevitable disclaimers: "The conventional rules, the enforced restrictions, which often set limits to the outbursts of natural feeling, had no existence for one so wholly the child of nature as Emily. She and Philip had loved each other in their childhood; before that childhood was fully past, they had parted; and as children they met again"[14]—Emily and Philip are, by my estimation, in their late thirties or early forties. Love in these books is inevitably founded on youthful affection, adult mutual respect, and a familial solicitude that gives several of the depicted unions muted incestuous overtones.[15] In his own works Joyce suggests that the appeal of these seemingly wholesome stories lies not so much in their relatively asexual plots and even less in their moral arguments, his characters enjoying instead the subliminally sexual feelings these fictions evoke. Not acknowledged as a presence, sensual desire is a gap in these texts, albeit clearly a provocative one. As Barthes suggests in *The Pleasure of the Text*, "Is not the most erotic portion of a body *where the garment gapes?* . . . it is intermittence, as psychoanalysis has so rightly stated, which is erotic: the intermittence of skin flashing between two articles of clothing . . . , between two edges."[16] Gerty and Stephen read romances that are characterized, figuratively speaking, by just such gaping intermittences, and as they imaginatively respond to these texts, they explore these apertures, making present what is hidden from sight. In the process they unconsciously revise the fictional artifact, so that the effect of these moral texts is radically different from their ostensible intent: attempting to suppress the sexual, the fictions only succeed in calling it forth. At the level of the unconscious, Gerty and Stephen perceive the sexual forces romance fiction elides, and in their fantasies, their private textual supplements, they provide the missing erotic elements. As readers, they make "didactic" texts "pornographical."

The potentially seductive impact of romance fiction is a well-established literary topos, available to Joyce through the works of "the divine comic Denti Alligator" (*FW* 440). In *Finnegans Wake* he pays an ironic

"I.O.U.," obliquely acknowledging his debt to the poet who damned Paolo and Francesca to hell for their kinetic response to the tale of Lancelot and Guinevere:

> Still he'd be good tutor two in his big armschair lerningstoel and she be waxen in his hands. Turning up and fingering over the most dantellising peaches in the lingerous longerous book of the dark. Look at this passage about Galilleotto! I know it is difficult but when your goche I go dead. Turn now to this patch upon Smacchiavelluti! Soot allours, he's sure to spot it! 'Twas ever so in monitorology since Headmaster Adam became Eva Harte's toucher, *in omnibus moribus et temporibus*, with man's mischief in his mind whilst her pupils swimmed too heavenlies, let his be exaspirated, letters be blowed! I is a femaline person. O, of provocative gender. U unisingular case. (*FW* 251)

A Dante scholar has recently exposed the hidden irony of Paolo and Francesca's textual arousal in canto 5 of *The Inferno*: the rendering of the legend they were reading before they submitted to "Galilleotto," the book as pander, was apparently a didactic condemnation of chivalric values, a moralistic version of the Arthurian tale composed for religious ends.[17] Paolo and Francesca's tragic misreading of their text is comically reduplicated in the above scenario—but here the reader is misinterpreting *The Inferno* itself, "the lingerous longerous book of the dark." The "good tutor" is clearly not interested in the epic's religious didacticism but is enjoying instead its extensive catalogue of evil temptations, its "most dantellising peaches," among which lies, of course, the sin of textual stimulation. In the hands of the lascivious teacher/toucher, Dante's text of moral instruction becomes a tool of sexual seduction. "Headmaster Adam" in this context probably refers to Milton's version of the Edenic forefather in *Paradise Lost*: educating Eve, he "would intermix / Grateful digressions, and solve high dispute / With conjugal Caresses, from his Lips / Not Words alone pleas'd her."[18] Consciously perverse, the Wakean instructor has "man's mischief in his mind whilst her pupils swimmed too heavenlies"—like the pilgrim in *The Inferno*, the student has apparently swooned after hearing "this passage about Galilleotto." Joyce adds another link to the chain of kinetic responses to narrative: the tale of Lancelot and Guinevere excites Paolo and Francesca, whose tale in turn moves Dante as pilgrim, whose tale effectively seduces the *Wake*'s "femaline" pupil, "waxen" in the hands of her "toucher."

"*Head*master Adam" seduces "Eva *Harte*" because of the inherent multivalence of language, the multivalence that allows fiction to be "misread," responded to reflexively, with no conscious consideration of the apparent aims of the author. But Joyce's irony is targeted not only at the kinetic readers who, wittingly or unwittingly, appropriate "innocuous" texts for seductive ends, but also at the authors who write these books, "the divine comic Denti Alligator" irreverently included. In his parody of the Paolo and Francesca scene, Joyce hints that the act of writing (as well as reading) about sin—even if only to condemn it—necessarily involves a sort of prurience, just as the transformation of the sexual into purely romantic or spiritual passion necessarily involves a knowledge of the very forces it denies. The writers of romantic or didactic fiction are partially blind to the impetus behind their art, like the young poet of *Portrait* who writes a dreamy ethereal villanelle inspired by an explicitly sexual fantasy. Early in his career, when a printer refused to print "Two Gallants," Joyce articulated his attitude toward politely sanitized literature in a caustic letter to Grant Richards:

> Is it the small gold coin . . . or the code of honour which the two gallants live by which shocks [the printer]? I see nothing which should shock him in either of these things. His idea of gallantry has grown up in him (probably) during the reading of the novels of the elder Dumas [author of *The Count of Monte Cristo*] and during the performance of romantic plays which presented to him cavaliers and ladies in full dress. But I am sure he is willing to modify his fantastic views. (*Letters* 2:132–33)

In his fictions Joyce stresses that repressive art is not only unrealistic or "fantastic" but also never as innocent as it pretends to be. In *Ulysses* Molly sounds unimpressed by *Ruby: the Pride of the Ring*, preferring texts with less disguised kinetic possibilities—the book turns out to be a moralistic reform novel about the atrocities of circus life.[19] Catching a glimpse of one of the illustrations of the sadistic circus master at work, Bloom thinks to himself, "Cruelty behind it all. Doped animals. Trapeze at Hengler's. Had to look the other way" (*U* 64/52–53). Despite this humane waking response to the picture, *Ruby* later provides graphic material for Bloom's masochistic fantasies in "Circe," didactic art once again turning pornographical. The unconscious responds quite differently than the waking mind does to various texts, invariably locating their repressed or perverse side.

• • •

The erotic possibilities of seemingly innocent texts are shown at their wildest extreme in the homework chapter of *Finnegans Wake*, where Joyce explores the associative potential of academic subjects, the potential that makes dry lessons highly kinetic. A wonderful piece of imitative form, 2.2 takes the shape of an annotated text, as if the thought of three children doing their lessons—perhaps scribbling in the margins of their books—produced a dreamtext that resembles a book marginally glossed by three youngsters. The three sets of marginalia each have a distinctive

tone and typeface to suggest three different individuals with three different handwritings. The chapter resembles one of those diverting library
books one occasionally finds, in which several previous readers have
taken the liberty of leaving their mark in the margin, of randomly jotting
down their opinions, impressions, and associations, regardless of how
personal or idiosyncratic. Shari Benstock writes, "the text [of 2.2] looks
very much like its scholastic counterpart, a monastic text with surrounding marginalia";[20] closer inspection reveals that the "scholarly" annotations bear a more marked resemblance to marginal graffiti with their tenuous and puzzling links to the material they comment upon. As Benstock
herself emphasizes, the associative supplements to the text seem governed
by a private logic, so that the reader is left with the often difficult task of
figuring out the connection between the notes and the text that has supposedly inspired them.

The chapter's form and content are structurally interconnected, for just
as the notes supplement the text proper, the children within that text
supplement the materials they study during their lessons. Much of the
marginalia in 2.2 is highly suggestive or blatantly sexual, particularly the
glosses that bear the signature of Issy or Shem, although the more abstract
and philosophical inscriptions attributed to Shaun have some provocative overtones as well ("PREAUSTERIC MAN AND HIS PURSUIT OF PANHYSTERIC
WOMAN" [FW 266]). The textual supplements within the text are analogously prurient, the children being kinetic readers par excellence, finding
their materials rife with erotic possibilities. The chapter shows the repressed underside of school lessons, revealing what might unconsciously
float through young students' minds as they read their books, their
thoughts secretly flying off on more interesting tangents.

Joyce gives us a brief waking version of this mental digressiveness in
his earlier fictions, when young Stephen sits in the classroom fantasizing
about the mysterious sin committed by the older boys at Clongowes.
Later in Portrait, the science teacher's offhand remark about "ellipsoidal
balls" provokes a ribald quip from Moynihan which in turn triggers in
Stephen's mind a vivid fantasy of a "sabbath of misrule" in which the
professors and priests themselves participate (P 192). This kinetic daydream appears, ironically enough, immediately before the young aesthete
delivers his theory of perceptual stasis. On the other side of the podium in
the "Nestor" episode, Stephen asks a student about Pyrrhus and receives
as a reply, "Pyrrhus, sir? Pyrrhus, a pier. . . . A thing out in the water. A
kind of a bridge. Kingstown pier, sir" (U 24/20). Through free association, the young scholar moves easily from ancient Tarentum to contemporary Dublin, from a remote and dusty historical incident to a local spot
for romantic trysts, certainly a more interesting topic for consideration.
Stephen's vision of youthful prurience as innate rather than acquired

("They knew: had never learned nor ever been innocent" [*U* 24–25/20–21]) returns in the inherent sexual precocity of the young students in the *Wake*.

The subjects the children study in the dream are allocated along sexually stereotypical lines, the boys learning history, geography, and mathematics, the girl sitting on the sidelines and acquiring more domestic skills: "Soon jemmijohns will cudgel about some a rhythmatick or other over Browne and Nolan's divisional tables whereas she, of minions' novence charily being cupid . . . will sit and knit on solfa sofa" (*FW* 268). Issy's few homework assignments are in the conventionally "female" domains of letter writing, penmanship, and English grammar. Traditional grammar lessons teach students about clausal conjunction and subordination, the correct hierarchical ordering of the parts of a sentence; but because they may also address the subject of verbal gender ("mascarine, phelinine or nuder" [*FW* 268]), Issy's text in 2.2 is transmogrified into a manual on the conjunction of men and women, on sexual rather than grammatical hierarchies and interrelationships. Chattily informal and highly ungrammatical, "gramma's grammar" is full of worldly wisdom on love and sex: it counsels alternately sexual deference, female submission ("mind your genderous towards his reflexives, such that I was to your grappa . . . when him was me hedon" [*FW* 268]); wary discrimination ("It's a wild's kitten, my dear, who can tell a wilkling from a warthog" [*FW* 269]); and practical attention to pecuniary concerns ("Lumpsome is who lumpsum pays" [*FW* 270]). Rather than finding in her primer any information about the rules of syntax, the young student reads instead a spate of pragmatic guidelines for attracting and selecting a suitable mate.

The twins' lesson in ancient civilizations is equally diverting and provocative: they have "conned the cones and meditated the mured and pondered the pensils and ogled the olymp and delighted in her dianaphous and cacchinated behind his culosses, [then find themselves] before a mosoleum" (*FW* 261). The Seven Wonders of the Ancient World are visible enough in this lesson, but so too is the sin in the park, or rather the version of it in which the young boys watch the father watching the tempting girls. The "pensils" refer to both the Hanging (or pensile) Gardens of Babylon and the Lighthouse at Alexandria, but the pensil-like Wellington monument in Phoenix Park is another phallic marker, doubling as the erect penis of the titillated father. Her "dianaphous" alludes to the Temple of Diana or to the temptresses' conveniently diaphanous apparel—perhaps "transparent stockings" (*U* 372/304–5) like those worn by the provocative Gerty ("dianaphous" also links back to "diaphane, adiaphane" [*U* 37/31], Stephen's intellectual speculations about visual transparency and opacity that mask essentially voyeuristic impulses). The "mured" and the "mosoleum" may be the Walls of Babylon and the

Mausoleum at Halicarnassus—or the Magazine Wall and the ancient burial grounds in Phoenix Park, the edifice from which the erring father falls (in the guise of Humpty Dumpty) and the grave in which he lands. Like the students in "Nestor," the ones in the *Wake* can always find in ancient history lessons something of a more personal interest, in this case paternal transgression. Whether reading about the Wonders of the Ancient World or spying on the father ("the olymp") in the park, the boys respond to their text with voyeuristic ogling and mocking laughter.

The increasingly kinetic progression of verbs in the the the passage ("conned . . . meditated . . . pondered . . . ogled . . . delighted . . . cacchinated") foreshadows the homework chapter's general movement. Rather than becoming bored with their studies, the twins find them more and more interesting, gradually discerning the sexual wisdom inscribed in even the most theoretical of texts. In *Portrait* Stephen naively assumes that a geometrical figure cannot excite desire, trigger kinetic impulses: "You would not write your name in pencil across the hypothenuse of a rightangled triangle. / —No, said Lynch, give me the hypothenuse of the Venus of Praxiteles" (*P* 208). In the Wakean night lesson, this highbrow assumption is comically critiqued when the young students find erotic significance not in a statue, a mimetic representation of the nude female form, but in abstract triangles themselves, interpreted in dream as stark metaphors for components of the female sexual anatomy.

The geometrical figure Dolph/Shem sketches for the benefit of Kev/ Shaun resembles the diagram for Euclid's first proposition or a mystical figure from Yeats's *A Vision*.[21] Enamored of the mother it figures forth, the young boys and their "triagonal delta" (*FW* 297) may also constitute a dream version of "Dante and the isosceles triangle miss Portinari he fell in love with" (*U* 637/521)—Stephen's rambling assessment of the poet in "Eumaeus."[22] But the twins, of course, also read the figure more kinetically, the circles becoming the mother's buttocks, the two triangles her vagina and uterus, the point "P" her vaginal opening which they confuse with her urinary and rectal ones. To designate this aperture, the text, like the nightletter, has been poked with a sharp instrument, here either the boys' compass or the father's penis ("Hear where the bolgylines, Yseen here the puncture. So he done it. Luck!" [*FW* 299]). Structurally similar to the ALP chapter (1.8) and to some reports of the sin in the park, the homework chapter has the father oriented toward the female (here the mother as opposed to the daughter) and the sons oriented toward both of them, secretly watching: "Elpis, thou fountain of the greeces, all shall speer theeward, from kongen in his canteenhus to knivers hind the knoll" (*FW* 267, footnote omitted). The sons will use the daughter to confirm the discoveries about female anatomy they make in the course of watching "Elpis" and her "kongen," later sneaking a glimpse at Issy while she urinates, after the fashion of the sexually curious children discussed by

Freud: "Whence followeup with endspeaking nots for yestures, plutonically pursuant on briefest glimpse from gladrags, pretty Proserpronette whose slit satchel spilleth peas" (FW 267).

In his exploration of various sexual theories of children, Freud argues that the male child often initially refuses to believe that his mother or sister does not have a penis, against all evidence to the contrary, as a result of his own fear of castration. This denial of anatomical difference works to prevent the curious child from figuring out the origins of human life. A second and related obstacle, Freud claims, is the child's ignorance of the womb and vagina, internal organs naturally difficult for the young speculator to imagine on his own.[23] During the Wakean nightlesson, the male twins overcome these hermeneutical problems, realizing the crucial difference between "The haves and the havenots: a distinction" (FW 295): this is a nicely equivocal phrase in the context of young boys learning to differentiate anatomically between the genders, for their discovery in 2.2 is that the phallusless woman does have a "whome." As Dolph adds the final triangle to his geometrical diagram, he articulates for his brother a theory of origins that resonates of one mentioned by Freud: "Alow me align while I encloud especious! The Nike done it. Like pah, I peh. Innate little bondery. And as plane as a poke stiff. Now, aqua in buccat. I'll make you to see figuratleavely the whome of your eternal geomater" (FW 296–97, footnotes omitted). Freud claims that one of the commonest and least misguided sexual theories produced by children is that "'the man urinates into the woman's chamber.'"[24] The various elements in Dolph's explication suggest that he has formulated this very hypothesis. He suspects that the man puts his "poke stiff" into the enclosed space within the female, the "innate little bondery," and then urinates so that the end result is "aqua in buccat."

Dolph has to educate his twin "figuratleavely" because the womb is unfamiliar, a component of the sexual other: he can approach the object only through indirections, through texts and analogies, like little Hans figuring it forth through vans, buses, and carts carrying freight.[25] Dolph's metaphors are more graphic, as he aims to convey the texture of the womb in addition to its structure. Trying to make his slower counterpart "vicewise," he gives him a series of instructions that evoke a dual-layered image of children at once learning their geometry and geography lessons and playing in the kitchen (see FW 286–87). Relying first on a cooking metaphor, Dolph tells Kev to "mull"—contemplate or heat up—"a mugful of mud," which the female footnote glosses as a reference to hot chocolate. The interpretation is characteristically precocious, and one step ahead of the text to which it is keyed, for it implies that the secret of sexual origins involves a mixing of substances, an integration similar to the process of "a spoon fist of sugans" dissolving in "a sotspots of choucolout." The marginal comment appended to the instructions that refers to "*The aliments of jumeantry*" suggests that the male annotator can imagine conception and birth only in terms of digestion and excretion: it conflates Euclid's *Elements of Geometry* with the alimentary canal of the young boys (*jumeau*: twins in French). The imagery of the instructions is pervaded with cloacal substances—pudding, puddles, bogs, mud, and goo. Like little Hans, Dolph produces an excremental version of the origins of human life. His metaphors are constrained by his male perspective—he is familiar with only male anatomy—and the compasses and coastal maps he calls on to supplement his figuration of the female reproductive system do not really bring him any closer to the mysterious "whome." Unequivocally male, Dolph's understanding of female anatomy is necessarily textual, figurative, or—if opportunity presents itself—voyeuristic.

In the final stages of his explication, Dolph appears to lift up the mother's skirt in order to confirm, for his brother's benefit, the actuality of the "redneck" leading up to the hidden "whome." The murky language of the dream, however, works against any such certainty:

> we carefully, if she pleats, lift by her seam hem and jabote at the spidsiest of her trickkikant (like thousands done before since fillies calpered. Ocone! Ocone!) the maidsapron of our A.L.P., fearfully! till its nether nadir is vortically where (allow me aright to two cute winkles) its naval's napex will have to beandbe. You must proach near mear for at is dark. Lob. And light your mech. Jeldy! And this is what you'll say. Waaaaaa. Tch! Sluice! Pla! And their, redneck. . . . (*FW* 297, footnote omitted)

The description of the supposed unveiling of ALP still contains all the geometrical terms used in her prior figurations (*trickkikant*: triangle in Danish, *winkles*: angles in German, Ocone, nadir, vortically, napex): it is possible that Dolph is simply altering his diagram. But regardless of whether the boys are examining the geometrical figure or the mother's body itself, the female still remains a text, the male twins her readers. They are simultaneously interpreters and voyeurs and, as such, remain at a distance from the object they seek to understand. Their observational viewpoint is betrayed in their surprised response to their investigations: "this is what you'll say [or see]. Waaaaaa. Tch! [watch]."

The male interest here in seeing the female genitalia may be the return of a lost moment from the very opening of *Portrait*, the dream recovery of that textually repressed misdeed that provokes the threat of punitive blindness ("the eagles will come and pull out his eyes" [*P* 8]). The academic context of this interest in 2.2 also links it to a slightly later moment in *Portrait*, that point when Stephen, immediately before a math lesson no less ("It was the hour for sums"), daydreams of going home to his mother and remembers in a fetishistic displacement "her feet on the fender and her jewelly slippers [that] were so hot and . . . had such a lovely warm smell!" This thought recalls, in turn, Dante's geography lesson about "the Mozambique Channel" and "the longest river in America" (*P* 11–12): in 2.2 mathematics are conflated with geographical mappings of rivers to produce a screen memory for infantile investigations of the female sexual terrain. The naughty boy of the homework chapter—"Dolph, dean of idlers, . . . retelling humself by the math hour . . . a reel of funnish ficts apout the shee" (*FW* 287–88)—can be read as a dream vision of young Stephen, likewise branded as an academic idler ("—Lazy idle little loafer! cried the prefect of studies" [*P* 50]). Stephen's schoolday fantasy of the home returns in the night lesson as a vision of the "whome," a common uncanny site in male dreams, Freud argues, at once strange and familiar.[26]

The ultimate focus of the children's studies being both of the parents ("Art, literature, politics, economy, chemistry, humanity" [*FW* 306]), the homework lesson culminates in a primal scene. The curious children, fascinated with the origins of life, are envisioned witnessing an act of intercourse, their "vectorious readyeyes" fixed on "those fickers which are returnally reprodictive of themselves" (*FW* 298). This climax is adumbrated early in the chapter when the children ascend to "the clarience of the childlight in the studiorium upsturts. Here we'll dwell on homiest powers, love at the latch with novices nig and nag" (*FW* 266). Jealous of the father's prerogative, the studious upstarts climb to the upstairs study to learn about the secrets of the parent's bedroom, that homey bower, through thinking about mathematical powers, exponential increase. They are apparently willing to peek through the keyhole to confirm their speculations. Margot Norris suggests that the practical educational benefits inherent in watching "love at the latch" are the twins' primary concern: "it is not the erotic but rather the procreative aspect of parental copulation that intrigues the Earwicker children"—they want to learn to become "fickers" themselves so that they can replace the phallic father and occupy the position of power.[27] But the economy of oedipal impulses serves the libido as well as the ego: the desire to supplant the father is motivated in part by the desire to possess the mother, by an impulse that Stephen would categorize as "pornographical." Indeed, the primal scene in 2.2 is an unambiguously kinetic text, as the twins' response to their seemingly miraculous lesson makes clear: "My Lourde! My Lourde! If that aint just the beatenest lay I ever see! And a superpbosition! Quoint a quincidence!" (*FW* 299). This primal scene gives credence to the eugenic theory of beauty Stephen cursorily dismisses in *Portrait*—the theory that "tells you that you admired the great flanks of Venus because you felt that she would bear you burly offspring and admired her great breasts because you felt that she would give good milk to her children and yours" (*P* 209). The eugenic theory has residual oedipal overtones: it implies that sexual longing is tied to desires for procreative power and subsequent generational continuance, all of which are at work in "the apprehension of [that] which pleases" (*P* 207). The voyeuristic young students in 2.2 may not salivate over the sexual scenario in the way the old men will in 2.4; nevertheless, their egotistical wish to be the powerful and potent father, to occupy his "superpbosition," is inseparable from their erotic feelings for the adored mother, "appia lippia pluvaville . . . first of all usquiluteral threeingles . . . the constant of fluxion, Mahamewetma, pride of the province" (*FW* 297).

During the primal scene, as during the exploration of the mother, it is unclear what the twins are looking at, which "text" they are reading, given the dual meaning of the word "fickers" (*FW* 298): are they actually watching "fuckers," witnessing a parental copulation, or simply envisioning the act through "figures," solving the mystery of human origins by imaginatively supplementing their abstract and theoretical mathematics text? The ambiguity remains irresolvable and works to stress the fact that the initial sexual experience is vicarious, observational. Children may start to piece together the facts of life through an actual primal scene, like Freud's Wolf Man; through fantasy and speculation, like little Hans; and through reading books that precipitate sexual stirrings, books that may be unequivocally dry, like the mathematics text of 2.2, or more suggestive, like the romances read by the young Stephen Dedalus. In Joyce's view, clearly influenced by Freud's, the ultimate source of children's sexual knowledge remains at once overdetermined and indeterminate, a variable conflation of experience, imagination, and ingested textuality, all brought to the service of an inherent interest in the taboo.

. . .

The ambiguous site of the primal scene—simultaneously the twins' speculative minds, the keyhole to the parents' bedroom, and the schoolroom text—suggests that the fantasist, the voyeur, and the reader are of imagination all compact. A hint of a connection between the three positions of vicarious pleasure appears as early as *Dubliners*, where the young boy in "Araby" reads a romantic novel by Sir Walter Scott, surreptitiously watches Mangan's sister (the girl he envisions as a romance heroine), and daydreams about her in the gloomy upstairs rooms. *Ulysses* explores the potentially masochistic pleasure of such vicarious sexual pursuits. The adulterous scenario Bloom randomly opens to in *Sweets of Sin* reminds him of the imminent tryst between Molly and Boylan. Scanning the book, he experiences a kinetic arousal, a perverse thrill, akin to the pleasure he derives from envisioning or watching his own cuckolding: Bloom's gratified perusal of the pulp novel in "Wandering Rocks" anticipates the imago of him peeking through the keyhole at the frolicking pair in "Circe."

In *Finnegans Wake* the structural analogy returns in more explicit form: in the Tristan and Iseult chapter, as in the homework lesson, reading, fantasizing, and peeping are hopelessly intertwined, conceived of as ultimately indistinguishable activities. Undergoing protean permutations linked by the observational point of view, the narrators in 2.4 appear as jealous voyeurs, scholarly textual exegetes, and nostalgic consumers of romance fiction. The geriatric four are alternately King Mark's barons spying on Tristan and Iseult's shipboard consummation; the various sea fowl hovering over the boat, watching the couple from a bird's-eye view; "foremasters in the rolls" (*FW* 385), the voyeuristic masts of the loveboat crossing the rolling sea (analogous to the voyeuristic bedposts of the marriage bed in 3.4); or Masters of the Rolls, aimlessly commenting on the records of the past, the official documents they are responsible for ("their role was to rule the round roll that Rollo and Rullo rolled round" [*FW* 389]). The chapter's numerous allusions to the sentimental plays of Dion Boucicault suggest that the four comprise a voyeuristic audience at a yearly revival ("the dear dear annual" [*FW* 384]) of *The Colleen Bawn* or *Arrah-na-Pogue*. They also apparently enjoy perusing sentimental fiction in bed, at an appropriately senile pace ("a letter or two every night, before going to dodo sleep atrance, with their catkin coifs, in the twilight, a capitaletter" [*FW* 397]), making it difficult to tell whether the old snoopers are spying on the young lovers, watching them on stage, reading about them in a book, or simply fantasizing about them. The four are "going to boat with the verges of the chaptel" (*FW* 395): they may be on the loveship watching the virgin of the chapel, Iseult the "maidenna" from Chapelizod, or they may have simply gone to bed with the romance—the verses of the chapter—and started to dream about its lovely heroine after compulsively dozing off during its love scene, like "narcolepts on the lakes of Coma" (*FW* 395). If they had their choice, these nostalgic old lechers would probably opt for virgins over verses as bedtime company, but having lost their virility and lapsed into sexual androgyny, the "four dear old heladies" (*FW* 386) are doomed to wishful thoughts rather than action, as the closing allusion to *Hamlet* emphasizes ("Their lot is cast. So, to john for a john, johnajeams, led it be!" [*FW* 399]). The impotent four must be satisfied necessarily with textual sweethearts, virgins composed from verses. On one level, they are the dream return of the old man in "An Encounter" who finds erotic pleasure in the textualized female, in mere discourse about young women. They have inherited his "pair of green eyes" (*FW* 395) and imitate the compulsive circles of his thinking and speech in the repetitive rounds of their combined narratives.

One of the central sources for 2.4 is Joseph Bédier's *The Romance of Tristan and Iseult*, a book Joyce explicitly recommended to Harriet Shaw Weaver while she was reading *Work in Progress* (*Letters* 1:241). Bédier's

tale is a composite and popularized rendering of the classic myth of triangular desire, but it is still tactful and unexplicit compared with what appears in the nightworld of the dream. Although less evasive than the romances read by Gerty and Stephen, Bédier's *Tristan and Iseult* leaves the
lovers' sexual consummation to the reader's imagination, true to both its
sources and the standards of popular nineteenth-century fiction. The
chapter entitled "The Philtre" ends with the obligatory but cursory remark, "And as evening fell, upon the bark that heeled and ran to King
Mark's land, they gave themselves up utterly to love."[28] In constructing
the *Wake*, Joyce elaborated the scene—or rather the one that is missing:
the four jealously watch the young Tristan "kiddling and cuddling and
bunnyhugging scrumptious his colleen bawn and dinkum belle . . . with
his sinister dexterity, light and rufthandling, vicemversem her ragbags et
assaucyetiams . . . palpably wrong and bulbubly improper, and cuddling
her and kissing her, tootyfay charmaunt, in her ensemble of maidenna
blue" (*FW* 384). All that appears of the romantic tale in 2.4 are its erotic
moments—the rest of the plot has dropped from sight. Joyce represents
the dreamer subjecting the myth to a sort of censorship in reverse, cutting
out the acceptable, elaborating the illicit, supplementing the story with
erotic fantasy.

Similarly kinetic revisions are performed on most of the *Wake*'s literary sources: the higher the original's pretensions are to innocent sentimentality, the perverser the transmogrification in the dream. The scene,
for example, in which Boucicault's Arrah-na-Pogue slips her brother a
secret missive in a kiss to help him escape from prison is reproduced in
reverse (male kisses female) and conflated with a rugby skirmish to produce the following effect: "with ripy lepes to ropy lopes . . . as quick, is
greased pigskin, Amoricas Champius, with one aragan throust, druve the
massive of virilvigtoury flshpst the both lines of forwards (Eburnea's
down, boys!) rightjingbangshot into the goal of her gullet" (*FW* 395–96).
Activating the obvious sexual potential of the "innocent" scenario, the
dreamer transforms the pragmatic exchange into a lurid french kiss or,
perhaps, coercive oral sex.

Looking on with "their mouths making water" (*FW* 386), the Four
read/watch/imagine the young lovers' rendezvous with graphically kinetic pleasure, but they seem to have trouble concentrating on it for any
significant length of time. As Michael Begnal observes, "strangely enough
it often seems that they are not always overtly interested in the romantic
proceedings. Though Luke may emerge with 'his kingly leer' . . . , for the
most part Mamalujo are relatively uninvolved in the shipboard drama,
and would rather think about their own times gone by."[29] Begnal's per-
plexity may be well-founded, but he misrepresents the relationship between "the shipboard drama" and the Four's "own times gone by": on

one level, the romance is the past of the old men, a sentimental vision of their own lost erotic vigor, a happy memory of the sexual triumphs of youth. This text of youthful erotic conquest is powerfully evocative, enabling the old men to relive their sexual prime while simultaneously calling forth a flood of related thoughts that divert them from their vicarious enjoyment of the sexual scenario. While the zany textual supplements of the children in 2.2 are full of erotic anticipation, recurrently pointing straight at the sexual possibilities of the lesson, the dull commentary of the Four is retrogressive and digressive, leading them away from the titillating text they strain their enfeebled ears and eyes to investigate. These nostalgic reminiscences become a self-generated Sirens' song, a self-seducing melody that celebrates former glories. Sentimental drama, music, and fiction in this section serve as the equivalent to the Sirens' song in popular textuality, as artifacts that provide pleasurable substitutes for experience itself.

In Joyce's fictions, the text becomes a fetish, an erotic substitute for sex, providing anticipatory thrills for the young, a refuge during the potential frustrations of middle age, and a nostalgic solace for the aged. During the lecture on the letter in 1.5, the fetishistic status of textuality is comically patent: the exegete compares the document's "quite everyday-looking stamped addressed envelope" to "the civil or military clothing of whatever passionpallid nudity or plaguepurple nakedness may happen to tuck itself under its flap" (FW 109). He dwells longingly on "the enveloping facts," arguing that they are central to an understanding of the document's "sound sense." Ignoring the envelope, the "clothing" of the letter, is like mentally undressing a woman upon initial introduction, like envisioning her

> plump and plain in her natural altogether, preferring to close [one's] blinkhard's eyes to the ethiquethical fact that she was, after all, wearing for the space of the time being some definite articles of evolutionary clothing, inharmonious creations, a captious critic might describe them as, or not strictly necessary or a trifle irritating here and there, but for all that suddenly full of local colour and personal perfume and suggestive, too, of so very much more and capable of being stretched, filled out, if need or wish were, of having their surprisingly like coincidental parts separated don't they now, for better survey by the deft hand of an expert, don't you know? (FW 109)

The prurient academician takes an obsessive fetishistic delight in his document's "outer husk," thinking of it as a piece of feminine attire, probably a pair of drawers, "full of local colour and personal perfume." His final "don't you know" echoes the verbal tick of Mr. Best from Ulysses, one of the bachelor librarians whom Stephen imagines fondling a misogynistic play, toying with it in a masturbatory way: "Unwed, unfancied, ware of wiles, they fingerponder nightly each his variorum edition of *The Taming of the Shrew*" (*U* 213/175). In the *Wake* the pleasure of the text becomes even more literal. An erotic object in and of itself, the text does not even have to be opened and read in order for it to be enjoyed.

The lecturer's confusion of clothing and textuality is not unlogical, personal attire creating a visual language in iself, providing another sort of semiotic fetish if properly arranged. Bloom is repulsed by the sloppily dressed Lizzie Twigg ("Her stockings are loose over her ankles. I detest that: so tasteless" [*U* 166/136]), excited by the nattily attired Gerty. Fetishism, in Bloom's case, has its roots in a necessary substitution of the cathected metonymic sign for the desired body or, in a double displacement, a substitution of the sign of the sign for the flesh itself: he claims that as a youth he could be aroused by "even *a pricelist* of [ladies'] hosiery" (*U* 548/447, emphasis added). This adolescent fetishism evolves into an active preference for the sign over the body, for text over sex, Bloom finding greater pleasure in garters, drawers, and petticoats than in straightforward nudity, which becomes in a sense a blank page; similarly, he opts for Martha's letters over a direct meeting with the woman herself. His unusual correspondence economically serves his voyeuristic and masochistic proclivities as well as his decidedly fetishistic tastes.

Through their clothing, many of Joyce's characters turn themselves into erotic texts, texts to engage sexual interest, texts to be read and enjoyed. Molly has spent "hours dressing and perfuming and combing" (*U* 742/611) in preparation for her afternoon tryst, and Boylan has carefully bedecked himself too, as Bloom has noticed after crossing his path three times earlier in the day: "Put them all on to take them all off. Molly. Why I bought her the violet garters. Us too: the tie he wore, his lovely socks and turnedup trousers" (*U* 368/302). Boylan's outfit has had its effect, impressing Molly visually and convincing her of his wealth ("lovely stuff in that blue suit he had on and stylish tie and socks with the skyblue silk things on them hes certainly welloff I know by the cut his clothes have and his heavy watch" [*U* 749/617]). She hopes that the liaison will expand her repertoire of seductive apparel, fantasizing about being bought a kimono, chemises, drawers, and corsets by her well-to-do lover. Mary Reynolds has discussed the connection between the musical tryst of Molly and Boylan and the textual seduction of Paolo and Francesca, pointing out that the sheet music for "Love's Old Sweet Song" Bloom finds on the piano becomes the equivalent of Francesca's seductive book.[30] Details elsewhere in the novel hint that the erotic textuality is also the carefully dressed pair of lovers themselves, garbed to seduce the eye.

Clothing and aromas serve as silent semiologies that in Joyce's fictions frequently announce sexual desires. Like Molly and Boylan, Gerty has dressed herself with extra care on June 16, "for she felt that there was just a might that he might be out" (*U* 350/287), her apparel and perfume constituting a mute appeal to the sexual other to be noticed. Bloom envisions her as an enticing female flower ("But it's the evening influence. They feel all that. Open like flowers, know their hours" [*U* 376/308]), and she will indeed return in the *Wake* as one of the floral temptresses, her silent but suggestive scent transformed into an actual voice: "And still nowanights and by nights of yore do all bold floras of the field to their shyfaun lovers say only: Cull me ere I wilt to thee!: and, but a little later: Pluck me whilst I blush!" (*FW* 15). The temptress's semiotic appeals to the other, evasively mute in waking reality, are rewarded not by a chance encounter with Reggy Wylie, but by the correspondingly silent attention of Bloom. His kinetic reading of her fashionable accouterments is followed by a more rational recognition of the unfulfilled sexual desires behind them: "Dressed up to the nines for somebody. . . . Out on spec probably" (*U* 368–69/302). As Bloom sees them, the linguistic supplements of provocative clothing duplicate artificially the physical supplements grown by mature animals ready to mate ("Dress they look at. Always know a fellow courting: collars and cuffs. Well cocks and lions do the same and stags" [*U* 369/302]). Perfumes, soaps, and lotions—and the body odors they attempt to hide—become the counterpart to the smells animals emit in estrus and use to identify each other:

> Know her smell in a thousand. Bathwater too. Reminds me of strawberries and cream. Wonder where it is really. There or the armpits or under the neck. Because you get it out of all holes and corners. Hyacinth perfume made of oil of ether or something. Muskrat. Bag under their tails. One grain pour off odour for years. Dogs at each other behind. Good evening. Evening. How do you sniff? Hm. Hm. Very well, thank you. Animals go by that. Yes now, look at it that way. We're the same. (*U* 375/307)

Bloom recognizes the finery and scents people put on to attract the attention of others as the cultural equivalent to the silent semiologies in nature that advertise sexuality. Analytic and pseudoscientific, his anatomy of desire demystifies it, perhaps in order to give the psychically disturbing attraction between Molly and Boylan a rational, comprehensible, and merely physical explanation.

Bloom's dissection of sexual semiologies returns in the ALP chapter (1.8) to expose the repressions and evasions built into his rational approach to desire. This section of the *Wake* contains a clear cluster of allusions to "Nausicaa": the seaside locale, the chiming of church bells, the descent of evening, blurring vision, optical illusions, the emergence of bats, and the chore of doing laundry, central to "Nausicaa"'s Homeric source.[31] The ALP chapter can be read as a nightmarish return of Bloom's twilight musings on Sandymount strand: a dream recognition that the scents and garments functioning as advertisements of desire can also create an evidentiary language of transgression. The laundresses notice in the female apparel they examine, not the holy scents of the incense from "Nausicaa"'s background Benediction service, but rather the perfumes and body odors that bespeak sexuality: "That's not the vesdre benediction smell. I can tell from here by their *eau de Colo* and the scent of her oder they're Mrs Magrath's. And you ought to have aird them. They've moist come off her. Creases in silk they are, not crampton lawn. Baptiste me, father, for she has sinned!" (*FW* 204). The compromising signifiers of male desire that Bloom fails even to think about—the probable stains on his shirttails after his masturbation—are foregrounded in dream and examined with prurient glee: "Look at the shirt of him! Look at the dirt of it! He has all my water black on me!" (*FW* 196). As they wash away the sins of the world, the laundresses simultaneously record and expose them in their gossip. The ALP chapter becomes, in a sense, "Nausicaa" in inverted form: the silent olfactory and visual semiologies are turned into audible speech; the private longings they signify are subjected to public discussion by intrusive and critical others; and the pseudoscientific speculations about the multiple discourses of desire are replaced by paranoiac visions of the multiple discourses of incrimination.

Clothing is cathected with anxiety throughout the dream because it often functions as the mask that hides identity but betrays desire, as the covering that reveals as much as it conceals. HCE dons costumes that articulate the secret longings of both the ego and the libido: "That's him wiv his wig on, . . . that's our grainpopaw, Mister Beardall, an accompliced burgomaster, a great one among the very greatest" (*FW* 587). HCE's disguise here bespeaks a self-aggrandizing wish to be a high-ranking official. Like those sometimes worn by attorneys and magistrates, the wig may serve as an accoutermental marker of his desired power and prestige; but it may also function as the trace of taboo libidinal impulses, as the signifier of transvestite or homoerotic inclinations that cause him to be identified with a wife ("wiv") and the homosexual Aubrey Beardsley ("Mister Beardall"). A related source of psychic fear is the clothing of the other, marked in dream as the agent of illicit sexual temptations. In the homework chapter a reference to the Edenic serpent ("This is the glider that gladdened the girl") is glossed by Issy as, "Tho' I have one just like that to home, deadleaf brown with quicksilver appliques, would whollymost applissiate a nice shiny sleekysilk out of that slippering snake charmeuse" (*FW* 271). The young girl would like to turn the skin of the poor serpent into a piece of attire, the mythic agent of seduction merging with the modern one—provocative garments. Thus in an early account of the dreamer's sin, the evidence against him is female apparel in the form of the maidservants' "published combinations of silkinlaine testimonies" (FW 34)—perhaps bloomers, like Gerty's, peeked at by a male voyeur.

Embedded in the semiotics of clothing, scents, and other cultural accouterments, sexual interchanges in Joyce's works become a highly theatrical affair, as Bloom's musings in "Nausicaa" suggest: "See her as she is spoil all. Must have the stage setting, the rouge, costume, position, music. The name too. *Amours* of actresses. Nell Gwynn, Mrs Bracegirdle, Maud Branscombe. Curtain up" (*U* 370/303). Cheryl Herr has pointed out that *Ulysses* exposes sexual identity itself as a theatrical phenomenon: the work "argues that sexuality is sheer theater, at least on the social stage on which we dramatically construct the selves we play."[32] In "Circe," in particular, sexual being emerges not as an essence but as a social fabrication, a cultural artifice, an elaborately staged masquerade. The Ulyssean portrait of theatrical sexuality returns in the *Wake* when the temptresses appear as "Skertsiraizde with Donyahzade . . . staged by Madame Sudlow as Rosa and Lily Miskinguette in the pantalime" and watched by "good Dook Umphrey" in an "all horserie show . . . from his viceregal booth" (*FW* 32). This screen memory of the dreamer's sin emphasizes that theater is often seductive, an exhibitionist act for a voyeuristic audience, and that seduction is often theatric, a performance contingent upon the proper props.

Joyce deconstructs the notion of desire as an independent essence, either metaphysical or physical; in his works, as in cultural reality, language mediates the most romantic of moments and the most carnal of acts. Representation frequently infiltrates memories of seductive stimuli, Bloom's thoughts of Molly's body in "Nausicaa," for instance, being immediately followed by a line from *Sweets of Sin* ("That's where Molly can knock spots off them. It's the blood of the south. Moorish. Also the form, the figure. Hands felt for the opulent" [*U* 373/305]). His earlier nostalgic recollection of his first encounter with his future wife is interwoven with the lyrics of a song, that "first night *when first I saw* her at Mat Dillon's" (*U* 275/226, emphasis added) containing a textual snippet of "M'appari" from *Martha*—"*When first I saw* that form endearing" (emphasis added). The song recounts, moreover, a visual seduction, an erotic moment triggered by the language of an endearing "form." Bloom's initial attraction to Molly is enmeshed in erotic signifiers of all varieties—visual, olfactory, and aural: the "yellow, black lace she wore"; the "full voice of perfume"; and the song called "Waiting" that allows Molly to announce her sexual wishes in the culturally sanctioned ritual of the parlor performance (*U* 275/226).[33] In *Finnegans Wake*, the sensory stimuli that kindle HCE's passion for ALP —"was it the twylyd or the mounth of the yare or the feint of her smell made the seomen assalt of her" (*FW* 331)—are connected to the body (the two lips of her mouth, the two lids of her eyes, her personal aroma) and the rhythms of nature (the twilight, the month of the year they met), but they are valenced nonetheless as signifiers endowed with kinetic meaning. Features of the human soma unmediated by the cultural supplements of clothing and perfume are relentlessly transformed into textuality, appropriated by *homo significans*. Desire in Joyce's works is kindled by representation itself and by representational resemblances: HCE imagines ALP as heaven on earth ("having an airth") because she looks like a stage actress with her "lovelyt face for a pulltomine" (*FW* 615), just as Molly initially finds Bloom handsome in part because of his resemblance to Lord Byron, the admired poet whose features she would have known only through reprinted images. The Bloom's sexual consummation of their highly textualized attraction is an intensely physical moment, permeated still by semiologies of desire, what Bloom fittingly calls the "language of flowers" (*U* 78/64): floral metaphors that seductively appeal to Molly's romantic and erotic longings ("he said I was a flower of the mountain yes" [*U* 782/643]) and metaphorically floral eyes that seductively speak to Bloom's ("Flowers her eyes were, take me, willing eyes" [*U* 176/144]). Joyce's works explore the inseparability of language and desire by recording the textual that constitutes the sexual, the semiotic that finally *is* the erotic.

"MY MULTIPLE MES":
THE SEARCH FOR THE SELF

DISCUSSING the inception of *Finnegans Wake* in the years 1922–1923, Richard Ellmann makes the following well-known claim about Joyce's conceptual framework for his final oeuvre:

> As Joyce informed a friend later, he conceived of his book as the dream of old Finn, lying in death beside the river Liffey and watching the history of Ireland and the world—past and future—flow through his mind like flotsam on the river of life. But this was perhaps only to indicate that it was not the dream of any of the more obvious characters in the book. . . . The characters would be the dreamlike shapes of the eternal, unholy family, Everyman, his wife, their children, and their followers, bobbing up and down on the river. In the twentieth century Everyman's avatar was to be Humphrey Chimpden Earwicker, keeper of a public house in Chapelizod. . . .[1]

Ellmann's assertion has an apocryphal air to it. He never mentions who the "friend" is or when Joyce supposedly made this statement, and he also fails to cite its source—did he hear it directly from the unspecified "friend" or from someone who supposedly heard it from the friend who supposedly heard it from Joyce?[2] Despite the unsubstantiated nature of Ellmann's claim, its influence can be felt in later critics' comments on the *Wake*: Sheldon Brivic, for example, writes that "*Finnegans Wake* is one of the most affirmative literary works since *The Divine Comedy*, but its affirmation depends upon a cosmic perspective and has about as much to do with the problems of everyday reality as Dante."[3] I interrogate Ellmann's assertion that Joyce "conceived of his book as the dream of old Finn" because there is ample internal evidence in the book itself and in Joyce's earlier fictions that *Finnegans Wake* should be conceptualized in an inverted way: not as the dream of a mythic figure who becomes in his twentieth-century incarnation an ordinary man, but rather as the dream of an ordinary man who envisions himself as a mythic figure, the giant Finn MacCool. Under the Wakean logic of associative substitution, this envisioned "identity" stands as only one in an ever-expanding series of fictional self-figurations ("entiringly as he continues highlyfictional" [*FW* 261]).

Joyce was fascinated throughout his literary career with the human predilection for fantasy and, more specifically, with the ordinary individual's wishful appropriation of heroic guises from history, myth, literature, or popular theater. Amid the noisy chaos of the Dublin markets, the protagonist of "Araby" imagines himself quixotically as an ardent young knight; against the backdrop of his family's declining fortunes in *Portrait*, Stephen plays the roles of Napoleon, the Count of Monte Cristo, and later Claude Melnotte from *The Lady of Lyons*. Joyce represents this escapist impulse as persisting into adulthood, although more conspicuously at the level of the unconscious: in the midst of Bloom's Circean trials we find the aggrandizing fantasy of the self as lord mayor of Dublin and ultimately king of the new Bloomusalem. The abundant mythic personae haunting the *Wake* can by read as the byproducts of this same psychic impulse that inflates the self through fictionalization. If one conceptualizes the dreamer as a mythic figure envisioning himself as a common mortal and not as a common mortal envisioning himself as a mythic figure, one misses the desirous impetus behind many of the dream imagoes.

The *Wake* explicitly states at points that the dreamer has two dominant personae—"tumulous under his chthonic exterior but plain Mr Tumulty in muftilife" (*FW* 261)—one of which assumes the inflated proportions of a god (chthonic: pertaining to deities) or of an imaginary giant embedded in the landscape (chthonian: dwelling underground), the other assuming the more realistic dimensions of a "plain" man in "mufti," an ordinary mortal—most frequently a publican—stripped of his dignifying uniforms and his elevating masks ("his chthonic exterior"). The postscript to the final version of the Wakean letter hints that the inflated vision of the self is an imago appropriated from geographical folklore: "Hence we've lived in two worlds. He is another he what stays under the himp of holth" (*FW* 619). Although the persona of the ordinary pubkeeper is no less figurative than that of the giant, the voice here implies that it approximates more closely the dreamer's waking status. The letter writer separates mythic idealization from mundane circumstance— the "two worlds" that frequently meld in the dream—by marking the legendary figure sleeping under Howth as a quixotic alter ego, an "another he."

Although the corporal and psychic sources of the oversized imagoes cannot be established with absolute certainty, several explanations are plausible. John Bishop has persuasively suggested that the dreamer's figuration of the self as a giant reclined in the local topography simply adumbrates the radically altered spatialities of the sleeping body: "sleep erases the boundaries by which, in wakefulness, we distinguish ourselves from the alien immensity of the surrounding world and set ourselves apart from it, as we were taught, in worried little subject-object relations"; in dream the external world has been "introjected and incorporated."[4] Another somatic source for the fantastical inflations may be located in the dreamer's sense of himself as being heavy, sprawling, and unable to move, like Gulliver in the land of the Lilliputians. They may be transmogrified visions of a body that has literally fallen, or visions that represent in a literal way metaphorically "fallen" states—a body in decline, on the road toward death, or a psyche that is guilt-ridden, obsessed with transgression. But the imagoes of the dreamer as physically large ("lights his pipe with a rosin tree and hires a towhorse to haul his shoes"[FW 137]) frequently translate into visions of being larger than life, of being a hero, god, king, or pope. The implicit equation of physical size and metaphysical import betrays the longing for prestige and significance that impels the various inflations. The gargantuan imagoes in the dream, in short, spring from a tangle of conflicting emotions, expressing sanguine hopes of being illustrious and enduring as well as fears of being flawed and mortal: in obedience to the dream's dialectical logic, they are driven by wishes while containing simultaneously residues of anxiety. As a "secondtonone myther rector" (FW 126), the Wakean dreamer shares with Joyce's earlier characters the desire to escape from a mundane, transient, and imperfect world. Far from having little to do with the problems of everyday reality, as Brivic suggests, the fantastical fabric of the Wake expresses very specific personal concerns—both physical and psychic—albeit in a disguised and deceptively impersonal form.

The imagoes of the publican find their origin in a similar psychic dialectic: measured against the mythic giant, they express a deflated self-estimation, yet they bespeak a patent desire as well. Becoming a successful businessman—and a hotelkeeper in particular—is, after all, one of Bloom's unfulfilled but professed ambitions, as Molly's soliloquy reveals: "Blooms private hotel he suggested go and ruin himself altogether the way his father did down in Ennis like all the things he told father he was going to do" (U 765/630). In the dream the publican periodically turns into the grocery magnate Adam Findlater, whom Bloom thinks of in Ulysses as the epitome of entrepreneurial prosperity (see U 58/48) but who also had the reputation of being a self-interested politico.[5] He was accused of being disloyal to Irish causes, as HCE often is, and of angling for a knighthood, that politically problematic laurel HCE visualizes receiving in 3.4 ("Arise, sir Pompkey Dompkey! Ear! Ear! Weakear!" [FW 568]). The mythic giant and everyday businessman are linked through their elevated status (as Irish hero and financial magnate) and through the verbal contiguity of their names—"the great Finnleader himself" (FW 214); but they also share the potential to become fallen giants, to end up as failures or "ruins," in every sense of the word—"The Reverest Adam

Foundlitter" (*FW* 420). The wishful visions of commercial enterprise in the dream ("our hugest commercial emporialist" [*FW* 589]) are always countered by fears of financial disaster, of ending up "leareyed and letter-ish, weeping worrybound on [one's] bankrump" (*FW* 590). At many points the dreamer can be conceptualized as Bloom, envisioning himself as the legendary giant in Howth he sees in "Nausicaa" and as the commercial giant he envies in "Calypso," but only to see himself ultimately following the downward trajectory of his father, fulfilling the expectations of a cynical spouse.

These shifting figurations indicate the way self-image in the *Wake* becomes as protean as the ever-changing landscape it is frequently superimposed upon, as transient and unpredictable as weather conditions ("the average human cloudyphiz . . . frequently altered its ego with the possing of the showers" [*FW* 51]). Self-image returns in dream in altered and destabilized forms: it becomes a text that is constantly being rewritten, a "traumscrapt" (*FW* 623) revised under the pressures of desire and anxiety. "He is exalted and depressed, assembled and asundered" (*FW* 136): this well describes the process whereby the dreamer is relentlessly constructed and deconstructed, in portraits sometimes glorified, at other times abased. These vacillating self-figurations are anticipated in "Circe," where Bloom's vision of himself, at the level of the unconscious, is represented as a protean stream of exalted and deflated imagoes. Hugh Kenner uses an appropriately theatrical trope to describe the process of self-transformation: "Bloom . . . plays parts and is instantly recostumed as the roles mutate. Costume is role, and self is a medley of allotropic roles."[6] Costuming in the *Wake* is even more fantastical and heterogeneous in its mutations: buildings, mountains, statues, eggs, machines, barrels, clouds, and rainbows—all serve as HCE's "apparel" in dream. When they assume more recognizably human contours, costumes are often explicitly marked as disguises ("dangieling his old Conan over his top gallant shouldier so was . . . he's like more look a novicer on the nevay" [*FW* 322]). These disguises make literal the larger problem of determining identity in the dream, of penetrating the fictive overlays that mediate self-image.

The *Wake* explores the self in language and the self as language: we confront a subject immersed *in* textuality and hence available to himself only *as* textuality, as the perpetual return of substitutive signs. The dreamer is known to himself—and to us—only indirectly, through the proliferative fictions, names, and imagoes his psyche generates; he is similar to the Shakespeare of Stephen's theory, the absent author known only through his verbal constructs, the characters, stories, and documents he has left in his wake. In "Scylla and Charybdis," Stephen fashions from these linguistic remains of the playwright's psyche a fairly coherent (though surely subjective) portrait of the artist; in the *Wake*, by way of contrast, the endless yarns that the dreamer composes and that compose the dreamer in no way add up to yield an identifiable character. In the answer to the opening question of 1.6 he is reduced to a gargantuan catalogue of metaphors, metonymies, and synecdoches: a paradigm, in a sense, of *Finnegans Wake* as a whole. Fritz Senn has discussed how in *Ulysses* Joyce makes Bloom "polytropic," like his Homeric precursor, by playing with his name throughout the book;[7] the Wakean dreamer is more literally polytropic, an ongoing series of multiple tropes. Language in its most circuitous and unreliable guises—figuration as opposed to literal description, speculation and story as opposed to straightforward fact—create whatever self the dreamer has: "By hearing his thing about a person one begins to place him for a certain in true" (*FW* 490). In the *Wake* language is exposed as an irrevocably self-alienating medium.

Like *The Odyssey*, the *Wake* is an epic of dispersal, but a dispersal that goes beyond Homer's ruined fleet of ships, a dispersal effecting most insistently the construction of identity itself, the attempt to formulate the self as a coherent whole. Maud Ellmann has argued that "as far as Joyce and Homer are concerned, identity can never rest in any single definition. . . . Instead, identity consists of the tales [the autobiographer] spins about itself in the attempt to recover its own origins."[8] This claim, though, tends to blur an important distinction between the classical and modernist epics. Odysseus does undeniably generate "a multitude of counterfeit identities"[9] that create an early version of ontological dispersion; but Ellmann is underestimating the significance of the middle section of *The Odyssey*, that Phaeacian night of self-reflective authentic narration, wherein the hero recollects his past and re-collects his self, verbally reconstructing what he has survived thus far and—implicitly—why: the prospect of home, of returning to Ithaca. Telling stories of the self becomes a means of getting back on course, of returning to one's initial trajectory. This brand of recollection/re-collection is precisely what is impossible in the *Wake*, the dreamer's dispersion being utterly irrevocable. The *corporal* defigurations and refigurations caused by the envisioned fall (the hump, the broken body, the changed physiognomy) provide an apt concrete image for the byproduct of fallen, meandering Wakean storytelling: incessant *verbal* defigurations and refigurations of the self. HCE's multifarious stories, names, and imagoes become the linguistic counterpart to his shattered physical form. The *Wake* records repeatedly how the dreamer "fell from story to story like a sagasand to lie" (*FW* 374–75). Represented as Ibsen's masterbuilder, he falls through space, like a sack of sand, past the stories of the skyscraper; as linguistic construct, he falls through time, suffering relentless revision as he passes from "story to story." Identity starts as a paradoxically truthful fiction that is quickly lost, as a "sagasand" (*sand*: true in Danish) that turns into a blatant "lie."

The attempts to define the dreamer in terms of vocation are as fruitless as those that try to do so through personal history, specific name, or fixed self-image. The search for "the genesis of Harold or Humphrey Chimpden's occupational agnomen" (*FW* 30) produces multiple possibilities, the verbal dispersion typical of the *Wake*: "we have for surtrusty bailiwick a turnpiker who is by turns a pikebailer no seldomer than an earwigger!" (*FW* 31). The alternatives are linked by partial klang associations (earwigger-earwicker-bailiwick-pikebailer-turnpiker), as are many of his other roles: the dreamer is a builder, a "bridgesmaker" (*FW* 126), or a tailor, a breeches maker, or a sailor, or a "soffsoaping salesman" (*FW* 45), or a mailman, or an owner of a pub, an "alamam alemon" (*FW* 331). An "occupational agnomen" may provide no source of identification at all, insofar as the word "Noman" whispers in agnomen and gives the supposedly specifying label a taint of anonymity.[10] An agnomen is also by definition an additional cognomen or an epithet—a potential linguistic excess working against nominal containment.

HCE's inability to re-collect his identity is a function of the evasive tactics of the dreamwork and, as such, reflects his guilt, his desire to remain unknown and unrecognized—even to himself. Evoking the literal residue of legal "redress," the inquisitors in 3.3 suggestively link identification with putting one's clothes back on, as if a person indecently exposed would naturally prefer to remain anonymous: they press their witness to "name or redress him and we'll call it a night" (*FW* 514). The command echoes that of the watchmen in "Circe" ("Come. Name and address" [*U* 455/371]), whose accusations impel their suspect to generate a roster of false identities, Bloom claiming—in Odyssean fashion—to be a dentist, a financier, a soldier, and a writer. In Homer's epic the hero's disguises are evidence of the conscious guile that ensures his survival; in Joyce's works they proliferate in the nightworlds, as byproducts of the unconscious guile that governs the formation of dreams.

The *Wake* is Joyce's most thoroughgoing attempt to interiorize the epic, to create an odyssey of psychic rather than physical trials. Epic traveling having been turned inward, the dreamer is forced to wander through a "labyrinth of . . . samilikes and the alteregoases of . . . pseudoselves" (*FW* 576). The work's digressive narrational style provides a formal enactment of wandering, symptomatic of the dreamer's inability to stay on course or even to get on course. The Wakean linkage of wandering with indeterminate selfhood has ample precedent, of course, in Joyce's earlier fictions and in some of the works that shaped them. Odysseus, the Count of Monte Cristo, the ironically named Frank from "Eveline," the Shakespeare re-created in "Scylla and Charybdis," D. B.

Murphy from "Eumaeus," even Leopold Bloom himself—their stories juxtapose absence from home or homeland with absence of certain identity, with disguises, potential posturing, aliases, forged histories, self-transformations. Identity is implicitly represented as a social fabrication, easily capable of being rewritten or revised. The sea that releases HCE from fixity of self is the dream itself, the unconscious construct that leads the subject away from the dry land of conscious individuality, that exposes waking determinate identity as a very tenuous fiction. As Margot Norris has written, "The question 'Who is the dreamer?' is a question properly addressed not to the reader but to the dreamer himself, who discovers in the dream that he is by no means who he thinks he is."[11]

The unconscious becomes an agency of ontological dispossession in Joyce's final dreamtext, an agency that leaves the individual bereft of definable selfhood. Joyce represents the self-alienating effects of the unconscious relatively early in his literary career, in the scene from *Portrait* where Simon and Stephen travel to Cork. Among the manifold dispossessions of the father—Simon's loss of property, prosperity, youth, and friends—Joyce carefully situates the ontological dispossession of the son: Stephen's loss of his very sense of coherent being through his experience of the intrusive force of unconscious thoughts. When the "monstrous reveries" spawned by the word *Foetus* force Stephen to wonder about their possible psychic origin (*P* 90), he feels an inexplicable rift in himself, sensing that he is inhabited by an unknown source of psychic activity: *"He could scarcely recognise as his his own thoughts*, and repeated slowly to himself: / —I am Stephen Dedalus. I am walking beside my father whose name is Simon Dedalus. We are in Cork, in Ireland. Cork is a city. Our room is in the Victoria Hotel. Victoria and Stephen and Simon. Simon and Stephen and Victoria. Names" (*P* 92, emphasis added). Stephen tries to use language to reorient himself, to reestablish his sense of selfhood, but the venture fails. His mechanical recitation drifts toward vacant verbality, the words Simon, Stephen, and Victoria remaining detached from any meaningful reference, insistently maintaining their status as mere "names." Immediately afterward, Stephen conjures up images of himself as a child, only to realize that that self "had faded out like a film in the sun. He had been lost or had wandered out of existence for he no longer existed. . . . It was strange to see his small body appear again for a moment: a little boy in a grey belted suit" (*P* 93). In this early scene from *Portrait*, Joyce shows the unconscious shattering the self's continuity over time as well as its coherence at the moment when the intrusive presence is felt.

The scene anticipates *Finnegans Wake* in several ways—in the concern with locating an internally divisive source of guilt, in the perceived lack of ontological coherence, in the futile reliance on language to make that coherence return. When Stephen is dispossessed of his identity in the present, however, he concurrently repossesses an identity from the past, if only in the form of a ghost, a self who "had been lost or had wandered out of existence." In "Scylla and Charybdis" Stephen will claim that ghosts are (among other things) discarded identities, the personae one assumed earlier in life: "—What is a ghost? Stephen said with tingling energy. One who has faded into impalpability through death, through absence, through change of manners" (*U* 188/154). In its implicit suggestion that an earlier self can "wander out of existence" by disappearing over time and becoming ultimately impalpable, his redefinition of a "ghost" posits the ontological discontinuity he has experienced directly in the second chapter of *Portrait*. The exchange that takes place in Stephen's mind in that scene—a present self lost, a ghostly former self found—links the trip to Cork, with its multiple revisitations of the past, even more strongly to the *Wake*: for Joyce's final dreambook is indeed a ghost story of sorts—a tale in which HCE's present self is rendered impalpable, turned into an elusive phantasm ("Like Faun MacGhoul" [*FW* 354]), but a tale in which his past selves return, in which the ghosts of that present indeterminate being once more freely walk the night. In the *Wake* wandering and return are not oppositional and temporally sequential, but rather identical and temporally simultaneous: the dreamer's wandering out of specific identity is also a return to previous selves, his ontological dispossession allowing a repossession of earlier phases of being. This simultaneity of wandering and return finds precedent not only in *Portrait* but also in "Circe," where Bloom explores the roles the male self may play over time: psychically released from middle-aged husbanddom, he becomes a carefree schoolboy, a sexually frustrated adolescent, an amorous young suitor, a hoary old man. Uncertain selfhood liberates the subject from fixed age and role, enabling the selves that have disappeared— "through death, through absence, through change of manners"—to be psychically relived and reinvestigated.

As a transcript of return, the *Wake* is perspectivally regressive, as Freud claims all dreamtexts are when he quotes the words of James Sully: "'Our dreams are a means of conserving . . . [earlier] successive personalities. When asleep we go back to the old ways of looking at things and of feeling about them, to impulses and activities which long ago dominated us'" (Freud's brackets).[12] Many of the anxieties and desires plumbed in the *Wake* are connected to the roles of father and husband, yet the book explores as well the psychic concerns of infants, schoolboys, adolescents, courting bachelors, widowers, and old men. Like all other markers of waking identity, age and familial role in dream are rendered indeterminate. Frequently the dreamwork superimposes different temporal perspectives, combining an early way of looking at an event with a later one:

the dominant vantage point of ALP's final monologue in Book 4, for instance, is that of a husband, imagining his wife speaking to him, yet at
points it shifts to that of son hearing the voice of his mother or to that of
an old man being addressed by his daughter. A similar perspectival ambiguity can be seen in the homework lesson of 2.2, where the young Dolph
and Kev (versions of Shem and Shaun) appropriate the sexual secrets of
the parents: the chapter makes sense as the anxiety dream of a father who
fears sexual usurpation and as the wish-fulfilling dream of a son who
covets paternal power and prowess. Scenes can be examined from oppositional perspectives simultaneously, because the return to "earlier successive personalities" is often synchronic in dream, outside the realm of
waking linear time. The *Wake*'s dominant patriarchal vantage, in short,
is mixed with perspectival residues of multiple other phases of being.

This complicated temporal perspective gives the male imagoes in the
dream a paradoxical status, turning them at once into self and other. The
ungrammatical structure of a sentence such as "*He am* Gascon Titubante
of Tegmine—sub—Fagi whose fixtures are mobiling so wobiling befear
my remembrandts" (*FW* 403, emphasis added) undermines the identity
of the imago in the very act of naming it, the voice labeling it as that of an
other ("He") while identifying with it simultaneously ("am"), so that its
precise status becomes imagistically destabilized ("mobiling so wobiling"). Patrick McCarthy emphasizes the temporal indeterminacy of the
dream figures when he points out that Shaun in 3.3 "has regressed to the
point where he is depicted as a wailing baby . . . lying on a hillock. On the
other hand, he is also an old man with a decomposing body and mind,
falling into senility, so that he represents both the beginning and end of
life."[13] Like that of the father HCE, the dispersion of the son Shaun is at
once physical and ontological: he complains in 3.1 that he is "hopeless off
course," like Odysseus adrift at sea, and that he would like "to isolate i
from my multiple Mes" (*FW* 410). The figurations of the son contain
unmistakable residues of those of the father, because, on one level, they
represent the same person: the dreamer inscribes himself in the dreamtext
as both father and son, like the Shakespeare of "Scylla and Charybdis"
who Stephen concedes is "all in all" (*U* 212/174). Because its two central
principles are rooted in Freudian claims about the status of the figures in
dream, Stephen's theory provides a helpful model for understanding the
complexities of characterization in the *Wake* (even if one rejects the argument about Shakespeare and artistic production in general). Stephen argues, on the one hand, that several individuals may be behind a given
character in the play, the ghost in *Hamlet*, for instance, containing facets
of Shakespeare, the betrayed husband, as well as his dead son ("through
the ghost of the unquiet father the image of the unliving son looks forth"
[*U* 194/160]). He points out correlatively that the individual author

writes himself into several different characters, scripting out oppositional
roles (ghost and prince, Iago and Othello, bawd and cuckold, ravisher
and ravished) that allow him to reenact unconsciously, in the act of writing itself, different positions in traumatic events from his own personal
past. The literary validity of these principles aside, they undeniably describe the relationship between dreamer and imagoes in *Finnegans Wake*:
any given figure in the dreamtext is semiotically overdetermined, and at
the same time the dreaming "author" is overdetermined in the text as a
whole, dispersed throughout it, even playing antithetical parts simultaneously. Any specific Wakean father figure, for instance, is always a conglomerate image, a visual and verbal hybrid created from a range of
sources; the dreaming patriarch HCE also invests himself simultaneously
in a wide array of persona—arguably every male character in the text.
Shem and Shaun are at once the other, the dreamer's offspring, as well as
the self, his own younger persona split into guilty and pseudovirtuous
components. Father figures in the text can be read as the self or as the
dreamer's father. The four old men are the dream's unreliable historians,
but also HCE's imago of himself as an octogenarian. The dream, in other
words, takes place "when you and they were we" (*FW* 403): this odd
grammatical construct hints at the way figures spoken of in the second
and third person can be incorporated into an indeterminate first person
because of their status as former selves, as returned ghosts, separated
from each other only by the passage of time. Identity in dream becomes a
plural construct, a matter of "we" or "Mes" rather than a unitary "I."

In "Scylla and Charybdis," Stephen decides that it is recollection that
binds the protean self, that creates the individual's waking sense of autonomy over the course of time: "But I, entelechy, form of forms, am I by
memory because under everchanging forms" (*U* 189/156). In the Wakean
nightworld memory breaks down, destroying the illusion of ontological
coherence. The dream becomes, in a sense, a text with an imperfect memory of itself, a text devoid of any absolute historical truths about the
dreamer, containing instead only mythic narratives and imagoes compet-
ing for validity. The chroniclers of the past, fittingly enough, are four
doddering, contradictory gospellers: as the "quobus quartet . . . flopsome
and jerksome, lubber and deliric" (*FW* 513), they are associated with the
psychic runes/ruins that suffer relentless devolution, with the internal
flotsam, jetsam, lagan, and derelict that undergo erasure over time.
Jacques Lacan has described messages from the unconscious as disappearing appearances, discoveries which are "always ready to steal away
again, thus establishing the dimension of loss":[14] this aptly describes the
countless reports of the dreamer's fall that are dug up and then buried,
presented and then dismissed, only to return later in altered form. If in the
Wake ancient psychic information is incessantly being recovered, it is

always later contradicted, discounted, or lost, a process imaged in the retrievals and subsequent burials of material in the "middenhide hoard" (*FW* 19). In 1.1 ALP, as the gnarlybird, gleans the litter/letter from the military rubbish after the battle of Waterloo, but in 1.4 the image is played in reverse when, in the guise of Kate Strong, she hides her "filth-dump" on the site of the conflict, "all over which fossil footprints, boot-marks, fingersigns, elbowdints, breechbowls, a.s.o. were all successively traced of a most envolving description" (*FW* 80). A text in itself, the battlefield is the perfect hiding place for another text, as it will act as a camouflage, obscuring the litter/letter among its "envolving" (evolving/involving) ruins: "What subtler timeplace of the weald than such wolfs-belly castrament [*castra*: military camp in Latin] to will hide a leabhar [book in Irish] from Thursmen's brandihands or a loveletter, lostfully hers, that would be lust on Ma, than then when ructions ended, than here where race began" (*FW* 80). The image provides a self-reflexive representation of the way the shards of the dreamer's personal history are obscured through their incessant mergence with other archaeological detritus of the self and its culture. In *The Odyssey* memory ultimately establishes the hero's identity: Odysseus proves to the doubting Penelope that he is indeed who he says he is by recalling that their marriage bed is immovable and passing her final test. In the *Wake* memory has been lost, for the fall of language naturally leads to the fall of certain knowledge: as inscriptions of the past, recollections become vulnerable to transmutation and erasure, turning the dreamtext into "a sequentiality of improbable possibles . . . for utterly impossible as are all these events they are probably as like those which may have taken place as any others which never took person at all are ever likely to be" (*FW* 110).

Returning through imperfect recollection to multiple earlier phases of being, the dream exposes the human subject as the victim of perpetual desire, never satisfied with a present role, eternally envious of the position of an other. This relentless desire is revealed most clearly in the absurdity of oedipal struggle in the dream: the son yearns to be the father, while the father in turn always yearns to be the son again, having forgotten the frustrations of the earlier self. At a transitional moment in 2.3, the son struggles to defeat the father and replace him—"*desprot slave wager and foeman foedal unsheckled, now one and the same person*" (*FW* 354). Rising to power, the son in the guise of the desperate wage slave and the feudal yeoman assumes the identity of the oppressive master, the despot or the foreman. In 3.1, however, the risen son finds the role of father burdensome, realizing that a "vacation in life" (*FW* 411) would be preferable to a vocation in life: "not what I wants to do a strike of work," Shaun complains, "but it was condemned on me premitially by Hireark Books and Chiefoverseer Cooks" (*FW* 409). Fatherhood is now seen not as a desired liberation from the shackles of sonship but as an inherited onus. The *Wake* dramatizes relentlessly the ironic truism of Goethe's that Stephen mentions in "Scylla and Charybdis"—"Beware of what you wish for in youth because you will get it in middle life" (*U* 196/161).

The contrasting perspectives on sex in the *Wake* also highlight the ironies of oedipal desire. In 2.2 the sons envy the "superpbosition" of the copulating patriarch (*FW* 299), but elsewhere thoughts of mating are enmeshed in ambivalence if not unequivocal anxiety. In 3.4 the sexual frustrations of married life are recollected grimly, the middle-aged copulator toiling away "in their bed of trial, on the bolster of hardship" (*FW* 558), trying desperately to satisfy his wife. Middle-aged sex returns here as a self-conscious ordeal, a chore, a marital debt ("O I you O you me!" [*FW* 584]), or—as the first narrator of the episode puts it—"Business" (*FW* 559). It is not surprising that the father resorts (or dreams of resorting) to the more passive pleasures of voyeurism. While the sons covet the father's position of active pleasure, the father prefers the sons' position of observational arousal.

In the chapter narrated from the perspective of senescence, however, the sexual conquests of a younger age are recalled romantically and enviously. If in 3.4 the four old men dissociate themselves from the toiling middle-aged lover, in 2.4 they nostalgically identify with him, but first transforming him into a suave young seducer and imaginatively projecting themselves into his enviable position: "they all four rememberd who made the world and how they used to be at that time in the vulgar ear cuddling and kiddling her, after an oyster supper in Cullen's barn, from under her mistlethrush and kissing and listening" (*FW* 384–85). As the disjunctive "kissing and listening" suggests, the four old men are uncertain if they are in the position of the participant or the audience. They are conveniently confused about where they are ("the past and present . . . and present and absent and past and present" [*FW* 389]) and who they are: the individual narrators in 2.4 recurrently refer to the four as "they," revealing their desire to dissociate themselves from the aged quartet, but they also sometimes use "us," conceding their unfortunate partnership in senility ("what do you think of the four of *us* and there *they* were now, listening right enough, the four saltwater widowers" [*FW* 387, emphasis added]). Former selves return transformed by the vagaries of memory, filtered through retrospective eyes of later selves that act as a highly distortional lens.

The ambiguous visions of sex in the dream are part of a larger exploration of the psychic ambiguities of marriage. The Norwegian sailor's repeated wanderings and returns in 2.3, for example, articulate contradictory feelings—a desire to rove endlessly countered by an urge to settle down. The sailor's question to the ship's husband, "Hwere can a ketch or hook alive a suit and sowterkins?" (*FW* 311), neatly encapsulates the oppositional impulses of the bachelor, in its simultaneous request for a new suit of sails for his ship and for a marriage suit, the hand of his "sooterkin" or sweetheart. Joyce uses the myth of the Flying Dutchman in this section in inverted ironic form: the endless wandering is not a loathed curse but rather the nervous reaction of a bachelor hesitant to marry. Joyce's comic reinterpretation of this legendary rover is close to Heinrich Heine's in *Memoirs of Herr von Schnabelewopski*. As Frank Granville Barker explains, "This fictitious gentleman recalls a play he once saw in Amsterdam on the subject of the Flying Dutchman. He recounts the action of the play in mocking vein, commenting on the Dutchman's failure to redeem himself through a faithful woman: 'Time after time he is glad enough to be saved from marriage, so back he goes to his ship.'"[15] Correlatively in the *Wake*, the need for a woman's love becomes not a redemption but a possible trap; as in the earlier myth, it is associated with mortality but as a plausible anxiety and a perverse desire. The urge toward matrimony is cast as a masochistic wish for crucifixion: "A Trinity judge will crux your boom" (*FW* 326) is the dream's ominous transformation of "At Trinity Church I Met My Doom," the famous song of matrimonial regrets. Elsewhere marriage is associated with bondage, with entrapping vines, belts, and halters ("For my qvinne I thee giftake and bind my hosenband I thee halter" [*FW* 62]). The dreamer fears his matrimonial jitters will be perversely cured only when he finally agrees to be "tied down": "Feeling the jitters? You'll be as tight as Trivett when the knot's knutted on" (*FW* 377). These anxiety-ridden visions play on the literal residue of negative words and clichés for marriage, such as wed*lock* or "tying the knot."[16] The vision of a hanging in 2.3—"Slip on your ropen collar and draw the noosebag on your head" (*FW* 377)—may well be the dreamwork's translation of the phrase "putting one's head in the sack," the trope used by Gallaher (*D* 81), Joyce's reluctant bachelor from "A Little Cloud."

As another simultaneous return to oppositional roles, 2.3 also probes the psychic concerns of the nubile young woman's father, represented as the ship's husband in the adventures of the Norwegian Captain and as the tavernkeeper in the barroom frame that continually merges with the tale. The Norwegian Captain is said to reek of "a beach of promisck" (*FW* 323), the accusation reflecting a native Irishman's fear of an invader plundering his promising shores or a worried father's fear of a promiscuous suitor breaking his word in a breach of promise. The father figure tries enticing the Norwegian Captain to settle by stuffing him with an elaborate homemade meal ("they plied him behaste on the fare. Say wehrn!" [*FW* 317]), which the rover devours and then runs off without paying for, much to the father's frustration: "—Stuff, Taaffe, stuff! interjoked it his wife's hopesend. . . . Come back to May Aileen" (*FW* 320). The father views the "prowed invisors" as an inevitability that one must exploit as best one can by turning the invader into a financially lucrative customer ("Kish met. Bound to. And for landlord, noting, nodding, a coast to moor was cause to mear" [*FW* 316]) or by forcing the daughter's admirer to become her husband. The Norwegian Captain is indeed eventually forced to pay for both his commercial exploitations and his sexual exploits when he is "fined" as and with "a faulter-in-law" (*FW* 325)—penalized as a thief with a fine and as an errant lover with a father-in-law.

But even though the father figure triumphs in the story of the Norwegian Captain, he is also recurrently defeated in the dream. The tale of the rover's reluctant marriage in itself is abruptly interrupted by the Butt and Taff skit vividly dramatizing the sons' patricide, as if the thought of becoming or being a father is inseparable from realizations of eventual impotence and defeat by the next generation. The "nowedding captain, the rude hunnerable Humphrey" (*FW* 325) is proleptically branded as "the now waging cappon" (*FW* 316), a label with overtones of an embattled capon, a castrated rooster. Fatherhood in the *Wake* is a role subjected to wildly varying interpretations: it is viewed with awed anticipation, nervous anxiety, and nostalgic longing; it is presented as a position of reverential honor, tedious responsibility, admired and envied potency, and vulnerable and flawed power. The symbolic site is occupied by figures at once authoritative and absurd, by gods, kings, mayors, popes, priests, saints, and conquerors, but also by the scattered Humpty Dumpty, the cuckolded King Mark, the persecuted and exposed Parnell, the mad and prurient Swift, and the voyeuristic Lewis Carroll. Frequently the dream produces self-contradictory visions of the patriarch, as in the imago of him as the duke of Wellington in 1.1, where the elaborate laudatory rhetoric detailing the hero's military apparel is punctured in a brief irreverent exposé: "This is the big Sraughter Willingdone, grand and magentic in his goldtin spurs and his ironed dux and his quarterbrass woodyshoes and his magnate's gharters and his bangkok's best and goliar's goloshes and his pulluponeasyan wartrews. This is his big wide harse" (*FW* 8). These ambivalent dream imagoes have their roots in countless visions of paternal authority from the earlier fictions. Bloom's thoughts are haunted by sympathetic memories of "poor papa," the pitiable victim of loneliness, an alien cultural milieu, and ultimately his own suicidal hand; in "Circe" he shows up, however, as a stereotype of a Jewish patriarch, hectoring and disapproving—as an imago out of popular melodrama (Mosenthal's *Leah the Forsaken*) that expresses a distorted filial fantasy of paternal domination. Over the course of *Portrait* and *Ulysses*, Stephen confronts a plethora of fathers, both real and symbolic, alternately impressive, pathetic, tyrannical, impotent, grandiose, or mundane—their objective reality interpretively tinged, in part, by the young artist's own mind. In a self-reflexive moment in the *Wake*, the artist Joyce creates the artist Shem creating a vacillating portrait of the pater, "one moment tarabooming great blunderguns (poh!) about his farfamed fine Poppamore, Mr Humhum, whom history, climate and entertainment made the first of his sept and always up to debt . . . and another moment visanvrerssas cruaching three jeers (pah!) for his rotten little ghost of a Peppybeg, Mr Himmyshimmy, a blighty, a reeky, a lighty, a scrapy, a babbly, a ninny, dirty seventh among thieves" (*FW* 173). Visions of the father in Joyce's works are intentionally infused with elements of the imaginary, the ineluctable wishes and fears of the filial psyche residually present in every patriarchal artist or dreamer.

• • •

In the Wakean dream, older selves reshape images of earlier ones in the process of imperfect retrospection; but just as surely, the perceptions of youthful selves inform and distort images of later ones, so that the paternal imagoes, for instance, are not only a father's fantasy vision of a father but also a son's. The dominant imago of the father as a giant is a dream shadow that roughly delineates not only HCE's present sense of himself, cathected with various anxieties and desires, but also a regressive memory from infancy of the father as a huge and imposing creature. In 2.1, one of the sections that recollects childhood trials, the patriarch is visualized not as the passive supine giant but rather as the menacing powerful one, whose thunderous voice scares the youngsters into the house at nightfall. The imagoes of ALP are similarly affected by ancient psychic impressions, subjected to the inevitable dream distortions. The dream reduction of the mother figure to a mere pinpoint, for instance—to "a pringlpik in the ilandiskippy" (*FW* 11) or "a tiler's dot" (*FW* 626)—is a metonymic and regressive representation of her, emerging from the infantile curiosity about her genitalia, in particular the vaginal aperture perceived as a "puncture" (*FW* 299). In the *Wake*'s extensive use of what Freud calls "the family romance," childhood fantasies and obsessions can be seen most clearly as residual determinants of the parental figures' contours throughout the dreamtext.

The family romance, as Freud defines it, is recorded in fantasies and dreams in which a child's parents are replaced by others of better birth. A form of wish fulfillment, a correction of actual life, it is motivated by a child's inevitable disillusionment with the parents he once assumed to be perfect. This psychic complex and the implicit dissatisfaction that impels it can be seen when young Stephen at Clongowes dreams that "his father was a marshal now: higher than a magistrate" (*P* 20) as a psychic defense against the students' snobbery about paternal occupations; or when Gerty fantasizes noble origins as a psychic escape from a squalid family life ("Had kind fate but willed her to be born a gentlewoman of high degree" [*U* 348/286]). Kenner's description of paternity in *Portrait* makes clear the wishful impetus behind substitutions of one parental figure for another: "fatherhood is a role rather than an estate; to shift fathers is for the son, too, to shift roles, to be no longer the son of a drunken bankrupt but heir to the vocation of the fabulous artificer."[17] Although Stephen accepts the chaos of his real father's household briefly in chapter 4, he ultimately disowns it, turning instead to the imaginary father of a classic family romance: his ecstatic appropriation of the mythic Daedalus is a later version of the fantasy of the father as a marshal, the powerful and exalted figure of a child's desire.

Freud characterizes the construction of the family romance as a regressive impulse that persists in the unconscious of many an adult mind, as a common nostalgic longing to return the parents to their idealized, prelapsarian state—one version of that paradise lost mourned throughout the *Wake*. As Freud explains,

> the whole effort at replacing the real father by a superior one is only an expression of the child's longing for the happy, vanished days when his father seemed to him the noblest and strongest of men and his mother the dearest and loveliest of women. He is turning away from the father whom he knows to-day to the father in whom he believed in the earlier years of his childhood; and his phantasy is no more than the expression of a regret that those happy days have gone. . . . We learn from [the] interpretation [of dreams] that even in later years, if the Emperor and Empress appear in [them], those exalted personages stand for the dreamer's father and mother. So that the child's over-valuation of his parents also survives in the dreams of normal adults.[18]

This wishful elevation of all-too-human parents runs throughout the *Wake*, where ALP and HCE are envisioned alternately as commoners and royalty—or sometimes as both simultaneously, as a king and queen lording it over an ordinary pub: "that royal pair in their palace of quicken boughs hight The Goat and Compasses" (*FW* 275). As John Gordon notes, "the testimony about [the mother's] ancestry conflicts: many times she is a mere tailor's daughter; at other times she is a queen or princess, a 'midget madgetcy' . . . who at the end declares regally, 'My people were not their sort.'"[19] The genealogy of the father is similarly equivocal, for he is rumored to be a "*Guilteypig's Bastard*" (*FW* 72) and at other points a man (or rock formation) of ancient noble origins and the ultimate social snob: "boasts him to the thick-in-thews the oldest creater in Aryania and looks down on the Suiss family Collesons whom he calls *les nouvelles roches*" (*FW* 129). In these dialectically opposed imagoes, wishes fight against the reality principle—and against fears of having not ordinary ancestors but actually low or illegitimate ones.

In a variation of the family romance, the child accepts the mother but replaces the father after learning the necessary uncertainty of paternity: "The child, having learnt about sexual processes, tends to picture to himself erotic situations and relations, the motive force behind this being his desire to bring his mother (who is the subject of the most intense sexual curiosity) into situations of secret infidelity and into secret love-affairs."[20] The fantasy enables the child to rid himself of a dissatisfactory actual father, but Freud argues it may serve an alternative function as well: it provides the psychic means of turning rival siblings into illegitimate pretenders. The ALP chapter of the *Wake* (1.8) contains precisely such a vision of a promiscuous mother with countless lovers—interestingly, it is narrated from the perspective of the embattled sons, transmogrified into the quarreling washerwomen. Their attribution of endless love affairs to ALP can perhaps be read as an attempt to bastardize the other and, implicitly, to legitimize the self. As the superimposition of the myth of Jacob and Esau onto Shem and Shaun suggests, birthright and ascendancy are at the heart of their rivalry. The Shem chapter (1.7) opens with the voice of Shaun denigrating his rival claimant by questioning his ancestry ("A few toughnecks are still getatable who pretend that aboriginally he was of respectable stemming . . . but every honest to goodness man in the land of the space of today knows that his back life will not stand being written about in black and white") and by situating him in an orphanage, a "garden nursery, Griefotrofio" (*brefotrofio*: orphanage in Italian), in an insinuation that he is not a true member of the family *(FW* 169). But in Book 4 Shaun himself is branded as "the fostard" (*FW* 603)—the bastard or fosterchild of indeterminate lineage and name. The classic uncertainty of paternity in the *Wake* leaves the son figures vulnerable to mutual accusations of illegitimate descent and fraudulent heirdom.

Lowly or flawed origins are dreaded in the dream because familial descent is interpreted not simply as a biological determinant of the self but also as a moral one, as an explanation of "character." Dream figures are repeatedly slandered through their alleged consanguinity with the insane ("*His Farther was a Mundzucker* [*Mondsucher*: lunatic in German]" [*FW* 71]) or, in an overdetermined slur, with lower-class American relatives in poor states of health ("his first cudgin is an innvalet in the unitred stables" [*FW* 320]). In the *Wake*, the claims of noble ancestry emerge as defensive gestures, denials of guilt, as they do in "Circe" where Bloom, under accusation, appropriates the nationality of the ruling class and alters his patrilineage, under the assumption that such elevations will establish his innocence: "My old dad too was a J.P. I'm as staunch a Britisher as you are, sir" (*U* 457/373). The Circean fantasies demonstrate, however, that a culturally stigmatized lineage can be not only turned into a moral onus, but also manipulated as a rationalization for moral errancy.

Bloom's hallucinatory defense lawyer turns bad genes to his client's advantage by arguing that Bloom is not responsible for his sexual aberrations because he has inherited an ineluctable predisposition to wander, in every sense of the word: "Intimacy did not occur and the offence complained of by Driscoll, that her virtue was solicited, was not repeated. I would deal in especial with atavism. There have been cases of *shipwreck* and *somnambulism* in my client's family" (*U* 463/378, emphasis added). Because the unconscious mind interprets genetics equivocally, the multiple references to the Jukes and the Kallikaks in the *Wake* take on a paradoxical signification, suggesting, on the one hand, incestuous interbreeding and a contaminating familial inheritance, but functioning, on the other, as an excuse for deviance, as an exonerating argument for genetic determinism. The dreamer fears that guilty impulses are somehow genetically transmitted, but he is also willing to use this possibility as a comforting rationalization of the "I-can't-help-myself" variety.

When the father is called upon to give his own estimation of his origins, it differs markedly from the assessment of his dubious wife: "as she would be . . . reanouncing my deviltries as was I a locally person of caves . . . I am, I like to think . . . confessedly in my baron gentilhomme to the manhor bourne" (*FW* 364–65). But the anxieties about being a "person of caves" or a "himpself"—a chimp-self and a humped self—permeate the dreamtext, particularly in 2.3, where the visions of descent from apes or other ignominious sources combine with visions of being physically misshapen ("that fellow fearing for his own misshapes, should he be himpself namesakely a foully fallen dissentant from the peripulator" [*FW* 313]). The fears of deformity expressed in the imagoes of the self as a caveman, the humpbacked sailor, Joe Biggar, or the puppet Punch, perhaps spring from an actual somatic state, the dreamer's sense of himself as fallen; but the physical condition takes on metaphysical consequences when it is interpreted as a signifier of lowness, as the mark of the social outlaw and misfit who cannot even be fitted with a suit of clothing. In the *Wake* the loss of clothes or the functional inability to wear them inscribes the dreamer's fear of dispossession, not only ontological but also cultural, in its suggestion of an embarrassing resistance to the appurtenances of civilized selfhood.

In its apprehensions about guilty lineage, the Wakean dream brings to the surface some of Stephen's repressed anxieties at the end of *Portrait*, anxieties betrayed only indirectly in his defensive pretensions and distastes. Despite his attempts to disown Simon as a father, Stephen clearly shares the patrilineal snobbishness about bloodlines and descent. In the final chapter in particular, he exhibits an almost Victorian arrogance toward lower origins and attempts, through his elaborate intellectual postures, to dissociate himself from what he considers to be inferior species.

He looks down upon the Irish peasant as a low and "other" form of life and dismisses his rival, Father Moran, as "a priested peasant, with a brother a policeman in Dublin and a brother a potboy in Moycullen" (*P* 221). During his discussion of his aesthetic theory, he also dismisses Darwinism, in a seemingly offhand intellectual gesture that perhaps bespeaks a decidedly Victorian phobia. His brief acknowledgment of his own animality is laughable in its priggish delivery and its dismissiveness: "—As for that, Stephen said in polite parenthesis, we are all animals. I also am an animal. . . . But we are just now in a mental world" (*P* 206). When the Wakean dream obsessively returns to this muted interest in descent, the truth of Darwinian theory is recognized: in the son's archetypal confrontation with the father embedded in the cad's meeting of HCE, the younger self comes face to face with "a markedly postpuberal hypertituitary type of Heidelberg mannleich cavern ethics" (*FW* 36–37). The quest for origins in the dream is revealingly described as "a meanderthalltale" (*FW* 19). The quest, moreover, becomes an erotic enterprise, as Darwin's investigation into the origin of the species is exposed as a displaced version of infants' curiosity about the origin of children, of their desire to explore physically the family tree: "delicted fraternitrees! There's . . . Erasmus Smith's burstall boys with their underhand leadpencils climbing to her crotch for the origin of spices and charlotte darlings" (*FW* 504). By conflating adult and childhood interests in origins here, the *Wake* suggests that Stephen's thoughts about genealogy in chapter 5—"Come with me now to the office of arms and I will show you the tree of my family, said Stephen" (*P* 202)—may simply be a disguised and acceptable form of his infantile voyeurism in chapter 1, his occluded sin that becomes in the dream the desire to see the mother's genitalia, the family tree's "crotch."

Stephen's ultimate appropriation of an avian father figure (the "hawklike man" [*P* 169]) creates parallels between *Portrait* and the myth of Christ, the story of the son descended from a god who at the annunciation takes the form of a bird. The myth of Christ incorporates the pattern of the family romance, infused with a religious ethos: it is, after all, the ultimate fantasy of high descent, which under Joyce's ironic pen becomes a very strange mixed marriage ("*I'm the queerest young fellow that ever you heard. / My mother's a jew, my father's a bird*" [*U* 19/16]) or a classic case of an upper-class man refusing to take responsibility for the child he sires with a lower-class woman: "Jesus is on strange terms with that father of his. His father seems to me something of a snob. Do you notice that he never notices his son publicly but once—when Jesus is in full dress on the top of Thabor?" (*SH* 117). In Joyce's works, the founding myth of Christianity bears a comic structural resemblance to the story told in "The Lass of Aughrim" and to those recorded in the romance tradition alluded to by Freud—those stories in which the lowborn son turns out to be the unacknowledged heir of the king or nobleman. The *Wake* contin-ues this irreverent treatment of Christianity, the search for the father often becoming a search for a god who has reneged on his paternal re-sponsibilities, in part by simply disappearing. The Wakean deity mani-fests himself as an absence, as an elusive and unlocatable being identified by only the vaguest of appellations (*"His Murkesty"* [*FW* 175], "the cloud Incertitude" [*FW* 178], "Heavenly blank" [*FW* 413], "dieobscure" [*FW* 431], "Theo Dunnohoo" [*FW* 439]). The spiritual father of the dream is neither transubstantial nor consubstantial, but instead insub-stantial, so that communion becomes a Barmecide feast: "But, lo, as you would quaffoff his fraudstuff and sink teeth through that pyth of a flowerwhite bodey behold of him as behemoth for he is noewhemoe. Finiche! . . . So that meal's dead off for summan, schlook, schlice and goodridhirring" (*FW* 7). In the *Wake* the construction of the family ro-mance is exposed as a futile venture, even the holiest of patriarchs turning out to be "fraudstuff," a figure whose pretensions to nobility merely mask a lack of both moral and physical "substance."

Another classic paradigm of the family romance is found in the myth of changelings, dramatized in the countless stories of two children—high-born and lowborn, good and evil, comely and deformed—switched in infancy by fairies, elves, gypsies, or other agents of mischief. This myth of ambiguous origins holds a clear fascination for Joyce, who scatters it throughout his works with interesting mutations in its implicit psychic import. At the Donelly's party in "Clay," Maria performs a song from a changeling story, the opera *The Bohemian Girl*: "I dreamt that I dwelt in marble halls" records the heroine Arlene's uncanny memory of her noble birthplace and home, prior to her abduction by the gypsies. As Norris has argued, Joyce uses the song to express Maria's sense of class displace-ment, her unconscious desire for superior birth and social milieu.[21] In Bloom's psyche, the myth becomes the vehicle for the articulation of a different sort of wish, the lost Rudy returning in Circean hallucination as a changeling child, as a victim of roguish fairies who left the weak son that died in the abducted and surviving one's place.[22] In a more ambigu-ous appropriation, the fantasy expresses a desire and an anxiety simulta-neously: Stephen's sense of himself as "fosterchild and fosterbrother" (*P* 98) in the second chapter of *Portrait* foreshadows, on one level, his at-tempts to disown his family and his imagined wishful descendance from the mythic Daedalus; but because this vision of himself comes in the midst of his guilt-ridden sexual awakening, he may also be feeling like the bad changeling child, the fraudulent heir whose ignoble origins provide an unconscious explanation for his overwhelming impulse to sin and fall.

By the time Stephen wanders along Sandymount strand in "Proteus," thinking extensively about familial and racial descent, he has become cynical about claims to lofty birth, his own included ("Houses of decay, mine, his and all" [U 39/33]). He rethinks the questions of his own origins indirectly by imaginatively visualizing a version of the myth of the changeling. Stephen first transforms the two women walking down to the sea into midwives carrying a hidden "misbirth with a trailing navelcord" (U 37–38/32); later he will imagine that they "have tucked it safe mong the bulrushes" (U 45/37), like the women who hid Moses, a changeling child of sorts. When he see the gypsies gathering cockles from the sea and labels them "the red Egyptians" (U 47/39), he psychically identifies them with the people who found the orphaned infant at water's edge and raised him as their own. That Joyce saw parallels between the story of Moses raised by the Egyptians and those of changelings raised by gypsies is made clear in a series of Egyptian references in the Buffalo Notebooks (6.B.1) that ends with the words "gypsy" and "Pharaoh."[23] In envisioning a rough facsimile of this myth of transferred parentage, Stephen works out a possible excuse for his own lack of filial loyalty.

In "Proteus" Stephen bifurcates his identity into guilty and innocent components ("Other fellow did it: other me. . . . *Lui, c'est moi*" [U 41/35]), the two parties in the changeling exchange that later become in his mind the true Irish son and the fraudulent outsider: "Then from the starving cagework city a horde of jerkined dwarfs, my people, with flayers' knives, running, scaling, hacking in green blubbery whalemeat. Famine, plague and slaughters. Their blood is in me, their lusts my waves. I moved among them on the frozen Liffey, that I, a changeling, among the spluttering resin fires. I spoke to no-one: none to me" (U 45/38). Stephen here affirms his Irish heritage ("Their blood is in me") and his distance from it simultaneously, uncertain about which member of the changeling pair he may be. Interestingly, the archaic meaning of "changeling" is a traitor, a turncoat, which may explain why this envisioned Irish Stephen of medieval Dublin remains characteristically aloof, or rather guiltily distant from his countrymen: the real heir to the Dedalus name may be a longlost double ("that I, a changeling") or Stephen himself, but still a changeling nonetheless, betraying with impiety and exile the Irish church, family, and state. His uncertainty about personal origins and identity is reemphasized in the doubled primal scenes in "Proteus," Stephen's visions of intercourse between parental figures of contrasting social class and nationality—first between Simon and May Dedalus (U 38/32), later between the gypsy couple (U 47/39). Through their shared association with the "winedark sea" carrying its load of children or thalassic spoils, the gypsy woman and May Dedalus will ultimately merge in Stephen's mind: "She trudges, schlepps, trains, drags, trascines her load. A tide westering, moondrawn, in her wake. Tides, myriadislanded, within her, blood not mine, *oinopa ponton*, a winedark sea. Behold the handmaid of the moon.

In sleep the wet sign calls her hour, bids her rise. Bridebed, childbed, bed of death, ghostcandled" (*U* 47/40). The disavowal of consanguinity here—the "blood not mine" that contrasts with the earlier "Their blood is in me"—remains ambiguously suspended in its referent: is Stephen rejecting the gypsy woman *or* the Irish mother who haunts him so insistently? Is he the lowborn son of wanderers, inherently resistant to the strictures of Catholic orthodoxy and national allegiances? Or simply the stubborn offspring of a once prosperous family, creating a convenient rationalization for the heretical behavior he fears contributed to his all too real Irish mother's death? Akin to the Wakean visions of descent from the Jukes and the Kallikaks, the family romance here in its inverted form—as a wishful fantasy of *ignoble* lineage—works as a psychic defense mechanism.

One residue of "Proteus" in *Finnegans Wake* can be found in the repeated envisioning of parental intercourse ("all the weight of that mons on his little ribbeunuch" [*FW* 332]; "everybug his bodiment atop of annywom her notion" [*FW* 475]; "somes incontigruity coumplegs of heoponhurrish marrage" [*FW* 607]). Through other specific allusions and imagistic echoes, the residual filial psyche in the dream returns to Stephen's musings about origins on Sandymount strand. The son figures in 1.8, for instance, narrate a scene of parental coupling that descends from images from "Proteus," poetically superimposed. The *Wake* combines Stephen's briefly imagined primal scenes with his vision of early invaders of Ireland—"Galleys of the Lochlanns ran here to beach, in quest of prey, their bloodbeaked prows riding low on a molten pewter surf" (*U* 45/37)—to produce a palimpsestic dream image of simultaneous territorial and sexual conquest: "with his runagate bowmpriss he roade and borst her bar. . . . When they saw him shoot swift up her sheba sheath, like any gay lord salomon, her bulls they were ruhring, surfed with spree" (*FW* 197–98). Stephen's thoughts about changelings also return in the *Wake*, where the enemy twins surface under the guise of "the old kings, Gush Mac Gale and Roaring O'Crian, Jr., both changelings, unlucalised, of no address" (*FW* 87): the twins can be read as the nightworld's counterpart to Stephen's bifurcated filial self. The supposedly virtuous Shaun is labeled "our rommanychiel" (*FW* 472), our gypsy lad, and in a related imputation of questionable descent, he becomes "the fiery boy" (*FW* 412), the offspring of the fairies posing as the heir apparent. The equation of the Christ-like son of Book 3 with the lowborn frauds of the changeling myth produces a dream vision of the Christian savior as the conscious hypocrite and whited sepulchre that Cranly describes to Stephen in their final conversation (*P* 242). In dream the uncertain origins of the sons stems from the untraceable descent of the father ("*Hail him heathen.* . . . *Courser, Recourser, Changechild.* . . . *Eld as endall, earth*" [*FW* 481]) who surfaces in the dream as both Irishman and outsider, native and invader. Stephen's visions in "Proteus" of alien alternative parents reappear in fairly clear form in the *Wake*, HCE manifesting himself as a scavenging gypsy rover (*FW* 12), as the "first pharoah, Humpheres Cheops, Exarchas" (*FW* 62: cf. "the red Egyptians"), and as the archetypal instigator of the changeling exchange, the leader of the fairies, "the king of Aeships [*Aos-sidhe*: fairy folk in Irish]" (*FW* 625). The dream, in a sense, clarifies what Stephen imagines the gypsy couple find along the shoreline, when ALP appears as a "zingari" (gypsy in Italian) who gathers from the sack of the maternal sea not only kindling but also discarded kids: "any of the Zingari shoolerim may pick a peck of kindlings yet from the sack of auld hensyne" (*FW* 112).

The *Wake* explores a historical version of the family romance in the visions of descendance from the great kings and noble leaders from Irish antiquity—as Mr. Deasy succinctly puts it, "We are all Irish, all kings' sons" (*U* 31/26). Stephen recognizes such a claim as another self-aggrandizing originary fiction ("Paradise of pretenders then and now" [*U* 45/38]) and as a nostalgic lie of a golden age of heroism that elides the bloody truth of a violent historical heritage. Historical memory in the *Wake* becomes as unreliable and transformative as personal memory, the archaeological ruins of "Emeraldillium" (*FW* 62) decaying like the runes of HCE's mind, throwing up only skeletal traces of the past, vulnerable to arbitrary (and self-serving) interpretation: "The house of Atreox is fallen indeedust (Ilyam, Ilyum! Maeromor Mournomates!) averging on blight like the mundibanks of Fennyana, but deeds bounds going arise again" (*FW* 55). In his Triestine lecture on "Ireland, Island of Saints and Sages," Joyce suggests that a nation's identity and history are inevitably reconstructed from the remnant "deeds bounds" of the past in the historical equivalent to the language of desire. In his characterization, a nation becomes a conglomerate "ego"—in every sense of the word—that spins grandiose stories about itself and its past, much in the way HCE often does in dream:

> Nations have their ego, just like individuals. The case of a people who like to attribute to themselves qualities and glories foreign to other people has not been entirely unknown in history, from the times of our ancestors, who called themselves Aryan and nobles, or that of the Greeks, who called all who lived outside the sacrosanct land of Hellas barbarians. The Irish, with a pride that is perhaps less easy to explain, love to refer to their country as the island of saints and sages. (*CW* 154)

In its vision of the forebear as Finn MacCool, Roderick O'Connor, or Brian Boru, the dream explores the wish to be the ultimate true-blue Irishman of glorious patrilineage; its psychic opposite is found in the fears of being of persecuted and punished for impure descent ("his teeth were shaken out of their suckets . . . for having 5 pints 73 of none Eryen blood in him" [FW 508]) or for being a racial misfit, for failing to conform to the nation's "personality" ("*Man Devoyd of the Commoner Characteristics of an Irish Nature*" [FW 72]). But the attempt to define the self in terms of racial descent is exposed as an absurdity: in his lecture as in his fiction, Joyce represents the national "ego" of Ireland as a racially heterogeneous one, as "a vast fabric, in which the most diverse elements are mingled, in which nordic aggressiveness and Roman law, the new bourgeois convention and the remnant of Syriac religion are reconciled" (CW 165). As Riana O'Dwyer writes, in seeking a pure racial heritage, "the searcher for an identity can never reach quest's end, because there is no end. There is no definitive Irishman because Irishness is a part of a process that has gone on before and will continue past the present moment."[24] In the *Wake* Mutt tells the invading Jute that the geological composition of Ireland is "puddinstone" (FW 17), conglomerate rock, and the "allaphbed" contains "miscegenations on miscegenations" (FW 18), ancestors who are racial hybrids, created from "our mixed racings" (FW 117). The father's heritage is richly eclectic, a racial patchwork quilt: "But it was all so long ago. Hispano-Cathayan-Euxine, Castillian-Emeratic-Hebridian, Espanol-Cymric-Helleniky?" (FW 263). In Joyce's fictions, personal identity and racial identity are simply myths of different proportions, both being cultural constructs artificially defined. Fatherhood remains indeterminate not only because of the uncertainty of biological paternity—that uncertainty articulated by Homer and echoed by Stephen Dedalus—but because the more general patrilineage of race becomes "a legal fiction" (U 207/170) as well.

The filial residue in the dream is strongest in the labyrinthine attempts to establish identity by discovering one's origins, by reuniting oneself with the father—the classic Telemachean mode of appropriating selfhood. In this return to the Homeric topos, the *Wake* imaginatively elaborates it, delving into parental origins of all varieties—anatomical, anthropological, social, racial, and geographical: "Or where was he born or how was he found? Urgothland, Tvistown on the Kattekat? New Hunshire, Concord on the Merrimake?" (FW 197). As the indeterminacies within these inquiries suggest, the paternal home of Ithaca is a nonexistent site in the dream, the father becoming the homeless Homer himself, the author of the great myth of reappropriated identity and origins returned to, who paradoxically remains anonymous and without a precise place of birth, rumored to have been born in seven different possible cities ("seven dovecotes cooclaim to have been pigeonheim to this homer, Smerrnion, Rhoebok, Kolonsreagh, Seapoint, Quayhowth, Ashtown, Ratheny" [FW 129]). The search for the home of the father is a search for the origin of the origin, infinitely regressive in its trajectory and infinitely plural in its possibilities.

In Joyce's revisionary dream epic, the father remains indeterminate in part because the desire to find him is in itself qualified, the quest for him being pursued with some residual hesitation. Despite the seeming obsessiveness of the quest, the truth of genealogy is both sought and avoided: "laid out lashings of laveries to hunt down his family ancestors and then pled double trouble or quick quits to hush the buckers up" (FW 134). This equivocal response to identifying ancestry is rooted in the complicated dialectics of the dreaming mind: the discovery of a fallen father is dreaded, because he is interpreted as a source of moral corruption; but from the perspective of a fallen worldly son, confronting a powerful authoritative father poses an equal, if different sort of psychic threat—one needs only to recall Stephen's response to Father Arnall or Bloom's to the Circean imago of Rudolph. When HCE meets a symbolic father in the form of the visiting king at the opening of 1.2, the confrontation induces disorganized behavior and nervous sweating ("Humphrey or Harold stayed not to yoke or saddle but stumbled out hotface as he was (his sweatful bandanna loose from his pocketcoat)" [FW 30]) as well as guiltily garbled speech patterns ("Naw, yer maggers, aw war jist a cotchin on thon bluggy earwuggers" [FW 31]). In the scurrilous Wakean rann composed by the son figures at the end of the chapter, HCE returns to his role as the father himself, paradoxically reviled for both his law and his lawlessness, for his socio-religious reforms and his moral deviancy. A far cry from a Telemachus, heartened to find a noble and powerful patriarch, the son within the dreamer regards heroic stemming as a heritage as psychically problematic as descent from apes. In the Joycean universe, where sons eventually discover their own capacity for moral wandering, the highborn authority figure of the family romance is ultimately accorded only the most hesitant of embraces. Closer descendants of Stephen or Bloom, filial figures in the *Wake* regard the fallen father as both an onus and a comfort, as a figure to be shamefully disowned or joyously claimed, in obedience to mutually contradictory psychic impulses: a lingering regressive wish for elevated lineage countered by a more realistic desire for both an explanation and excuse for a hopelessly flawed nature. In the *Wake*, the father's fall is cursed and yet also celebrated in a relieved refrain of "o felix culpa!"

· · ·

The attempt to find the origins of the self in the dream merges with the relentless attempt to locate the origins of sin, to define the nature of an elusive primal transgression committed by or against the father. In 1.2 we hear one of the earliest versions of the sin in the park (at once Eden and Phoenix Park) followed by its passage through the rumormill of Dublin and its final emergence as the rann, the song attributing multiple crimes to the father that bear little or no resemblance to the initially narrated incident. The sequence of events suggests that the father is the victim of a communal scapegoating ritual led by men who are versions of the son, appearing *in utero* to the dreamer ("Lisa O'Deavis and Roche Mongan . . . as an understood thing slept their sleep of the swimborne in the one sweet undulant mother of tumblerbunks with Hosty" [FW 41]). But this account of the father's defeat is unwritten at the outset of 1.3 with the report of the disappearance of the various scandalmongers who participated in the overthrow: "Therewith was released in that Kingsrick of Humidia a poisoning volume of cloud barrage indeed. Yet all they who heard or redelivered are now with that family of bards and Vergobretas himself and the crowd of Caraculacticors as much no more as be they not yet now or had they then notever been" (FW 48). In a lengthy series of interviews in 1.3, further accounts are generated and then subverted, as "many, we trow, beyessed to and denayed of, are given to us by some who use the truth but sparingly" (FW 61). "Beyessed to and denayed of"—this is the process of assertion and retraction, of narrative weaving and unweaving that every hypothesis about an originary transgression undergoes. Vanishing with a single jerk at the narrative thread, the texture of the dream resembles the handiwork of Penelope's loom, that duplicitous ephemeral fabric that is ceaselessly spun out and unraveled.

The individual idiosyncratic accounts of the father's fall come fast and furious throughout the dream, evoking fables of transgression through both specific allusions and broader structural analogies. The version of 1.2 resonates of the fraternal conspiracy postulated by Freud in *Totem and Taboo* ("*totam in tutu*" [FW 397]) that becomes the anthropological counterpart to the myth of Oedipus, itself a variant of the religious allegory of Original Sin. But by stressing the indeterminacy inherent in these accounts of primal transgression, Joyce produces in the *Wake* a marvellously inconclusive paradigm of guilt. These myths of originary culpability leave ultimate blame unfixed: does it lie with an overautocratic father? or with the rebellious heirs who resent his domination? with a flawed and errant father? or with the heirs who find his weakness an excuse for his deposition? In the dream Adam and Eve only reinforce the generational ambiguity as to the source of guilt, serving as prototypes of children with an "eatupus complex" (FW 128) and of culpable parents who "pawned our souls . . . and bequeathed us their ills . . . and turned out coats and removed their origins and never learned the first day's lesson" (FW 579).

By emphasizing the ambiguity inherent in intergenerational theories of guilt, Joyce creates in the *Wake* a circular and evasive structure of blame that prevents ultimate responsibility from being located with any certainty or stability. Given the indeterminacy of the dreamer's familial role, it is logical to speculate that the son in HCE blames the father, while the father in him fingers the son. The equivocal dialectic can be economically expressed in a single phrase such as "How Buccleuch shocked the rosing girnirilles" (FW 346). The condensation combines the son's patricidal gesture (how Buckley shot the Russian General) with the father's rumored penchant for exhibitionism: how buccleuch, the cleft rump of HCE (bucca: cheek in latin, cleuch: a cleft or ravine in a hill in Scottish)[25] shocked the blushing ("rosing") girls. Where causality in the Wake is not circular it is hopelessly labyrinthine—"So this was the dope that woolied the cad that kinked the ruck that noised the rape that tried the sap that hugged the mort?" (FW 511). Echoing the assertions of the various Wakean witnesses, critics tend to try to stabilize the dream's primal transgression, even those that affirm its radically decentered structure. In The Decentered Universe of "Finnegans Wake," for instance, Norris argues that "the search for 'facts,' the 'objective' truth, is a red herring that conceals the real issue: the universal guilt resulting from the oedipal relationship to one's parents, the Original Sin descended from Adam and Eve."[26] But guilt stemming from intergenerational conflict, indeterminate within itself, is only one alleged source of the "hubbub caused in Edenborough" (FW 29), one rumor among many. In its obsessive and regressive search for originary sin, the Wake explores the entire gamut of transgression, a gamut articulated in part in the catalogue of abusive names for HCE in 1.3. The possible cause of the fall may be fraud ("Hoary Hairy Hoax"), treachery ("Informer"), shady business transactions such as bribery, usury, or blackmail ("Coocoohandler" [Kuhhandel: shady business in German]), drunkenness ("Tight before Teatime"), sexual avarice or bigamy ("Wants a Wife and Forty of Them"), rape ("Sower Rapes"), or even murder ("Moonface the Murderer"). Other appellations in the list suggest the father's only crime is homeliness ("Funnyface"), an unspecified difference from others ("Peculiar Person"), an unconventional vocation ("Artist"), or simply physical mortality, old age ("Old Fruit," "Terry Cotter," "Dirt"), perhaps accompanied by a touch of lunacy ("Flunkey Beadle Vamps the Tune Letting on He's Loney" [FW 71–72]).

Although it may seem odd to liken the dispersed to the compact, the diffuse to the concise, I would argue that the central discursive structure of the Wake—the fall obscured by its accounts—is seminally embedded in two of Joyce's earliest pieces of writing, the first being "The Sisters." In this inaugural short story, Father Flynn's taint remains permanently elusive, shrouded by what Phillip Herring has aptly called "the gnomonic nature of the story's language . . . elliptical, evasive, and sometimes mysterious."[27] A paradigm in miniature of the sprawling Wakean dream, the story provides narrative presence that only adumbrates an absence, supplying information about the fallen father that is excessive yet lacking: the elliptic suggestions of old Cotter, the confused speculations of the dreaming boy, and the final disclosures of Eliza, who enumerates the symptoms of her brother's infirmity but not a definitive cause. As in the case of HCE, it remains unclear if the priest's lapse is ethical, sexual, psychological, or simply physiological, the common and inevitable decline into weakness and senility.

A similar narrative construct reappears in the first chapter of *Portrait*, where the students pray to God to keep their school safe from "*the snares of the enemy*" (*P* 18) that supposedly caused the initial fall of man but soon after learn that several of the older boys at Clongowes have transgressed. Appropriately enough, one of the punishments is expulsion—a perfectly realistic detail whose symbolic resonance was probably not lost on Joyce. Suspecting that the wrath of the masters will be felt by all and resenting the principle of guilt by association, Fleming unwittingly articulates the problem raised by the concept of Original Sin: "—And we are all to be punished for what other fellows did?" (*P* 43). But in its fundamental indeterminacy, the schoolboys' transgression departs from the Edenic paradigm: although its moral nature is as clear as the reprisal, the specific contours of the lapse remain mysterious, at the level of hearsay, as in "The Sisters" and *Finnegans Wake*. Cecil Thunder confidently asserts that "they had fecked cash out of the rector's room," Wells challenges his authority, reporting that they had drunk the altar wine, while Athy announces with quiet assurance, "You are all wrong," and claims that the truants were caught "smugging" in the square (*P* 40–42)—a deliberately obscure activity, as puzzling to young Stephen as Athy's earlier question in the infirmary, which he posed and then refused to answer. This third report sounds authoritative, but it fails to halt the imaginative interest in the mysterious crime. Fantasizing in the schoolroom, Stephen vividly constructs yet another possibility: "Perhaps they had stolen a monstrance to run away with it and sell it somewhere. That must have been a terrible sin, to go in there quietly at night, to open the dark press and steal the flashing gold thing into which God was put on the altar. . . . But God was not in it of course when they stole it" (*P* 46). Like the other boys, Stephen confuses speculation with certain fact, as his train of thought slides easily from the tentative "Perhaps they had stolen a monstrance" to his final, more assertive "when they stole it." In his mind the sacred vessel is gone and on its way to the pawnshop, but in the reader's the transgression must remain opaque. Stories of sin in Joyce's works are hopelessly obscured by speculative fictions—"Totalled in toldteld and teldtold in tittletell tattle" (*FW* 597).

In their search for an originary transgression, the Wakean citizenry investigate all forms of textual evidence—museums, monuments, letters, textbooks, dirty laundry, legal testimony, journalistic reports, family trees, rubbish heaps, mastabas of the dead and other archaeological ruins that provide a sort of "photography in mud" (*FW* 277). These pursuits are all isomorphic variants of one another: the analogical framework of the *Wake* collapses the nice distinctions the waking mind makes between legal inquiries, scholarly investigations of the past, leisurely sightseeing, and the tedious task of scouring someone else's clothes, revealing the essentially voyeuristic thrust behind all. If "the publication of private events is the thematic equivalent of sexual exhibitionism,"[28] then the prior investigation of them is the thematic equivalent of sexual voyeurism: two of the crimes recurrently attributed to the father are ironically enacted by his detractors in the very process of muckraking. The keen interest in transgression betrayed by Father Flynn's mourners, the schoolboys in *Portrait*, and their counterparts in the *Wake*, amounts to a disguised and sublimated form of transgression in itself: in Joyce's works, to pursue guilt is to incur guilt, to reveal one's own unlawful impulses. The contamination inherent in the search for guilty secrets is announced by the gossiping washerwomen at the opening of 1.8: "Tell me all. Tell me now. You'll die when you hear" (*FW* 196). Because guilty speculations involve an indirect participation in guilt itself, Stephen's sense of incipient incrimination after his humiliating pandybatting has a certain psychic logic to it: his fear that there might be "something in his face which made him look like a schemer" (*P* 53) may express a subliminal awareness of vicarious complicity in sin.

The Wakean dreamer is plagued by a less doubtful sense of ineluctably guilty being. But the attempts to locate that contaminating originary sin inevitably take his internalized investigators in the wrong direction, away from anything resembling an event. Interpretation, hypothesis, exegesis, speculation—these replace a logos of guilt rather than locating one. The dreamer wants to know "Why have I fallen? Where, when, and how?"— but the consequence of this fall is a linguistic and ontological dispersion that prevents the question from being answered with any certainty. In Christian mythology, the fall functions as the logos of the postlapsarian world, as a rational explanation of the chaotic; it implies a movement into transience, instability and decay, yet it is held itself as a stable origin. In the Wakean dream, Joyce implicitly critiques this mythic structure by subjecting the originary primal parents to decentering linguistic play ("Alum on Even" [*FW* 86], "alum and oves" [*FW* 393], "atoms and ifs" [*FW* 455], "atman as evars" [*FW* 596]) and by unwriting the coherence and unity of the fall itself. In a fallen world, Joyce implies, it becomes impossible to sift an originary sin out of the resulting chaos. In its dispersion and multiplicity in the *Wake*, the fall is rendered as a hopelessly fallen concept.

In place of a specified fall with a specified cause, the dreamer can generate only paradigms of descent—falling leaders, falling excrement, falling sleet, snow, and rain, falling fortunes, falling bodies, falling apples, falling buildings and civilizations. The myths and fables that ostensibly posit origins of human sinfulness not only fail to offer any truths about the source of the dreamer's guilt but actually help to bar it from him. Imposing further encrustations of text on the already textual (the various individual accounts), they put both dreamer and reader at a further remove from anything resembling an event. The *Wake* is extreme in its metaphoricity—a metaphoricity that is suggestive, interpretable, by no means meaningless—but a metaphoricity that is endlessly plural and contradictory in what it suggests. As resistant to coherent assemblage as Humpty Dumpty, the accounts and figurations of the fall cannot be reconciled to produce a logical and unitary cause. The incessant attempts to move from a chaotic multeity to a unitary logos are a vain battle against the verbal equivalent of the Second Law of Thermodynamics.

The *Wake* is Joyce's most systematic deconstruction of the waking notion of identity, of all the means by which the conscious subject constitutes and defines itself: name, self-image, vocation, age, role, memory, nationality, parentage. It also enacts a thoroughgoing assault on the concept of an origin—of self, of sin, of race, of language. In *The Interpretation of Dreams*, Freud suggests that all dreams have what he calls a navel, "a tangle of dream-thoughts which cannot be unravelled," which have no definite endings, which reach down into the unknown.[29] In the *Wake* this navel is the mystery of the navel itself, of our bond to a past which forever eludes us. As material substance, human records of the past are vulnerable to devolution over time as well as inaccuracies and mistakes in the very process of transcription ("For that . . . is what papyr is meed of, made of, hides and hints and misses in prints" [*FW* 20]). A mutable commodity, language obscures rather than conveys beginnings, eliminating any certain knowledge of the past, be it personal ("the flowers of speech valed the springs of me rising" [*FW* 318]) or historical ("As they warred in their big innings ease now we never shall know" [*FW* 271]). The *Wake* explores the impossibility of recovering origins within a medium that perpetually transforms both itself and the multiple histories it purports to record; embedded in language, the question of origins will never be answered. Once language starts its inscriptive wanderings, origins forgo the possibility of return.

Chapter 4

"THAT OTHER WORLD":
THE JOURNEY TOWARD DEATH

AS THE FUNEREAL overtones of its title suggest, *Finnegans Wake* is not only a regressive wandering through a past, but also an anticipatory wandering into the shared future of every mortal being: dying and death. In Joyce's earlier funereal fictions, such as "The Sisters" or "Hades," the narrative unravels from the vantage of the survivors, the individuals ensconced in the world of the living. Bloom concedes the otherness of death in his life-affirming thoughts at the end of the funeral rites: "I do not like that other world she wrote. No more do I. Plenty to see and hear and feel yet. Feel live warm beings near you. Let them sleep in their maggoty beds. They are not going to get me this innings. Warm beds: warm fullblooded life" (*U* 115/94). When Joyce reexplores "that other world" in the dream, he returns to the perspective elided in his earlier fictions—that of the dying man who will ultimately end up as the corpse. Suspended between life and death, trying to look both backward and forward, the dreamer occupies that strange unfixed psychic vantage approximated in the disturbing reassurance to the doomed man in *Measure for Measure*: "Thou hast nor youth nor age, / But as it were an after-dinner's sleep, / Dreaming on both. . . ."[1]

The dream attempts to explore what it might feel like to abandon being, to un-become, as it were, to submit oneself to dissolution, both psychic and physical. Dwelling extensively on both anticipated death and recollected life, the Wakean psyche discovers an imaginative means of reconciling these seemingly oppositional temporal trajectories. As a "fish-abed ghoatstory" (*FW* 51), the *Wake* merges the return of former ghostly selves with the putative experience of drowning, as if the psychic sensation of watching one's life pass before one's eyes induces associative corporeal fantasies of death by water, of immersion in the female element:

> a stream, alplapping streamlet, coyly coiled um, cool of her curls (*FW* 57)

> her waters of her sillying waters of and there now brown peater arripple (may their quilt gild lightly over his somnolulutent form!) (*FW* 76)

> He lay under leagues of it in deep Bartholoman's Deep (*FW* 100)

Focusing on the presence of the body in the *Wake*, John Bishop has argued that these recurrent visions of a man immersed in water have an immediate and realistic somatic source, their ultimate point of reference being the dreamer himself, who in sleep becomes aware of his own over-whelmingly liquid being.[2] Yet specifics make it clear that this reexperience of the liquid soma is inseparable from ontological anxieties and desires. The images of immersion, for instance, often contain clear over-tones of helplessness and confinement: "his ship thicked stick in the bot-tol of the river and all his crewsers stock locked in the burral of the seas" (FW 84–85). A miniature ship in a bottle of water, a ship stuck at the bottom of the river, the cruising crew trapped in the barrel of a boat in burial at sea—the fears of watery entrapment and premature interment of the living are unmistakably present in this overdetermined vision. In a dialectical reversal, the sea turns into a comforting watery cradle ("Rock-abill Booby in the Wave Trough" [FW 104]) or, by retrogressive associa-tion, the amniotic fluids of the womb: "Don't you know he was kaldt a bairn of the brine, Wasserbourne the waterbaby?" (FW 198). Inextrica-bly associated with mother love in the dream, water love is given a regres-sive origin in the recollection of the comforts of intrauterine existence. Because the sea is envisioned as the ontological alpha and omega, as the blissful womb and the suffocating tomb,[3] the dreamer is alternately hydrophile (like Bloom) and hypdrophobe (like Stephen). In the Wake infancy and death are frequently linked ("a cradle with a care in it or a casket with a kick behind" [FW 98]) because imaginative regression to the womb becomes another way of exploring the process of un-becoming: it is an undoing of the self, a return to a stage prior to identity, death's complementary point of ontological insubstantiality.

The visions of watery confinement in the dream express a larger recur-rent claustrophobia, implicitly connected with anxieties about interment. Summarizing the analogous claustrophic images in 1.4, Rose and O'Han-lon note that "[HCE's] cell, which in the preceding chapter changed from house into tavern into shack into hotel into telephone booth, is now described as a cage, then as a tent, then as a mill. Later, it becomes a teak coffin and after that a stone grave which itself turns into a mine."[4] Wakean males are also incarcerated in numerous boats (such as the "burialbattell" [FW 479] in 3.3), an ink bottle, a jail cell that doubles as a watery lough ("how long was he under loch and neagh?" [FW 196]), a sarcophagus that merges with the Vatican ("prisoner of that sacred edi-fice" [FW 100]), and barrels that turn into uncomfortable and ill-fitting clothes ("A strange man wearing abarrel" [FW 351]). As a telling slip makes clear, entrapment in relatively roomy spaces—like the gated yard in 1.3—still bespeaks fears of eventual inhumation, of being "clodded" with dirt like Paddy Dignam in "Hades": "just thenabouts the iron gape . . . was triplepatlockt on him on purpose by his faithful poorters to keep him inside probably and possibly enaunter he felt like sticking out his

chest too far and tempting gracious providence by a stroll on the peo-
plade's eggday, *unused as he was yet to being freely clodded*" (FW 69,
emphasis added). The impulse to escape the claustrophobic confine, expressed here in desire for a stroll, reiterates the restlessness of the corpse
in 1.1, who has to be cajoled into dormancy and later actively pinned
down by his mourners.

I read the claustrophobia in the *Wake* as the obsessive return of a brief
thought that occurs to Bloom as he watches Dignam's interment:

> The gravediggers took up their spades and flung heavy clods of clay in on the
> coffin. Mr Bloom turned away his face. And if he was alive all the time?
> Whew! By jingo, that would be awful! No, no: he is dead, of course. Of
> course he is dead. Monday he died. They ought to have some law to pierce
> the heart and make sure or an electric clock or a telephone in the coffin and
> some kind of a canvas airhole. Flag of distress. Three days. Rather long to
> keep them in summer. Just as well to get shut of them as soon as you are sure
> there's no. (U 111/91)

Although Bloom momentarily identifies with the dead man in the coffin,
the confining contours of which induce a brief sensation of panic, he ultimately betrays his allegiance to the living when he shifts his thoughts to
the inconvenience and impracticality involved in waiting for a corpse to
revive. "Hades" functions as an extended exploration of the difficulties of
thinking death from the vantage point of life. Although Bloom has a very
unsentimental attitude toward death, silently mocking the concepts of
afterlife and resurrection ("Once you are dead you are dead" [U 105/
87]), when he tries to envision it he often reflexively attributes to the dead
the cognizance of the living. Thinking about "love among the tomb-
stones," he assumes that human lovemaking must be "tantalising for the
poor dead" (U 108/89), making them jealous. During the Catholic funeral ritual he concludes, "Makes them feel more important to be prayed
over in Latin" (U 103/85). Bloom can conceive of death only as an actively experienced boredom and dampness ("The dead themselves the
men anyhow would like to hear an odd joke or the women to know
what's in fashion. A juicy pear or ladies' punch, hot, strong and sweet.
Keep out the damp" [U 109/90]). When he passes by one of the crypts in
Glasnevin he wonders to himself, "Who lives there?" (U 114/94). Because
it is obviously difficult for the living to imagine nonimagining, to feel
nonfeeling, Bloom's attempts to fathom the nonsensation of death result
in non sequiturs: "Well, it is a long rest. Feel no more. It's the moment
you feel. Must be damned unpleasant" (U 110/91).

Following its Homeric model, the "Hades" episode involves a confrontation with the death of the other; the *Wake*, by way of contrast, explores
a confrontation with the death of the self. Unlike Odysseus or Bloom,

HCE does not simply meet the dead, rather in dream he frequently *is* the dead. In *Joyce's Book of the Dark*, Bishop emphasizes the preoccupation with death in the *Wake* yet refuses to conceptualize the sleeper as a dying man: "Joyce's own stated interest was always in the human experience of the night, the evidence of the *Wake* itself suggesting any prolonged scrutiny of events presumed to befall the stiff inside the coffin inevitably opens into a meditation on the state of sleep."[5] But this reduction of death to metaphor, to a mere vehicle for thinking about the sleeping soma, is a denial of sorts, a little like those produced by Wakean figures themselves, who frequently try to evade death's imminent reality. If anything, sleep becomes a metaphor for death in the *Wake*, but ultimately an inadequate one. HCE's precarious physical condition is hinted at throughout the dream: in the explicit images of large man with waning vital signs ("His braynes coolt parritch, his pelt nassy, his heart's adrone, his bluidstreams acrawl, his puff but a piff" [*FW* 74]); in the concrete visions of the self as history, artifact, a thing of the past; and in the more intangible anxieties betrayed in the representations of filial overthrow, funeral rituals, and claustrophobic confinement. As I will suggest later in the chapter, the feared loss of selfhood in "that other world" is also inscribed in the dream in odd rhetorical strategies and linguistic experimentations. If "Hades" examines death from the perspective of the living, *Finnegans Wake* explores it from the perspective of the dying. One can conceptualize HCE, on one level, as an aged Bloom, whose sense of death is naturally sharper than it is in middle age; but the dreamtext, like "Hades," exposes the difficulties inherent in human attempts to conceptualize the beyond, regardless of how imminent it may feel.

As a dying man, the dreamer is still within life, his thinking shaped by the preoccupations of this world. Thoughts of death in the *Wake* are insistently subjected to ironic anthropomorphisms, infused with the conceptual categories of the living human form. Envisioning death as claustrophobic confinement, for instance, involves recourse to an experience of human spatial sensitivity and orientation; envisioning it as sleep involves an obvious assumption of its temporary nature. Another distinctly experiential metaphor for death is extreme intoxication, a surrender of bodily control to overpowering fluids, a surrender that merges with the fantasies of drowning: "fearsome where they were he had gone dump in the doomering this tide where the peixies would pickle him down to the button of his seat and his sess old soss Erinly into the boelgein with the help of Divy and Jorum's locquor and shut the door after him to make a rarely fine Ran's cattle of fish" (*FW* 316). But like sleep, the journey out of waking selfhood "with the help of Divy and Jorum's locquor" is, more often than not, a wandering with a return. Joyce explores how literally unimaginable "that other world" is by constructing a work that relentlessly attempts to think death, only to end up thinking life instead: a necro-centric perspective is a contradiction in terms.

How can a dying man, still within mental subjectivity and bodily feel-ing, think something that is radically outside these constructs? Because they anthropomorphize death to an extreme, ancient Egyptian funeral rituals are perfectly suited to the *Wake*'s exploration of the inherent limits to worldly conceptualizations of the beyond. Like a dying pharaoh, the dreamer envisions taking supplies and sustenance with him on his jour-ney: the "inhumationary bric au brac for the adornment of his glasstone honophreum" includes snuff, sheets, hatboxes, beer, water, smoked sau-sages and other savories (*FW* 77). Protective of property, an anonymous voice announces an injunction against disturbing the dead and his burial mound: "And let him rest, thou wayfarre, and take no gravespoil from him! Neither mar his mound! The bane of Tut is on it. Ware!" (*FW* 102). The Egyptology here, however, works in ambiguous ways. In its assump-tion that the dead can be roused by intruders and that he needs his worldly hoard, the injunction betrays a hope that death will be exactly like life; but to be undisturbed by the living is also to be ignored by them, to be forgotten—one of the strongest anxieties running throughout the dream. The funerary gifts for the journey are also ambiguously coded, turning frequently into devious enticements to die, bribes offered by in-sincere mourners.

Thoroughly embedded in the concerns of this world, funeral rituals often reveal more about the surviving participants than they do about the departed they purport to honor. As Freud argued most extensively in *Totem and Taboo*, elaborate mourning and solicitous preparation of the dead for burial may hide very different feelings—hostility toward him, even relief and satisfaction that he is gone. In "Hades" Bloom publicly pities Dignam's widow, while privately speculating that she might be feel-ing some sanctimonious pleasure on the occasion of her husband's alco-holic demise:

—A sad case, Mr Bloom said gently. Five young children.
—A great blow to the poor wife, Mr Kernan added.
—Indeed yes, Mr Bloom agreed.
    Has the laugh at him now. (*U* 102/84)

The sincerity of the death ritual in the *Wake* is envisioned as being simi-larly dubious, marked by a contrast between surface formalities, such as inquiries about the cause of death, and more self-interested concerns that remain unspoken: "one asks was he poisoned, one thinks how much did he leave" (*FW* 133). The dreamer hears his mourners assuring him that that his burial has been performed with a punctiliousness that is suspi-ciously excessive ("we have performed upon thee . . . all the things which the company of the precentors and of the grammarians of Christpatrick's ordered concerning thee in the matter of the work of thy tombing" [*FW* 26]). They promise him they will maintain his grave site and decorate it with expensive memorials and flowers—but flowers that turn out to be opiates to keep him dormant ("offerings of the field. . . . Poppypap's a passport out" [*FW* 25]). The unconscious mind recognizes, with uneasy clarity, the suspect impetus behind elaborate propitiatory funeral "honors."

The participants in the imagined death ritual in the dream indulge in sorrowful keening punctuated by boisterous joviality: "Sobs they sighdid at Fillagain's chrissormiss wake, all the hoolivans of the nation, prostrated in their consternation and their duodisimally profusive plethora of ululation. . . . And the all gianed in with the shoutmost shoviality" (*FW* 6). The mourners respond to the death of the father with the behavioral ambivalence that characterizes the totem feasts described by Freud. After the totem animal that signifies the primal father is slaughtered and eaten, it is "lamented and bewailed. . . . But the mourning is followed by demonstrations of festive rejoicing: every instinct is unfettered and there is licence for every kind of gratification."[6] The ambivalence of the rite betrays the ambivalence of its celebrants, the admixture of guilt and joy felt at the father's death, for the totem feast is simultaneously an act of atonement, a request for forgiveness, and a celebration, a riotous cannibalistic reenactment of the primal patricide: "The importance which is everywhere, without exception, ascribed to sacrifice [in primitive ritual] lies in the fact that it offers satisfaction to the father for the outrage inflicted on him in the same act in which that deed is commemorated."[7] Freud and Joyce seem to have discovered almost simultaneously that communion is a contemporary form of this primitive meal, Stephen recognizing in *Ulysses* the ritual's clear cannibalistic undercurrents, and Bloom concluding that they are what would make modern Christianity appealing to savages ("Rum idea: eating bits of a corpse. Why the cannibals cotton to it" [*U* 80/66]).

In *Finnegans Wake* the death watch and the communion service are always conflated, so that the wake comes to resemble perfectly a primitive totem rite, containing all its contradictory elements—the lamentation and the festivity, the pious atonement and the greedy consumption: "Earwicker is not only the corpse but also the meal; and both in the social and in the Eucharistic sense he is the Host."[8] His mourners have a decided "eatupus complex" (*FW* 128), gathering around his supine form only to consume it, "socializing and communicanting in the deification of his members, for to nobble or salvage their herobit of him, the poohpooher old bolssloose" (*FW* 498). The dead father laid out on his bier is "taboo" in the antithetical sense mapped out by Freud, being both attractive and frightening, revered and loathed, mysteriously sanative and dangerously contagious, the masses flocking to his wake "for the lure of his weal and the fear of his oppidumic . . . like lodes of ores flocking fast to Mount Maximagnetic, afeerd he was a gunner but affaird to stay away" (*FW* 497). HCE often appears as various animals, the commonest form of the taboo tribal totems[9]—"our family furbear, our tribal tarnpike" (*FW* 132)—and has recurrent fantasies of himself as food: "makes a delictuous *entrée* and finishes off the course between sweets and savouries" (*FW* 128). The fantastic visions of being eaten are the dreamer's disquieting premonition of a more realistic human fate: providing food, not for people, but for worms and maggots. The anxiety is the veiled subtext, I would argue, of those imagoes that represent a gigantic supine being, crawled on by multiple tiny creatures sometimes explicitly identified as insects ("Men like to ants or emmets wondern upon a groot hwide Whallfisk which lay in a Runnel" [*FW* 13]).

The wake in the dream becomes so riotous that it rouses the corpse, although the image of Tim Finnegan rising from his bier surely represents a psychic wish more than an actual likelihood. The myths of resurrection that permeate the *Wake*—the allusions to the Christian concept of heaven or to the Norse one of Valhalla, the secular ballad of Tim Finnegan itself, the Phoenix motif and countless other scraps of Egyptology—all work to mitigate the stinging reality of personal death, as Norris has convincingly argued.[10] The biological contingency of the self's origins can be conceded in the dream, yet the inevitability of its demise is vehemently disputed: "We may come, touch and go, from atoms and ifs but we're presurely destined to be odd's without ends" (*FW* 455). As Freud has written, "It is true that the proposition 'All men are mortal' is paraded in text-books of logic as an example of a generalization, but no human being really grasps it, and our unconscious has as little use now as ever for the idea of its own mortality."[11] Hence the dreamer envisions himself miraculously escaping his confines, like Harry Houdini ("is escapemaster-in-chief from all sorts of houdingplaces" [*FW* 127]) or simply faking death in order to avoid it, like a huge, fleshly, pragmatic Falstaff ("by such playing possum our hagious curious encestor bestly saved his brush with his posterity" [*FW* 96]).

The countless oversized imagoes of the dreamer—as a Falstaff, a mythical giant, a whale, or a mountain—have a further psychological impetus in the context of his pervasive anxieties about death. Physical massiveness is represented in the dream as a personal defense against death's finality, as an unconscious attempt to stave off the ultimate diminution of the human form:

in so hibernating Massa Ewacka, who, previous to that demidetached life, had been known of barmicidal days, cook said, between soups and savours, to get outside his own length of rainbow trout and taerts atta tarn as no man of woman born, nay could, like the great crested brebe, devour his three-scoreten of roach per lifeday, ay, and as many minnow a minute . . . was, like the salmon of his ladderleap all this time of totality secretly and by suckage feeding on his own misplaced fat. (FW 79)

According to the sanguine logic of this passage, HCE's resurrection is made possible by his former voracity, the temporary nature of his burial ensured by his obesity, the accumulated fat becoming an emergency food supply: as a defense against putrefaction he has practiced "portrifaction" (FW 78). Death is wishfully transformed here into hibernation, a snug and temporary winter's sleep in which the vital processes continue. Eating as an unconscious defense against mortality may explain the size of the two men in "Hades" who have to deal with death day in and day out—the "prosperous bulk" of John O'Connell, the cemetery's caretaker (U 107/88), and the bloated form of Father Coffey, the priest performing the funeral ritual. A perceived irony perhaps motivates the obsessive interest, on Joyce's part, in representing overweight clerics, from the "tub of guts" (P 33) in the opening chapter of Portrait, to "Aquinas tunbelly" (U 47/ 39) of "Proteus," to the voracious Shaun of 3.1 in the Wake: men who consciously believe in the immortality of the spirit are nonetheless concerned with preserving the substantiality of the flesh, the unconscious logic being that if the spirit does not perdure maybe a massive body will.

Just as fears of being eaten countercheck fantasies of compensatory eating, anxiety-ridden images of decomposition ("Load Allmarshy!" [FW 17]) frustrate wishful visions of perdurance and resurrection. The father can return after death only through cycles of natural renewal, his enormous rotting body turning into fertilizer ("being humus the same roturns" [FW 18]), like the hefty carcass of the epicure, "invaluable for [a] fruit garden," that Bloom thinks of in "Hades" (U 108/89). When this vision returns in the nightworld, the dreaming subject is the overfed corpse itself, sustaining the country's crops through bodily decay ("on the bunk of our breadwinning lies the cropse of our seedfather" [FW 55]). In the most unsavory visions of his future, the dreamer sees himself as excrement, a logical variant of fertilizer. An overdetermined image, the pervasive dung in the dream is at once the evidence of the father's sin, which by some accounts is defecation ("It may half been a missfired brick . . . or it mought have been due to a collupsus of his back promises" [FW 5]); the sign of his mortal nature that causes the soldiers in 2.3 to hesitate to kill him after realizing he will die of his own accord; his ultimate destiny and hence the legacy he leaves to future generations ("he dumptied the whole-borrow of rubbages on to soil here" [*FW* 17]). The fallen son that takes the father's place in Book 3 suffers a similarly excremental fate, descending into a toilet bowl instead of ascending to heaven: "he spoorlessly disappaled and vanesshed, like a popo down a papa, from circular circulatio" (*FW* 427). Just as the evanescent trace of the fallen father is a "'Stench!" (*FW* 17), Shaun leaves behind a dubious perfume, "a reek . . . waft on the luftstream. He was ours, all fragrance" (*FW* 427). The excremental imagoes bespeak the vulnerabilities of the human soma, but the indignities posed by the prospect of death are arguably even more threatening to the human ego. The obsessive visions of the self as dung supply a metaphor for not only an anticipated physical decay, but also a dreaded ontological status: the *Wake* reverberates with anxiety about not mattering, not signifying, about being, in short, "shit"—a concern that first surfaces, in veiled form, in the story appropriately called "The Dead."

• • •

Throughout "The Dead," Gabriel Conroy is preoccupied with cultural difference—so much so that he can even detect it in the muffled sounds of dancing feet in another room:

> He waited outside the drawing-room door until the waltz should finish, listening to the skirts that swept against it and to the shuffling of feet. . . . The indelicate clacking of the men's heels and the shuffling of their soles reminded him that their grade of culture differed from his. He would only make himself ridiculous by quoting poetry to them which they could not understand. They would think that he was airing his superior education. He would fail with them just as he had failed with the girl in the pantry. He had taken up a wrong tone. His whole speech was a mistake from first to last, an utter failure. (*D* 179)

Gabriel's self-reproaches seem to suggest that he wants to mute cultural difference, that he wishes to speak to the fellow guests on their level. But his speech, as eventually delivered, exposes the spuriousness of this desire: with its classical allusions and inflated rhetoric, it works as an assertion of difference, a pompous advertisement of intellectual superiority. Gabriel's need to distinguish himself springs from his insecurities, from his self-conscious anxieties about how others estimate him: his desire for cultural significance, in other words, is directly proportional to his fear of insignificance—not merely cultural but also ontological. By the end of "The Dead," however, when he experiences a fleeting premonition of his eventual death, his desired difference from others genuinely recedes, as individualized selfhood momentarily evaporates: "His own identity was fading out into a grey impalpable world: the solid world itself which these dead had one time reared and lived in was dissolving and dwindling" (*D* 223). Gabriel briefly abandons himself not simply to insignificance but rather to nonsignificance, to a state that obliterates signifying differences altogether. Writing about death in another modern short story, Norris has defined it ontologically as "an erasure of difference, a transition from difference to lack of difference, for is it not the case that in life we are all different while in death we are the same—or, to put it another way, is death not precisely the inability of the living to sustain their difference from the dead?"[12] The faintly falling snow unites the quick and the dead in the final image of *Dubliners*, adumbrating this failure of differentiation that all individuals ultimately succumb to and that Gabriel briefly envisions.

Death is the great leveler, the eraser of human uniqueness, as Bloom senses in "Hades" when he contemplates the waste and absurdity inherent in the custom of individualized coffins. But because he can never totally abandon the perspective of the living and its attendant presupposition of differential individuality, Bloom then imagines a corpse being "particular" about its accommodations, assuming the dead to share the categories and values of the living:

> Poor Dignam! His last lie on earth in his box. When you think of them all it does seem a waste of wood. All gnawed through. They could invent a handsome bier with a kind of panel sliding, let it down that way. Ay but they might object to be buried out of another fellow's. They're so particular. (*U* 109–10/90)

The un-particularity of death, its disquieting indifference and nondifference, is inadvertently adumbrated in burial monuments, all inscribed with the same banal and formulaic euphemisms. When Bloom mentally composes epitaphs for "So and So, wheelwright" or the man who traveled for cork lino (*U* 113/93), he expresses a desire for memorials that record human difference and individuality. Personalized and idiosyncratic, the inscriptions he imagines are tributes to the living, the differentiable—not to the dead. Observing the funeral ritual, Bloom tries to focus on signifying distinctions ("A tiny coffin flashed by.... A mourning coach. Unmarried. Black for the married. Piebald for bachelors. Dun for a nun" [*U* 95–96/79]) only to note ultimately other markers of dreary sameness ("Paltry funeral: coach and three carriages. It's all the same" [*U* 100/83]). His thoughts in "Hades" record a recurrent effort to maintain difference in the face of nondifference, but the effort never succeeds, the depersonalized nature of the rite insistently betraying the depersonalized nature of death ("Said he was going to paradise or is in paradise. Says that over everybody" [*U* 104/86]).

The concept of death as the obliteration of individual difference and significance returns in the *Wake*; it helps to explain, for instance, the dying dreamer's lack of identity. The voice that warns the dreamer, "First you were Nomad, next you were Namar, now you're Numah and it's soon you'll be Nomon" (*FW* 374), insinuates that HCE's guilty peregrinations through endless roles foreshadow the dissolution of identity in death. While maintaining traces of distinctiveness, the minimal verbal differences in the warning (Nomad/Namar/Numah/Nomon) enact this dissolution at the level of language, in the medium used to name and define the self. The final self-negating appellation "Nomon" combines the Homeric "Noman" with the Euclidean "gnomon," by definition the remainder of a parallelogram after the removal of a smaller one containing one of its corners. The geometrical shape of a "gnomon" can be visualized as a form that has started to disappear—an apt figure for a dying man, for a someone becoming a "no man." Joyce's retrospective narrator in "The Sisters" seems to recognize as much (if only unconsciously), recalling his obsession with the strange word in the context of the fallen priest's dying and death. The Wakean dreamer's tendency to name himself only through the initials HCE provides a further linguistic enactment of dissolving selfhood: at the level of the letter, he is a mere trace of his former self, a skeletal verbal residue, a "gnomon" of a fully named being.

The excess of names that flesh out those initials HCE has a paradoxical effect, the appellative excess finally yielding an appellative lack: the oversignification of the self in the *Wake* constitutes a de-signification of the self, an erasure of identity, uniqueness, singularity. Dying is figured rhetorically as an unnaming, as a reverse baptism, as a loss of one's particular verbal tag. This de-signification of the self in dream works itself out on several interrelated levels: as a loss of one's name, one's personal signifier; as a loss of one's identity and meaning, one's sense of signifying individuation; and—most disturbingly—as a loss of one's consequence, one's importance, one's significance in relation to others.

Shortly after he fantasizes his own demise in "Circe," Bloom has a vision of his funeral that provides a prototype for a recurrent scenario in the *Wake*. The anonymous "voices" of his mourners are bland, platitudinous, uncertain as to who he is, and clearly apathetic about his departure from their midst: "(*sighing*) So he's gone. Ah yes. Yes, indeed. Bloom? Never heard of him. No? Queer kind of chap. There's the widow. That so? Ah, yes" (*U* 544/444). The greatest threat to the dreaming ego in the *Wake* is precisely this stance of perfect indifference, this absence of respect or even disrespect from the perduring other. The dreamer's lack of a stable signifier reflects his lack of a stable sense of significance, name and estimation being intimately connected. Although he hopes to leave behind a good name for himself (such as "the heroest champion of Eren" [FW 398]), he fears that he does not possess a requisite amount of import to command and ensure memory, to be named and recollected at all. In his earliest proleptic vision of his wake in 1.1, HCE imagines the mourner who speaks to him giving him assurance that he will be well remembered, that people will reminisce about him fondly ("Your fame is spreading like Basilico's ointment. . . . The menhere's always talking of you" [FW 25]). But the focus of this monologue suddenly shifts away from the dying dreamer to the world of the living he is departing—"Everything's going on the same or so it appeals to all of us, in the old holmsted here" (FW 26)—the shift hinting that his friends and family are very much preoccupied with their own concerns, that he is fading from memory already, that he is rapidly becoming a "no man" and a "gnomon": the assertions of the discourse are undermined by its trajectory. In a strange memory of nonmemory, HCE recollects the land of the living only to envision himself being forgotten.

This anonymous speech that closes 1.1 is a catalogue of optimistic assertions and promises that express antithetical disturbing thoughts. What sounds on the surface like a calm reassurance that all is well in "the old holmsted," for instance, is in fact a disquieting hint that the dreamer's presence there has always been marginal: he is clearly neither missed nor needed. The cheery descriptions of the daughter and wife getting along fine in the world of the living produce not so much a sense of relief and comfort as a sharply felt pang of longing and desire. Immediately after the news of the daughter's supposed career as an exotic dancer is reported ("She's making her rep at Lanner's twicenightly. With the tabarine tam-tammers of the whirligigmagees. Beats that cachucha flat. 'Twould dilate your heart to go"), the dreamer tries to rise, only to imagine himself being pinned down by his mourners ("Aisy now, you decent man, with your knees and lie quiet and repose your honour's lordship! Hold him here, Ezekiel Irons, and may God strengthen you!" [FW 27]). The evocation of the wife's youthful head of hair has a similar effect, precipitating a second moment of restiveness: "Her hair's as brown as ever it was. And wivvy and wavy. Repose you now! Finn no more!" (FW 28). The thought of disappearing from the midst of one's family and friends engenders a desire to reassert one's presence. The dreamer's implicit response to the imagined monologue exposes its devious rhetoric of sham consolation.

The fear of becoming an anonymous cipher is generated in part by the grim realization of human substitutionality. HCE envisions himself forgotten and unmissed because he senses that he may be replaced by another who will easily assume his functions: "For, be that samesake sibsubstitute of a hooky salmon, there's already a big rody ram lad at random on the premises of his haunt of the hungred bordles, as it is told me. Shop Illicit, flourishing like a lordmajor or a buaboabaybohm" (*FW* 28–29). With its hint that someone bigger, more impressive, and more qualified will take the dreamer's place, the ominous announcement roughly echoes one Bloom hears in "Circe" from the sadistic Bello: "(*sarcastically*) I wouldn't hurt your feelings for the world but there's a man of brawn in possession there. The tables are turned, my gay young fellow! He is something like a fullgrown outdoor man" (*U* 541/441). Since one's position can always be filled by another, the human disposition to define the self in terms of role—within the family, workplace, society, or state— leaves the ego vulnerable to fears of facile succession. At the level of the unconscious, the impersonal and artificial nature of cultural roles—their status as a "part" that is "performed"—awakens a sense of personal insignificance often repressed in conscious thought, where roles—even onerous ones—usually carry connotations of responsibility, duty, and personal significance rather than its opposite. In the context of the dreamer's fears about substitutionality, only highly ambiguous consolation can be heard in the voiced assertions that others can imitate HCE, reproduce his mannerisms in an "act" ("Mick Mac Magnus MacCawley can take you off to pure perfection" [*FW* 25–26]; "Stout Stokes would take you offly" [*FW* 619]). While such "take-offs" constitute a tribute of sorts and ensure remembrance, they also suggest that the self can be reduplicated—and in perhaps implicitly insulting form. Physiological reduplication of the self is similarly threatening to the ego, as Stephen Dedalus argues during his dissection of Shakespeare in "Scylla and Charybdis": "The images of other males of his blood will repel him. He will see in them grotesque attempts of nature to foretell or repeat himself" (*U* 195–96/161). In HCE's dream the descriptions of "other males of his blood" who resemble him are often couched in misleadingly mawkish terms—"Whene'er I see those smiles in [Kevin's] eyes 'tis Father Quinn again" (*FW* 562)— perhaps to disguise the anxiety behind the image. This form of suspicious sentimentality first surfaces in *A Portrait of the Artist*, when Simon cries at the sight of Stephen dressed like a little man for his first Christmas dinner "because [Simon] was thinking of his own father" (*P* 30)—and also presumably of his own younger self whom his son has supplanted. But the prospect of supersession in the *Wake* can also produce soberer visions of the moribund self as a flawed and useless automobile, invariably followed by a newer model ("he . . . was recalled and scrapheaped by the Maker" [*FW* 98]), visions akin to Bloom's in "Hades," where decaying internal organs are likened to worn-out and discarded machinery ("Lots of them lying around here: lungs, hearts, livers. Old rusty pumps" [*U* 105/87]). The process of endless mechanical production and reproduction supplies the impersonal vehicle for thoughts of more personal replaceability.

The dreamer's horror at the prospect of "after his life overlasting . . . being reduced to nothing" (FW 499) leads to fantasies of compensation, of psychically gratifying substitutes for the self. Freud's comment in "The 'Uncanny'" on the compensatory impulse propelling various themes and forms of representation sheds interesting light on their counterparts in the Wake:

> the 'double' was originally an insurance against destruction to the ego, 'an energetic denial of the power of death,' as Rank says; and probably the 'immortal' soul was the first 'double' of the body. This invention of doubling as a preservation against extinction has its counterpart in the language of dreams, which is fond of representing castration by a doubling or multiplication of the genital symbol; the same desire spurred on the ancient Egyptians to the art of making images of the dead in some lasting material.[13]

The dreamer suffers from the castration complex—in the revisionary Lacanian meaning of the term—insofar as he is plagued by a general sense of lack. This feeling may have its origins in HCE's realization of the ultimate insubstantiality of the body pitted against the onslaught of time, but the consequence of the perceived physical vulnerability is metaphysical in its import: a feeling that he is missing something as a person, that he is not consequent enough to perdure. He hopes to be immortalized in a constellation but fears he will only end up with his head ignominiously buried in shit ("Your heart is in the system of the Shewolf and your crested head is in the tropic of Copricapron [koproi kaprôn: pig shit in Greek]" [FW 26]). The recuperative strategies employed in the dream to deal with anxieties about lack, both bodily and reputational, are precisely the three mentioned by Freud: a wishful belief in immortality; a multiplication of the self's signifier, of its compensatory "phallus"; and numerous representations of the self's image recorded in some preservative medium.

HCE's multiple signifiers in the dream that ultimately only negate selfhood have an ambiguous psychic status: they also function as a compensatory assertion of identity, a production of identity in wishful excess as it were, as if numerous appellations provided a defense against the possibility of a lone one being forgotten. HCE's numerous nominative signifiers are replicated in his abundant representational signifiers, in those envisioned substitutive markers that leave a record of the self: statues, monuments, relics, coats of armor, photos, movies, ballads, newspaper reports, and epics. The Wake at many points becomes a self-reflexive narrative about narrative, containing numerous references to storytelling particularly dense in 1.2 ("the best authenticated version . . . has it that it was this way" [FW 30]; "They tell the story" [FW 35]; "as the aftertale hath it" [FW 38]; "the tale rambles along" [FW 41–42]). These tales within tales contribute to the larger recurrent vision of the self being replaced by textuality: the *Wake* turns into a whirlpool of excessive discourse, the receding center of which is the dreamer himself. But the endless tales about the self are often reduced to mere traces of narrative, mere fragments of coherent sound and information—hearsay, echoes, noise. The degeneration of temporal constructs, such as stories, into rumor or cacophony parallels the degeneration of spatial constructs, such as monuments, into ruins or junk.

The compensatory records of the self imagined in the dream are ultimately an inadequate defense against the power of time to level meaning, to obliterate signifying differences. Inscribed in materiality, those records are as vulnerable to erasure and ultimate nonsignification as the corporeal self they attempt to memorialize:

> How charmingly exquisite! It reminds you of the outwashed engravure that we used to be blurring on the blotchwall of his innkempt house. Used they? ... I say, the remains of the outworn gravemure where used to be blurried the Ptollmens of the Incabus. Used we? (*FW* 13)

The linguistic erasure here is recorded on two levels: within the dream imagoes of HCE as the washed-out, blurring engraving and the worn-out, blurring tombstone ("gravemure"), and within the dream rhetoric, the second sentence being an effaced or blurred version of the first, containing verbal traces of its structure and diction (reminds/remains, outwashed/outworn, engravure/gravemure, blurring/blurried, innkempt house/Incabus). The process of dying and being forgotten is figured in dream as the disappearance of visual forms and verbal inscriptions. Language undoing itself, effacements of meaning, tales vanishing through retraction—these are Joyce's rhetorical strategies for approximating that unwritable "other world," for signifying nothing.

Exactly how the ephemeral textual remains and markers of the self will be interpreted after death by the perduring other is the dream's most recurrent obsession, the self's reputational "wake" being beyond its control or knowledge ("the earthball where indeeth we shall calm decline, our legacy unknown" [*FW* 79]). HCE has anxiety visions of the populace writing an insulting epitaph in his memory that expresses their desire to be rid of him: the "councils public" present him with "a stone slab with the usual Mac Pelah address of velediction ... : We have done ours gohellt with you, Heer Herewhippit, overgiven it [*overgeven*: give up in Dutch], skidoo!" (*FW* 77). The fragmented stories about HCE that surface in the dream only to be later revised or forgotten are frequently highly unflattering. The "sigla H.C.E." on exhumed holographs, for instance, first receive a grandiose interpretation ("An imposing everybody he always indeed looked" [*FW* 32]), but then a more slanderous construction of their significance emerges ("A baser meaning has been read into these characters the literal sense of which decency can safely scarcely hint" [FW 33]). The prototype for the reputational wake in the dream is found in "The Sisters," where Father Flynn leaves behind a trail of scandalous speculation. As Phillip Herring writes, in the ritual dialogue of condolence that closes the story, "One expects to learn nothing, yet the shocker comes when the sisters deviate from traditional inanity to reveal information about their brother that the priest would have wished left unsaid."[14] The compromising conversation is the model for HCE's dominant and most disturbing fantasy: being talked about and accused of crimes when one is helpless to defend oneself. The defamatory voices that reverberate throughout the dream reflect HCE's fear that he will be known only for his sins, as if he were Father Flynn reincarnated, overhearing the gossip at his own death watch.

The self's enduring significance is precarious because entirely dependent upon the memory of others: not only might others remember the self in unflattering and undesirable ways or forget to remember at all—others too are only mortal and hence inadequate to ensure personal perdurability. As Bloom senses in "Hades," the self's reputational legacy can die twice, first when it fades from living remembrance, secondly—and most finally—when those who did once remember die: "People talk about you a bit: forget you. Don't forget to pray for him. Remember him in your prayers. Even Parnell. Ivy day dying out. Then they follow: dropping into a hole, one after the other" (U 111/91). A vision of this secondary death is more elaborately imaged in the *Wake* when at the beginning of 1.3 all the carriers of HCE's dubious acclaim in 1.2 suddenly vanish one by one: Frisky Shorty becomes "the decentest dozendest short of a frusker . . . [who] disappeared . . . from the sourface of this earth"; Peter Cloran, who turns into "Paul Horan" and later "Orani," is referred to in the past tense ("He was."); O'Mara, now "A'Hara (Okaroff?)," is also reported to have perished; and Hosty reappears as "Osti-Fosti" but only to disappear with the rumor that "no one end [of him] is known" (FW 48–50). The transience of these spreaders of the dreamer's infamy is etched into their very names, all of which resurface in altered form. The nominal erasures adumbrating their bodily disappearances suggest their own vulnerability to uncertain remembrance. Joyce sets up a regress of vanishing acts: the deceased HCE verbally disappears with the obliteration of the rumor carriers, who do not simply die, but also are verbally erased and forgotten in their turn.

Even perduring monuments offer no protection against anonymity, for they easily turn into empty signifiers, markers whose meaning is lost on the average human being ("Sir Philip Crampton's memorial fountain bust. Who was he?" [U 92/76]). In the *Wake* lasting memorials often only record embarrassments, errancy, or weaknesses: the illustrious Wellington monument turns into the father's erect phallus, and his museum (or "museyroom" [FW 8]) only saves for posterity a record of his humiliating defeat and fall. When HCE's memorials are reduced to junk or random trash ("upshoot of picnic"; "*Dig him in the rubsh!*" [FW 261]), they become markers which fail to "signify" in both senses of the word: they neither produce an intelligible message nor confer an iota of prestige.

Dying is conceptualized in the *Wake* as an odyssey of irrevocable and manifold dispossession. The octogenarians of 2.4 have experienced loss in a devastatingly thorough way: loss of property, spouse, clothing, occupation, health, gender identity, sexual potency, mental acuity, and control over bodily functions. The *Wake* dramatizes countless skirmishes between male rivals over physical possessions (territory, money, women) and metaphysical commodities (power, social prestige, familial legitimacy); but the futility of the warfare is recognized in the recurrent visions of time as the leveler of amassed goods and acclaim, in the imagoes, for instance, of the self as dispersed physical detritus. The dream contains the wisdom that dispossession often brings, the wisdom heard earlier in Stephen's thoughts in "Nestor"—"Vain patience to heap and hoard. Time surely would scatter all" (U 34/28)—against the ironic backdrop of Deasy's advocacy of material accumulation and the students' struggle for the prestige of victory.

Death involves also a dispossession of visual presence, as Bloom realizes during Dignam's burial when he sounds the literal and morbid residue of a common figure of speech: "The clay fell softer. Begin to be forgotten. Out of sight, out of mind" (U 111/91). The most viscerally frightening aspect of death—the decay and disappearance of the human form—is put "out of sight" in two ways, literally through the almost unique ritual of burial ("Only man buries. No, ants too. First thing strikes anybody. Bury the dead" [U 109/90]), figuratively through psychological repression. In the dream the anxieties associated with disappearance are negated in wishful imagoes of reappearance, visual return. At the end of 1.8, an apparition of HCE emerges amid the scandalous gossip of the washerwomen, the visual absence reasserting traces of presence: "Is that the great Finnleader himself in his joakimono on his statue riding the high horse there forehengist? Father of Otters, it is himself! Yonne there! Isset that? . . . Holy Scamander, I sar it again! Near the golden falls. Icis on us! Seints of light! Zezere!" (FW 214). HCE identifies throughout the *Wake* with heroes and leaders that come back after long absence or presumed destruction: The Flying Dutchman, Odysseus, Osiris, King Arthur, Rip van Winkle. These figures return, moreover, not only within their stories and myths, but also in the larger scheme of recorded history: the dreamer's appropriation of them bespeaks a desire for similarly legendary status, for literary if not bodily immortality. *Finnegans Wake* exposes the profoundest psychic impetus behind heroic identifications in a way that *Ulysses* does not. The self-inflating Circean imagoes of Bloom as the nation's savior spring merely from his random daydreams about municipal improvement and his desire to be accepted as legitimately Irish. The unpresumptuous Bloom, of course, also secretly shares the common human longing for renown. In the *Wake* this wish to be significant is generated by the fear of being—not simply insignificant—but rather nonsignificant; fantasies of fame and distinction become defensive protests against the dreaded collapse of ontological difference effected most absolutely by death.

If dying in the *Wake* is figured as the disappearance of signifying differences, escape from dying is figured as their reemergence. Suggestively, it is only at the wishfully envisioned moment of awakening that HCE starts to regain a sense of individuation. Immediately before he imagines his wife trying to rouse him from his comatose sleep, he hears her differentiating him from Finn MacCool ("Hence we've lived in two worlds. He is another he what stays under the himp of holth" [*FW* 619]), so that the return of self and the return to life become temporally linked. Although his identity is never totally clarified or fixed, the contours of a distinguishable person start to come into focus within the discourse of the fantasized monologue that follows. Ironically, however, the dreamer regains personal significance, individuating meaning, only to be reduced to insignificance: he emerges as a figure that is domestic, familiar, more particularized than anywhere else in the *Wake*—but as a figure that is also quintessentially ordinary. HCE's paradoxical dream vision of himself as an "everyman" and a "no man" creates the perfect trope for death itself: every differentiable being's ultimate capitulation to nondifference, anonymity, nothingness.

Chapter 5

"SEE OURSELVES AS OTHERS SEE US":
THE ROLE OF THE OTHER
IN INDETERMINATE SELFHOOD

ULYSSES has a curiously hesitant opening, and like hesitancies elsewhere in Joyce's fictions, this one functions to betray. Buck Mulligan steps up onto an open-air stage of sorts, carrying his shaving equipment; he intones a Latinate phrase from the Mass—and then suddenly halts. The exact motive behind this pause remains ambiguous. Does Mulligan start his mock ritual for the benefit of a wholly imaginary eye, only to realize that an actual eye is preferable and readily available? Or does he interrupt his theatrics when he realizes that the actual eye he has posited from the start is in fact wholly imaginary, that he has no audience, that he must summon forth his weary tower mate to watch the show? The second explanation seems more likely, but in either event the significance of that halt is largely the same: the gestural hesitancy betrays Mulligan's interest in the eye of the other, his desire for an other to witness and, he hopes, to appreciate his early morning performance. This brief opening pause hints at a concern that preoccupied Joyce throughout his literary career, most prominently in *Ulysses* and *Finnegans Wake*: the self-conscious subject, the subject intensely aware of and sensitive to the other's eye. When Stephen looks in the mirror later in "Telemachus," he thinks to himself, "As he and others see me. Who chose this face for me?" (*U* 6/6); instead of identifying with the image, he immediately envisions it as something looked at by other subjectivities. Like many other Joycean characters, Stephen is highly self-conscious, afflicted by "an obsessive sense of being watched, even when, as in 'Proteus,' there is no one present to do the watching."[1] Bloom, too, is preoccupied with the eye of the other, wondering at lunch hour, when he sees a man wolfing down food in the Burton, "Am I like that? See ourselves as others see us" (*U* 169/139).

The Robert Burns poem that Joyce alludes to in these words suggests that, much as we may try, we never do see ourselves as others see us: "O wad some Power the giftie gie us / To see oursels as ithers see us! / It wad frae monie a blunder free us, / An' foolish notion: / What airs in dress an' gait wad lea'e us, / An' even devotion."[2] The basic point that captured Joyce's attention in Burns's poem has also been explored in psychoanalytic thought. Because the conscious subject is irremediably limited, self-perception involves misperception, *méconnaissance*, the subject's field of vision inevitably containing a scotoma, a dark or blind spot. As Jacques Lacan writes in his lecture on the gaze, "No doubt, in the depths of my eye, the picture is painted. The picture, certainly, is in my eye. But I am not in the picture. . . . if I am anything in the picture, it is always in the form of . . . the stain, the spot [i.e., the scotoma]."[3] Several points in this lecture inform my own study of Joyce's interest in the attempt to transcend the limits to self-perception by seeing the self through the eye of the other.

Lacan's relevance to the Joycean corpus may not be merely coincidental, for his lecture shares a common theoretical source with at least one of Joyce's fictions, his final dreambook *Finnegans Wake*. Lacan elaborates on and responds to several works, including Freud's case history of the Wolf Man ("From the History of an Infantile Neurosis"); Joyce carefully studied this Freudian text, took notes on it, and worked explicit elements of it into the *Wake*.[4] Joyce and Lacan were both keenly interested in intersubjective vision, and perhaps they were drawn to the Wolf Man's case history because of what it suggests about the self in relation to the eye of the other. After briefly outlining my understanding of a few of Lacan's contentions and showing their coincidence with several features of Joycean texts, I confine my focus in this chapter to Joyce's contrasting representations of intersubjective perception in his waking and night worlds and to his exploration of the negative and positive psychological functions of the other's gaze. An examination of these issues provides a clue to the logic of the *Wake*'s highly idiosyncratic structure, a problem that has long baffled critics; it also sheds some light on the sexual dynamics of intersubjectivity as Joyce represented them over the course of his career.

In discussing intersubjectivity in conscious and unconscious life, Lacan suggests that dreaming involves a crucial alteration in the subject's relation to the other's eye:

> we are beings who are looked at, in the spectacle of the world. That which makes us consciousness institutes us by the same token as *speculum mundi*. . . . in the so-called waking state, there is an elision of the gaze, and an elision of the fact that not only does it look, *it* also *shows*. In the field of dream, on the other hand, what characterizes the images is that *it shows*. . . . So much is [this insistence on showing] to the fore . . . that, in the final resort, our position in the dream is profoundly that of someone who does not see. The subject does not see where it is leading, he follows.[5]

This insistence on "showing" gives dreams a dramatic and impersonal quality, despite their obvious subjectivity, as Freud implies in *The Inter-*

pretation of Dreams: "a thought ... is objectified in the dream, is represented as a scene, or so it seems to us, is experienced. ... the thought is represented as an immediate situation with the 'perhaps' omitted, and ... transformed into visual images and speech."[6] In the process the self sometimes becomes its own spectacle, an object of its own theatrical viewing. The seemingly "scenic" and "objectified" status of the dreamtext may help to explain why Joyce chose the dramatic mode for "Circe" and why he constructs *Finnegans Wake* as a "drema" (*FW* 69), as a series of densely complicated tableaux and speeches, with a central or singular narrative I/eye glaringly absent.[7] What the unconscious theatrically "shows," on one level, are images of the self and its desires that the subject does not want to recognize and that are hence elided in waking life. By day, for instance, Bloom may not fully acknowledge that he plays a role in his own cuckolding and derives pleasure from his complicity, but in the unconscious fantasies of "Circe" this guilty truth is vividly revealed to him: he envisions himself as pander to Molly and Boylan, servilely waiting on them and heeding his rival's instructions to "apply your eye to the keyhole and play with yourself while I just go through her a few times" (*U* 566/462). Bloom's vision also dramatizes the possibility that Molly and Boylan are very much aware of his voyeuristic presence, that they are watching him watch, that the viewing subject is also the viewed object. Joyce creates in Bloom a paradoxically blind voyeur, one whose visual acuity and curiosity are matched by psychic scotomas that blot out those images working to show the self as it would not wish to be seen.

More important, Lacan's formulation suggests that the key truth usually elided in waking life is the gaze itself, the gaze of the other that makes attitudes of "deviance" deviant to begin with, the gaze that causes various desires to be shameful and embarrassing, shame and embarrassment being strictly intersubjective responses. Dramatizations or "showings" of this normally elided gaze can be found in the case history of the Wolf Man and throughout Joyce's works. What is made both visible and literal in the Wolf Man's dream of the watching wolves in the tree is the gaze of the other, in this instance of the father himself. But of course in the primal scene for which the dream supposedly provides a screen, the father is not watching the child at all; the child only imagines the father's gaze, leveled at him, the subject, in a taboo position (the position of the voyeur)—the position that the dream's key reversal carefully censors and yet betrays by turning the viewing subject into viewed object.[8] Although on deeper levels the son's dream may indeed express his anxieties about castration, its projection of a wholly imaginary gaze as actual more obviously dramatizes the subject's enthrallment to the other. A similar projection appears in *Portrait* when Stephen, affected by Father Arnall's hellfire sermon, has a paranoiac vision of his bedroom as a cave filled with judgmental inhabitants: "Faces were there; eyes: they waited and watched. . . . Murmuring faces waited and watched; murmurous voices filled the dark shell of the cave" (*P* 136). Like those in the Wolf Man's case history, these prying eyes can be read both as a momentary externalization of the self's conscience and as an inverted image of the self's voyeuristic transgressions: shortly after this hallucinatory vision, Stephen reminds himself, "He was in mortal sin. Even once was a mortal sin. It could happen in an instant. But how so quickly? *By seeing or by thinking of seeing*" (*P* 139, emphasis added). Lacan translates into theory what Joyce and Freud represent in fiction and case history, emphasizing both the factitiousness of the gaze ("The gaze I encounter is, not a seen gaze, but a gaze imagined by me in the field of the Other") and the subject's absurd enthrallment to it: "the level of reciprocity between the gaze and the gazed at is, for the subject, more open than any other to alibi."[9] The subject is always aware of the gaze, is always watching the gaze—reflexively, not intentionally or consciously—but the gaze is not necessarily watching the subject. Hence Lacan likens the gaze to ocelli, the eyelike spots on some forms of wildlife—for example, leopards, ocelots, and various butterflies—that potential predators often mistake for eyes but that of course see nothing at all. These ocelli-like eyes will reappear with a vengeance in the hallucinations of "Circe" and again in *Finnegans Wake*, where others are recurrently marked as "wickedgapers" (*FW* 366) and "peersons" (*FW* 60).

The waking subject's reflexive watching of the gaze can be seen most patently in "Lotus Eaters," where Bloom is guiltily self-conscious, marching soberly through the episode's sleepy, soporific atmosphere; he remains visually alert, carefully checking to make sure that no one he knows sees him enter the post office or walk down a back lane to read Martha's most recent letter. When he retrieves the post-office-box card from his hatband but hides the gesture by pretending he has taken off his hat to wipe his brow, Bloom is putting on an act for an imagined other, performing for a gaze not actually there. Elsewhere in the novel, however, Bloom considers himself relatively indifferent to what others think of him, curious about the other's point of view only as a source of potential insight into himself, although he does admit, significantly, that he is sensitive to the good opinion of the opposite sex. In "Nausicaa" when an unnamed gentleman he has seen earlier passes by again on the strand, Bloom thinks to himself, "Walk after him now make him awkward like those newsboys me today. Still you learn something. See ourselves as others see us. So long as women don't mock what matter?" (*U* 375–76/307). As his thoughts about "parallax" suggest, Bloom in waking life sees alternative points of view as part of an intellectual pastime, as providing an interesting exercise in envisioning the way an object or person changes when looked at from a different vantage point.[10] Attuned to perceptual relativity, he is usually willing to concede the validity of others' opinions, to "look at it other way round" (*U* 380/311). In "Circe," however, parallactic vision is replaced by the paranoiac, the opinions and perspectives of the various phantasms being not an intellectual interest, but a personal psychic threat, the gaze of the other being an agency not of insight but rather of exposure: in accordance with Lacan's argument, the gaze here is revealed as not simply looking but also showing. On the level of the unconscious, Bloom is very much concerned with what the other thinks of him, with how the other sees him, as his dialectical fantasies of persecution and grandeur imply.

Over the course of "Circe," the human other gives way to the nonhuman: the nymph from the picture over Bloom's bed; the statue from the museum; the babbling waterfall, murmuring yew trees, and ruminating calf from Bloom's high school field trip to Poulaphouca; the nannygoat from his romantic outing to Howth Head—all enter the stream of phantasms as witnesses to Bloom's polymorphous desires. These nonhuman accusers once again betray the gaze as imaginary, emphasizing the way that human self-consciousness is constituted and mediated by factitious ocelli: eyes in pictures or on statues do not really look, of course, while those of animals do see but without moral censure. The calf from Poulaphouca and the nannygoat from Howth are surely indifferent to the potential indiscretion of masturbating in the woods or making love in the open air—such an activity is embarrassing only to a human being envisioning a judgmental eye. Like the dream in the Wolf Man case history, Bloom's unconscious fantasies show forth this elided gaze, his repressed and even denied enthrallment to that imaginary but ever-present other.

Finnegans Wake inherits the paranoiac ambiance and perverse imagoes of the "Circe" chapter, the fallen dreamer picturing himself in almost every conceivable posture of "deviance": as voyeur, exhibitionist, sadist, masochist, self-contrived cuckold, furtive adulterer, lecherous desirer of the daughter, homosexual desirer of the sons. Joyce represents the dream as the site of negative epiphanies, a conception of dream he shares with (and perhaps derives from) Freud. He may have borrowed from the Wolf Man case history in particular one possible unconscious interpretation of Christmas, the season of the epiphany, although he partially recasts its psychic significance to suit the dominant paternal perspective of the *Wake*. Freud speculates that his patient had the wolf dream on Christmas eve (also the eve of his fourth birthday) after falling asleep "in tense expectation of the day which was to bring him a double quantity of presents."[11] The wish for material gifts from the father screens a wish for sexual gifts from the father, and in his dream the boy constructs an imaginary precondition for obtaining this erotic satisfaction by recalling from the primal scene the female's position and her genitalia. Because the patient equates—unconsciously and erroneously—female sexual pleasure with a prior and necessary castration, the dream memory translates "gifts" as "punishment," turning the wish into an anxiety. Joyce's Christmas motif in the Wakean dream is similar insofar as Christmas gifts consistently turn into their psychological opposite and insofar as Christmastime epiphanies seem precisely designed to shock and disturb. ALP's knapsack, which doubles as Santa Claus's sack of goodies (*FW* 209), may be a Pandora's box of sorts or a dangerous document one hesitates to open ("My colonial, wardha bagful! . . . All that and more under one crinoline envelope if you dare to break the porkbarrel seal. No wonder they'd run from her pison plague" [*FW* 212]). Exploring a dreaming father's fears, Joyce makes Christmas the occasion for "youlldied greedings" from oedipal offspring (*FW* 308), for dramatic realizations of relentless generational succession and personal mortality: in the *Wake* the traditional season of the son's birth is frequently associated only with the father's death. Epiphany takes the form of both psychological exposure, a showing forth of repressed truths and perverse desires, and physical exposure, a showing forth of normally concealed bodily parts. When the dreamer envisions his back buttons popping off his pants (cf. Bloom's "*back trouserbutton snap[ping]*" [*U* 552/450] in "Circe"), a voice suddenly exclaims, "How culious an epiphany!" (*FW* 508).

Resembling "Circe" in structure as well as in theme, *Finnegans Wake* inverts waking subject/object relations, recurrently representing the subject as spectacle, as the object of the other's eye. In 2.3 a vision of the pub customers staring at a hunting picture on the wall (*FW* 334) is followed by the Butt and Taff skit, also presumably watched by HCE's clientele, on the screen of a TV set: the two pieces of dreamtext seem homologously connected, for the televised drama turns into a hunting story, with the target being the dreamer himself. Adaline Glasheen likens the television set to the mousetrap in *Hamlet*, to the play the prince stages for Claudius and Gertrude:[12] the analogy is apt, for the set functions as an agency of exposure, as a medium that openly dramatizes embarrassing possibilities, unflattering and threatening images of the self—the father letting down his pants and defecating in public, the spying sons then shooting this vulnerable authority figure. The content and form of the dreamtext here are psychically related, both expressing fears of being shot—by a gun in the skit itself and by a camera in its televised structure. Later in the dream HCE's bedroom turns into a movie set (*FW* 558–59), the mise-en-scène for a particularly frustrating session of intercourse. Despite all the athletic frenzy of the scene, HCE's efforts are indeed strained, and his wife is imagined laughing at his performance (*FW* 583). The possibility of being poorly reflected in his wife's gaze spawns a vision of being exposed to a more general gaze, HCE fearing that his humiliating sexual showing—

"the coming event" indicative of the father's decline—will be widely pub-
licized: "The man in the street can see the coming event. Photoflashing it
far too wide. It will be known through all Urania soon" (*FW* 583). The
dreamer is threatened by actual eyes as well as by mechanical ones ("hitch
a cock eye, he was snapped on the sly" [*FW* 363]), dreading an "exposure" of the self in every sense of the word.

Given the fear of cameras in the dream, it is not surprising that the
potentially scandalous nightletter takes the shape of a photo negative, the
written exposé transforming into a visual one. HCE is figured as a cam-
eraman whose equipment is turned upon him to bring about his down-
fall ("you were shutter reshottus and sieger besieged" [*FW* 352]) or as
Charles Dodgson snapped in intimate self-portraiture with his little friend
Alice ("And there many have paused before that exposure of him by old
Tom Quad, a flashback in which he sits sated . . . [with] the tata of a tiny
victorienne, Alys, pressed by his limper looser" [*FW* 57]). These visions
are part of a larger dream pattern that represents HCE as representation—as a picture, a monument, a statue, or an exhibit in a wax museum.
In the Wakean nightworld, the self is often imagined both as a figurative
object, as a person looked at by intrusive eyes in intersubjective perceptual relations, and as a literal object, as a nonhuman thing examined by
human others. The dreamer's subjectivity is not simply threatened and
preempted by the subjectivities of others, it is inscribed imagistically as
nonexistent, defunct. In the context of the pervasive anxieties about
human mortality, these visions of the reified self become attempts to
imagine death, to think within subjectivity what it is like to be without
subjectivity, to conceptualize that moment when the self is utterly and
irrevocably replaced by figuration—figuration left to the hermeneutical
whims of an unknown other. The gaze is inscribed as a potential perpetu-
ity that follows the self beyond the bourn, although, as I suggest later,
such an inscription records a wish as well as an anxiety.

In a similarly reifying dream imago, the corporeal self is imagined as
physical territory, invaded physical territory—literally invaded in the visions of homosexual rape, figuratively in the fantasies of the body as investigated terrain. Blending somatic and external worlds, the dreamer frequently perceives the self as inflated or gargantuan: visits to his property
turn into tours of his body which then becomes a landscape that others
walk on and explore. This conflation of private and public premises is
best seen in the sequence where the four old men investigate the father's
physical plant—his house and tavern—as well as his physical form (3.4).
Imagining the four watching his large shape at work on the marriage bed,
the dreamer suddenly envisions himself as Phoenix Park, the "second position of discordance . . . [in which] the male entail partially eclipses the
femecovert" (*FW* 564) turning into an overhead view of the park's land-

scape. His rectum becomes a gorge, cave, or well into which visitors throw an echo, while some suspicious welts and bruises on his bottom turn into belts of trees or silver mines: "The black and blue marks athwart the weald, which now barely is so stripped, indicate the presence of sylvious beltings" (FW 564). The gargantuan imagoes of the self limn for the reader the dreamer's implicit physical condition, his sense of being ponderous, fallen, inert; but the fantasy of being a terrain traversed by others may have a psychic rather than a somatic origin. If the *Wake* is structured largely around myths of "trespass," expressing unconscious desires to transgress lawful boundaries,[13] then the visions of intruders tromping over the body's territory, violating the self's physical boundaries, literalize the trope. If the prime trangressor is in fact HCE, who in dream explores his own unlawful impulses, then a guilty subject/object reversal has occurred, the trespasser defensively representing himself as the trespassed against.

HCE's continual sense of the self as a viewed and explored object is connected to his elusive transgression that flickers across the surface of the dream in an endless array of forms. This mysterious fall, which HCE wants both to remember and to forget, usually involves one older man, two younger women, and three younger men, and in its most abbreviated form it is designated simply by the numbers one, two, three. Although the structure and nature of the temptation are protean, representationally unstable, the two young women and three young men often haunt the dream as unwanted witnesses to transgression, taking shape as meddlers, spies, intrusive fusiliers and forest rangers:

> it seemed he was before the eyots of martas or otherwales the thirds of fossilyears (FW 40)

> The two childspies waapreesing him auza de Vologue but the renting of his rock was from the three wicked Vuncouverers Forests bent down awhits, arthou sure? (FW 88)

> A pair of sycopanties with amygdaleine eyes, one old obster lumpky pumpkin and three meddlars on their slies. (FW 94)

> *Fickleyes and Futilears* (FW 176)

Joyce often represents the young men metonymically as eavesdroppers (fossily*ears*, futil*ears*) and also stresses their role as witnesses and voyeurs ("widness thane and tysk and hanry" [FW 316]; "peep of tim boys and piping tom boys" [FW 385]). What is psychically disturbing to the dreamer is not committing any particular sin but being seen in the act of sinning. This threat is clear even when the fall becomes literal, when it takes the form of tipsy Tim Finnegan crashing down from his ladder:

"wan warning Phill filt tippling full. His howd feeled heavy, his hoddit did shake. (There was a wall of course in erection) Dimb! He stottered from the latter. Damb! he was dud. Dumb! Mastabatoom, mastabad-tomm, when a mon merries his lute is all long. *For whole the world to see*" (*FW* 6, emphasis added). At points, however, the dreamer suspects that his watchers are unreal, that the threatening eyes are merely ocelli. He envisions himself predominantly as viewed object but also occasion-ally as a viewing voyeuristic subject observed only by an impervious uni-verse, only by "the clouds aboon"—the clouds above and the clouds alone: "aither he cursed and recursed and was everseen doing what your fourfootlers saw or he was never done seeing what you coolpigeons know, weep the clouds aboon for smiledown witnesses" (*FW* 29). HCE's transgression is appropriately described as "the fairest sin the sunsaw" (*FW* 11)—as a sin seen by the prying oedipal offspring or maybe only by the sun, by oblivious and indifferent nature.

Instead of momentarily disappearing, the gaze more frequently multi-plies, compounds itself, forming voyeuristic regresses wherein one party is watched by another party, who in turn is watched by another party, who in turn is watched by still another. The regression of gazes drama-tizes the self-consciousness of the human subject of desire: the image of the self in a position of desire seems to spawn automatically a representa-tion of the gaze, imagined as the eye of another prurient and desirous viewer, who is thus always reflexively conscious of yet another gaze. More patently, the voyeuristic regress exposes the vulnerability of the voyeur, the way in which the pruriently viewing subject, presumably safe in a position of furtive pleasure, may unknowingly also be the viewed object of yet another I/eye, or of the I/eye it is itself secretly viewing (one recalls Bloom's Circean vision of Molly and Boylan). Power is the psychic issue in images that combine seeing with being seen, for they question the self's control over its own assumed position as subject. Joyce explores the limits of this control in his early play *Exiles*—and already in the context of devious intersubjective watching. Richard tolerates Robert's dalliance with Bertha because he is able to observe its progress and thus feel some control over its course. He secretly exults in revealing his knowledge to Robert and in watching his rival's confusion, embarrassment, and dis-belief ("You knew? From her? . . . You were watching us all the time?" [*E* 75]). But Joyce's notes on the play hint that Richard could have been even more ingeniously duped, that his position in the visual dialectic is not as secure as he might like to think: "In the last act (or second) Robert can also suggest that he knew from the first that Richard was aware of his conduct and that he himself was being watched and that he persisted because he had to and because he wished to see to what length Richard's silent forbearance would go" (*E* 157).

One of the sources for the *Wake*'s complicated configurations of intersubjective watching is Bédier's *Romance of Tristan and Iseult*. Commenting on Bédier's rendering of the romance, Glasheen writes, "Ten thousand emotional miles from Wagner's, [it] is an ur and unslick bedroom farce peopled all with tricksters."[14] Much of the farcical quality derives from the elaborate spying and counterspying of the major characters. The four jealous barons are constantly trying to catch the young lovers in a compromising position and goad King Mark into joining their voyeuristic pursuit of the pair; but Tristan and Iseult, having superior visual acuity, are never caught. The couple always detect their unwanted company and adjust their behavior accordingly. In one scene King Mark hides in a pine tree, ready to surprise the lovers in an illicit embrace, but they notice his reflection in the water of a well. Instead of abandoning themselves to desire, they engage in an artful conversation bemoaning King Mark's unwarranted jealousy and the barons' villainous deception of their lord.[15] Later the pair kill one of the wily barons after Iseult perceives his shadow on the curtain of the window through which he planned to watch their tryst.[16] Tristan and Iseult elude their pursuers because, when watched, they are always secretly watching back. What appealed to Joyce in Bédier's book, I suspect, is its representation of the human as the ontological fraud, trapped in a manipulative theater of desire; but Joyce, unlike Bédier, captures the irony of the human penchant for performance. Joycean figures, with "eyes all over them" (*U* 371/304), become parodic versions of the spotted beast, their ocelli warding off an other that is often merely a psychic construct.

The spying and counterspying in the *Wake* become most complicated in 2.4 (the Tristan and Iseult chapter), where all the central figures from Bédier's account appear in an intricate tableau of intersubjective gazing. The four scoptophiliac ancients, analogues of King Mark's barons, are added to the familiar one-two-three configuration—the older man, the pair of young women, and the triad of young men—giving the voyeuristic regress a further dimension: "How it did but all come eddaying back to them, if they did but get gaze, gagagniagnian, to hear him there, kiddling and cuddling her, after the gouty old galahat, with his peer of quinnyfears and his troad of thirstuns, so nefarious, from his elevation of one yard one handard and thartytwo lines, before the four of us, in his Roman Catholic arms, while his deepseepeepers gazed and sazed and dazecrazemazed into her dullokbloon rodolling olosheen eyenbowls by the Cornelius Nepos, Mnepos. Anumque, umque. Napoo. / Queh? Quos?" (*FW* 389). The confusion indicated by the final puzzled interrogatives is well warranted, although in the context of the whole episode, the contours of the scenario are not impenetrable. The four ancients are apparently either watching the older man watch the young lovers or else reading a version of the famous myth of triangular desire in a book by Cornelius Nepos, a Roman historian and letter writer.[17] In either event, the "gouty old galahat" spies on the couple from some point of elevation, perhaps a tree, after the fashion of King Mark, or one of the masts of the boat, the site of the initial consummation.[18] His name appropriately suggests Galehoult, the pander who in some versions of the Lancelot and Guinevere story arranges the lovers' illicit union: in the analogous myth of Tristan and Iseult, King Mark plays the pander himself, promoting his own cuckolding by appointing Tristan his proxy in love. But the verbal ambiguities and syntactical disjunctions destabilize the scenario, making it difficult to sort out who is watching whom and who (if anyone) is simply being watched. The dualistic young female appears as a "peer of quinnyfears," but exactly who she is peering at remains characteristically uncertain. The "troad of thirstuns" gazes adoringly into her "olosheen eyenbowls," whose sheen suggests a mirrorlike surface, a duplicitous reflector that perhaps enables the gazer to see the voyeur, like the well in Bédier's account. The afterthought "Anumque," which means "and the old woman" in Latin, hints that the maternal ALP has joined the party of oglers. While the accusative case suggests that she is probably a voyeuristic object, her appearance elsewhere as a devious viewer ("his ambling limfy peepingpartner" [FW 580]) leaves her status within the visual dialectic highly ambiguous. Another possible witness of HCE's possible voyeurism, the mother compounds the paranoiac, though potentially illusory, threat of the other's gaze.

In *The Decentered Universe of "Finnegans Wake,"* Margot Norris explains the way the theme of the fallen father subverts the traditional attributes of patriarchal authority, dislocating in the process the androcentric hub of religious, social, and familial orders: the fallen dreaming father "is named rather than namer. He is uncertain of name and identity, unlocatable rather than a center that fixes, defines, and gives meaning to his cosmos. He is lawbreaker rather than lawgiver. As the head of the family, he is incestuous rather than the source of order in the relations of his lineage."[19] The subversion, I would add, continues on a level that is at once visual and psychological. Instead of being an omnipotent and all-watchful patriarch, the fallen father fears he is watched by others, others who have devious designs on him ("he conscious of enemies" [FW 75]). Instead of being omniscient, he possesses limited—and hence uncertain—vision and knowledge. Far from divine, his visual capacities are frequently directed toward prurient and worldly voyeuristic ends, and they are threatened moreover by craftier forms of voyeurism. The very presence of the father's multiple voyeurs—however imaginary they may be—betrays his all too human status as thrall to others' eyes, his enslavement to intersubjective self-perception. The self-defined and self-created patriarch of Christian mythology becomes in the *Wake* the flawed father whose humanness is measured by the extent to which he derives his identity from the other.

The human enthrallment to the eye of the other provides a clue to the logic behind the *Wake*'s larger narrative orientation, its odd, dispersed mode of telling that has been the source of much debate. Michael Begnal, who has identified and characterized several of the voices in the *Wake*, summarizes some of the critical perspectives on the book's structure after explaining his own view of the matter: "The single-dreamer theory, which names Humphrey Chimpden Earwicker as the sole narrator, overlooks the use of multiple point of view [*sic*] . . . and creates more critical problems than it overcomes. When one realizes that several people are dreaming together, it becomes much easier to individualize them and to redefine them in greater depth."[20] But if one rejects "the single-dreamer theory" on the grounds of the *Wake*'s multiplicity of perspectives, one misses the work's central ontological paradox, the degree to which the individualized self is founded upon and determined by the other. In contrast to the carefully controlled and usually identified subjectivities in Joyce's earlier fictions, the *Wake*'s countless narrating I/eyes often remain nameless, in a dreamtext constructed around the hypothetical gazes of a seemingly infinite series of others. Within this decentered structure of multiple perspectives, HCE is logically identified as the dreamer, not because he is the central "speaker," but rather because he is the central "spoken of": with a compulsive predictability, the topic of discussion returns to him—or, if not to him, to a familial extension of him, to his wife, his sons, or his daughter. Frequently, though, these family members themselves compose the other, their voices constituting much of what there is in the dream of distinguishable, personalized speech. In the course of dreaming these various voices, HCE betrays not only his ambivalent feelings toward his nearest and dearest but also—more prominently—his fears about their own potentially ambivalent feelings toward him. In her essay on ALP, Norris writes that "we must understand the dreaming male figure in order to understand the female figure. Yet Joyce, paradoxically, sets up a hermeneutical spiral in *Finnegans Wake* through which the best insights into the condition of HCE (presumably the male dreamer) are given by Anna Livia in her final monologue."[21] This "hermeneutical spiral," I would argue, characterizes the structure of not simply the final monologue, but the entire dreamtext: although HCE does envision himself speaking at several points, most of the information (or misinformation) we are given about him is mediated, delivered through imagined others. What we confront in the *Wake* is the subject's image of himself as he imagines it appears to other I/eyes, to alien subjectivities. The human enthrallment to the gaze, in short, is a technical as well as a thematic concern in the *Wake*, a concern vividly dramatized in the book's idiosyncratic but revealing narrative form.

Because one's image in the eye of the other is elusive and unknown, the dream's fabric is contradictory and protean, resistant to any sort of fixity or consistency. The changing visions of the dreamer that are produced by even the identifiable and individualized speakers betray the uncertainty of his estimation of their estimation, of his perception of their perception; the self-image reflected through the discourse of wife, sons, or daughter is invariably incongruous, dispersed—as irrevocably fractured as Humpty Dumpty's ubiquitous shell. The wildest inconsistencies occur when one tries to reconcile not a single other's vision of HCE but the vision of the aggregate others in the dream. The dreamer has as many identities as there are others, as the attempt to specify his name at the end of 1.2 suggests: "Some vote him Vike, some mote him Mike, some dub him Llyn and Phin while others hail him Lug Bug Dan Lop, Lex, Lax, Gunne or Guinn. Some apt him Arth, some bapt him Barth, Coll, Noll, Soll, Will, Weel, Wall but I parse him Persse O'Reilly else he's called no name at all" (*FW* 44). HCE's fluctuating identity is a function of its mediated status: this is made clear in the contrasting versions of the elusive nightletter, which is written to and about the dreamer, but which also is the dreamer ("a huge chain envelope, written in seven divers stages of ink" [*FW* 66]). We are told that "closer inspection of the *bordereau* would reveal a multiplicity of personalities inflicted on the documents or document" (*FW* 107): the singular document becomes multiple documents because its text varies according to who is imagined creating or reading it. The letter changes in form and content every time it returns in the dream because it is produced by "the continually more and less intermisunderstanding minds of the anticollaborators" (*FW* 118). The nightletter is another imago of the self as a textual artifact, as an artifact not simply explored and discussed by others but also actually written and defined by others.

• • •

Amid all the paranoid visions of being investigated, read, and spied on, there are some scenarios in the *Wake* in which being gazed on is a pleasure, a desire. At one point, for example, the dreamer imagines himself lord mayor of Dublin welcoming the king of England to Ireland and presenting him with the keys of the city (*FW* 568). The ceremony is witnessed by a crowd of "peeplers entrammed and detrained on bikeygels and troykakyls and those puny farting little solitires" (*FW* 567). The encrusted references to trams, trains, and cycles with varying numbers of wheels perhaps suggest the modes of transport used to arrive at the ceremony; but the metonymic one-two-three, the furtive watching implied in the word "peeplers," and the allusion to farting (flimsily disguised as the sound of air leaking from a tire) all link this grandiose event, with its pleasurable moment of self-consciousness, to the elusive sin, with its embarrassing moment of self-consciousness. The two scenes, in other words, are versions of each other and yet psychological opposites, expressing respectively the positive and negative possibilities of the gaze: the ceremony watched by a throng of impressed spectators is simply the wishful inversion, the gratifying transformation, of a culturally stigmatized act watched (or heard) by an intrusive and unwelcome audience.

Through both specific details and larger patterns, this Wakean fantasy of public grandeur is connected to Bloom's Circean vision of himself as lord mayor of Dublin, a vision that escalates to dreams of being crowned Leopold the First, king of the new Bloomusalem. The most salient feature of these fantasies of acclaim is the excess of cultural signifiers of significance itself: resplendent clothing, symbolic jewelry, phalanxes of titled men, a superabundance of fanfare. Bloom also assumes numerous titles, "emperor-president and king-chairman, the most serene and potent and very puissant ruler of this realm," and multiple names, "Leopold, Patrick, Andrew, David, George, be thou anointed" (U 482/393). This excess of literal signification, frequently associated with majesty, finds its approximate Wakean counterpart in the proliferating appellations for HCE, appellations that inflate in rank and length simultaneously (as if longer names were more impressive than shorter ones): "rich Mr Pornter, a squire. . . . handsome Sir Pournter. . . . Lord Pournterfamilias" (FW 570). Attributes of excess that are potentially ambiguous—such as excessive weight—are invariably encoded favorably in these scenes. When the imagoes of the self physically inflate, Bloom and HCE turn into men (like Henry VIII or Edward VII) whose massiveness functions as a positive register of their substantiality, import, and power (and not as a negative signifier of, say, a metabolic disorder, a pathological oral fixation, or a gluttonous impulse): in "Circe" Bloom "uncloaks impressively, revealing obesity" (U 487/397) and in 3.4 of the Wake "one sees how he [HCE/Mr. Porter] is lot stoutlier than of formerly" (FW 570). In context these details of excess and the excess of these details ultimately betray themselves as compensatory signs, as wishful tokens of overestimation designed to mask fears of underestimation, as counters to the anxieties about disparagement and disrespect that run strongly through both "Circe" and the Wakean dream.

HCE's massiveness is interpreted by the other as a pregnancy, his body envisioned as the repository of several male heirs: "One would say him to hold whole a litteringture of kidlings under his aproham. . . . yes indeed, he has his mic son and his two fine mac sons and a superfine mick want they mack metween them" (FW 570). This image can be read as the Wakean return of the maternal fantasy in "Circe," during which Bloom gives birth to male octuplets. As critics have noted, Joyce accentuates the children's status as socioeconomic signifiers: with their faces made of valuable metals, their auric and silvery names, their highbrow interests, and their impressive jobs (*U* 494/403), Bloom's eight sons are overdetermined cultural markers expressing his "petit bourgeois wish for status, power, and wealth,"[22] his "parental dream of vicarious upward mobility."[23] Gender too plays a role in the valences of this imago. In a moment of psychic powerlessness in his confrontation with the other, Bloom imagines himself as female—through a stereotypical association that will resurface when he meets Bella/Bello. But to recoup his losses, he appropriates an androcentric signifier of female desirability (i.e., pregnancy) that will also strategically play on the sentiments of the other: the Circean delivery is an attempted deliverance, a defensive maneuver to gain "clemency" and "compassion" when the crowd starts to turn on the leader it exalted moments before (*U* 494/403). Bloom then proceeds to produce an excess of sons (as does HCE) in part because it is the male gender that signifies within androcentric semiotics. In his manipulative efforts to ward off a potentially critical eye, Bloom reveals his thorough internalization of the en-gendered sign.

Amid cheering, lavish celebrating, and citywide bell ringing, Joyce's "inflated" protagonists deliver ceremonial speeches that echo one another in both structure and content:

([*Bloom*] *uncloaks impressively, revealing obesity, unrolls a paper and reads solemnly*) Aleph Beth Ghimel Daleth Hagadah Tephilim Kosher Yom Kippur Hanukah Roschaschana Beni Brith Bar Mitzvah Mazzoth Askenazim Meshuggah Talith. (*U* 487/397)

he [HCE] shall aidress to His Serenemost by a speechreading from his miniated vellum, alfi byrni gamman dealter etcera zezera eacla treacla youghta kaptor lomdom noo (*FW* 568)

The nonsensical erudition suggested by the concatenated Hebrew and Greek words is paradoxical and finally self-subverting rhetoric. On one level each "speech" aims to make a statement: Bloom attempts to assert his place in a Judaic tradition—obviously only imperfectly remembered— and HCE attempts to stake his claim in a classical one. But at the same time, of course, their oratories are pretentious babble: the true rhetorical end of these honorific rituals is not so much to communicate as it is to impress (one is reminded of Gabriel's after-dinner speech in "The Dead"). Because the ultimate signifier of significance is not the position of honor and the attendant regalia but the gaze that recognizes their symbolic value, the other—more specifically, the sexual other—plays a pivotal role in these fantasies. The Circean visions of the self in positions of prestige and power occur shortly after the scene in which all eyes are turned against Bloom, after the nightmarish trial where he is accused of almost every possible transgression—mainly by indignant women. During Bloom's hallucinatory reign as lord mayor, the women have an antithetical function, his prime accusers becoming now his prime admirers: "*All the windows are thronged with sightseers, chiefly ladies*" (*U* 479/ 391). As in the *Wake*, the fantasy of acclaim, of being watched by awed onlookers, is a psychic reversal of a fantasy of humiliation, of being watched by prying and hostile eyes belonging predominantly to the opposite gender. The role of the sexual other is more veiled in the *Wake*, but the final parenthetical appositives in the description of HCE as Lord Mayor—"Meynhir Mayour, our boorgomaister, thon staunch Thorsman, (our Nancy's fancy, our own Nanny's Big Billy)" (*FW* 568)—hint that this dream of public veneration is linked to desires for female approval. Women play paradoxical roles in these male fantasies: physically degraded or semiotically devalued, they are yet perspectively powerful, their gaze functioning frequently as the arbiter of male value itself.

The gaze in its more gratifying form functions in Joyce's works as the final signifier of significance, as that which fulfills the self's desire to be acknowledged and recognized, to be a somebody rather than a nobody. In situations of romantic rivalry it has the power to mark the desirable, the preferred, the sexually significant. This function can best be seen in "Nausicaa," an episode structured around a gaze: the young women on the strand make almost every gesture self-consciously, with the aim of catching the eye of their mysterious onlooker. The gaze plays a powerful role in the chapter, for it is with his gaze that Bloom will signify which woman he finds most attractive, most appealing, and relegate the unsuccessful rivals to the realm of sexual negligibility; the prospect of this signifying gaze sparks the jealousy and catty competiveness that emerge as the episode develops. It is the eventual focus of Bloom's gaze on Gerty that drives Cissy to perform so frantically and shamelessly, with the hope of capturing at least a little bit of regard for herself: she makes bold and provocative comments, runs after the twins "with long gandery strides" (*U* 359/294), hoping to show a little bit of skin and petticoat, and eventually even approaches Bloom directly to ask the time. This last gesture, however, may be not an attention getter at all but an act of vengeance, her way of punishing the onlooker for not choosing her as the image of desirability. The gesture interrupts—and seems aimed to interrupt—Bloom's incipient masturbation: he is forced to take his hand out of his pocket when she approaches. After Bloom thwarts Cissy's desire for sexual recognition, she vindictively tries to thwart his desire for sexual gratification. If this chapter is a modernist rerendering of the Judgment of Paris, as Norris has argued, then Cissy clearly assumes the role of the vengeful

Juno, the sore loser of ancient legend. Joyce revises the sexist myth, however, not only by exposing its primordially corrupt model for the judgment of beauty and desirability,[24] but also by allowing one of the "goddesses" to return as a counter gaze in Circean hallucination, by transforming the reified female object into a critical female subject: Gerty wins the contest and the right to judge the judge as a "dirty married man" (*U* 442/361).

Although less literal than the one in "Nausicaa," the gaze as the signifier of the desirable appears earlier in Joyce's works at the end of "The Dead." At the close of the party when Gabriel watches his wife listening to Bartell d'Arcy's singing, he responds with inward joy to her flushed cheeks and shining eyes because he assumes that she is thinking of him, that her inward gaze is secretly focused on him. En route to the Gresham Hotel, he composes a fantasy script in his mind in which the object of her gaze is revealed, dramatically enacted: "When the others had gone away, when he and she were in their room in the hotel, then they would be alone together. He would call her softly: / —Gretta! / Perhaps she would not hear at once: she would be undressing. Then something in his voice would strike her. She would turn and look at him. . ." (*D* 214, Joyce's ellipsis). The revelation that this desirous gaze is wholly imaginary, that Gretta's thoughts are in fact turned backward toward her earlier lover, precipitates an ego-shattering vision of the self, a vision of the self as ludicrous, clownish, and negligible. Gabriel's self-image is predicated on Gretta's gaze, its imagined presence kindling sexual confidence, desire, its revealed absence leading to deflated self-esteem, sexual humiliation. The antithetical visions of the self produced by Gretta's gaze are reflected in the chevalglass of the hotel room: before Gabriel hears her story, he sees a paterfamilias with a "broad, well-filled shirt-front" (*D* 218); afterward the image is revised, shrinking to one of a mere "pennyboy[,] . . . the pitiable fatuous fellow he had caught a glimpse of in the mirror" (*D* 219–20).

This feeling of negligibility at the end of "The Dead" prefigures an important moment at the end of *Finnegans Wake*, the moment when HCE suffers an ontological diminution that is dramatized through images of physical diminution: the dream woman ALP is heard dolefully confessing to her spouse, "I thought you were all glittering with the noblest of carriage. You're only a bumpkin. I thought you the great in all things, in guilt and in glory. You're but a puny" (*FW* 627). ALP's waning estimate of her husband is conveyed through the figures of Cinderella's carriage changing back into a pumpkin, of an impressive nobleman being exposed as a bumpkin, or of HCE—whose dominant mythic guise is the giant Finn MacCool—shrinking until he is only a puny. One can see perfectly in the final monologue the mediated nature of the dreamer's sense of self: when

ALP's attitude toward HCE is positive, supportive, and loving, he is the gargantuan albeit somewhat clumsy man, threatening to trample on her feet; when her attitude turns more cynical and indifferent at the very end of the dream, he all of a sudden becomes small, physically and ontologically insignificant. Shortly before this image of self-diminishment, ALP concedes that her vision is fading, that she can no longer see clearly the dreamer whom she is envisioned speaking to ("Illas! I wisht I had better glances to peer to you through this baylight's growing" [FW 626]): this disappearance of her eye foreshadows the disappearance of her voice, the voice that sustains the dreamer's very being, the voice that assures him that the other is still there. If Joyce opens his book of the emerging son, *A Portrait of the Artist*, with the voice of the other creating the self, with the discourse of the father bringing the young Stephen into being, he closes his artistic career with a reverse but complementary narrative gesture: his book of the dying father ends with the abrupt cessation of the voice of the other, a cessation logically signaling the mediated self's death.

While the gaze of the other may be a threat, a feared intrusion, or—to borrow a Lacanian trope—an evil eye, it is also an egotistical construct, a construct of desire, whose vanishing leads to another sort of fear—a fear not of a critical other, but of an indifferent other, whose stance exposes not the subject's guilts or flaws but his potential insignificance or negligibility. What is dreaded most in the *Wake*—even more than the gaze visualized as an agency of exposure—is the gaze visualized as an utter absence. Thus the dying dreamer's obsessive interest in his "wake" may betray a fearful and even paranoiac concern with his reputational legacy, with the opinion of the imagined perduring other; but the envisioned "wake" simultaneously expresses a wish to be remembered, to escape anonymity and oblivion, to maintain one's significance through posterity. Contingent on being preserved at least in the mind's eye of the other, the wake is perhaps yet another form of the gaze, a form that bespeaks most clearly the desire to negate the possibilities of insignificance and nonsignificance, of indifference and nondifference, those possibilities disturbingly figured forth in death itself.

Chapter 6

THE RETURN OF THE REPRESSED:
MALE VISIONS AND RE-VISIONINGS OF
THE FEMALE I/EYE

JOYCE'S WORKS contain male visions of the female that are patently sexist. Bloom turns the servant girl in Dlugazc's into "a stallfed heifer" (*U* 59/ 48) and thinks of Gerty MacDowell, "still she was game" (*U* 372/304)— a probably unintentional double entendre, revealing nonetheless. Stephen classifies Emma Clery as "the most deceptive and cowardly of marsupials" (*SH* 210), while Boylan sees a shopgirl as "a young pullet" (*U* 228/ 187) and treats Molly like a horse, slapping her on the rear. This male tendency to reduce women to the level of the beast returns in the *Wake* when ALP becomes a domestic fowl or a mare for HCE to ride ("The galleonman jovial on his bucky brown nightmare" [*FW* 583]). In a seemingly opposite perceptual transformation, men exalt the female by visualizing her as a fine work of art, a perfect aesthetic image. The most familiar example of this, of course, is Stephen's enraptured vision in *Portrait* of the Virgin-like girl on the strand (who, in her resemblance to a bird, retains a residual link to those visions of the woman as animal). He interprets her look as being "without shame or wantonness," despite the "faint flame [that] trembled on her cheek" (*P* 171)—the dim but discernible trace of disconcerted self-consciousness or subliminal erotic excitation. A similar aestheticized image of the female surfaces in the *Wake*, when another budding artificer invites his audience to view a young woman he has created, stripped of all desire: "Every admirer has seen my goulache of Marge . . . which I titled *The Very Picture of a Needless-woman*" (*FW* 165). The perceptual transformations of the female into meat, sheer animal presence, and art, sheer beatific image, differ insofar as one debases her and the other idealizes her; but the psychic impetus and effect of the transformative gestures are precisely the same. In their similar elisions of female humanness, both types of visions spring from a male resistance to acknowledge the subjectivity of women. They work to perpetuate the convenient conceptual categorization of woman-as-object, be it in the shape of the animal prey to be kinetically pursued or the aesthetic image to be statically admired.

Joyce was keenly aware of the way the dichotomy subject/object is superimposed on the categories male/female: the androcentric hierarchies represented in his works are frequently reflected in perceptual paradigms. But it is important not to confuse Joyce's representation of ways of seeing with Joyce's own way of seeing: for his works offer a recurrent subversion and critique of those androcentric perceptual patterns that function to reduce women, in visual terms, to the status of the object and, in political terms, to the status of the abject. This chapter focuses on the ways in which Joyce exposes the limitations of male vision, on his strategies for revealing the scotomas and distorting biases that afflict male I/eyes that have internalized androcentric assumptions. Unconscious thought and insight are of particular importance in this exposé because they often operate as a sort of corrective vision, an other way of seeing. Women have a paradoxical status in the revealing epiphanies, fantasies, and dreams of Joycean males: within these psychic structures, females become objects in the male mind, mere imagoes; yet it is within these imagoes that women frequently reappropriate their subjectivity—their eyes, pens, and voices, their potential as viewers, writers, and speakers. In the male unconscious as Joyce represents it, we find clear residues from waking perceptual modes of female objectification; but we also confront, more frequently, a return of the repressed, illuminating re-visionings of the female I/eye.[1]

Joyce's mythic method is well documented, but his ironic rewritings of classical stories with implicitly androcentric biases—one of his strategies for critiquing traditional male visions of the female—has received, in comparison, scant attention. Joyce frequently aligns his characters with archetypal figures, but only to question and to recast the sexual power structures inherent in the identification. Gabriel Conroy in "The Dead," for instance, suffers from the Pygmalion syndrome: an urge to transform the female into an artistic image that embodies distinctly male desires. His reflex when he sees his wife pensively listening to Bartell d'Arcy's singing is to deny her subjectivity, her patent responsiveness, by envisioning her first as an abstract symbol and then as a picture he would like to paint, as a framed, contained, and named image—the work of the male artist's controlling imagination and ego: "There was grace and mystery in her attitude as if she were a symbol of something. He asked himself what is a woman standing on the stairs in the shadow, listening to distant music, a symbol of. If he were a painter he would paint her in that attitude. Her blue felt hat would show off the bronze of her hair against the darkness and the dark panels of her skirt would show off the light ones. *Distant Music* he would call the picture if he were a painter" (D 210). Because Gabriel cannot see Gretta's face (D 209), Adrienne Munich sees in this vision "a familiar figure of the Silent Woman, the woman without a head and therefore speechless"; she also finds an implicit allusion to Browning's "My Last Duchess," the poem in which the jealous Duke responds to his wife's elusive will and lively subjectivity by murdering her into art.[2]

I find as well a reference to the myth of Pygmalion and Galatea, for the aesthetic image eventually comes to life for Gabriel: the "colour on [Gretta's] cheeks" that floods him with joy and longing (*D* 212) is reminiscent of Galatea's blush that confirms her metamorphosis from cold ivory statue to warm human flesh, from inaccessible masterpiece to attainable erotic object. The myth of Pygmalion's "ivory girl"[3] is also residually present in Stephen's transformative vision of the birdgirl, whose skin looks like ivory and whose cheek is similarly tinged by that revealing flame of color. Joyce's use of this classic myth of male desire is ironic and subversive, particularly in the signification of the blush—Gabriel, like Stephen, misinterprets it, albeit in a different way. If Stephen's reading of the female on the strand elides her desire (by ignoring the meaning of the flame that marks it), Gabriel's reading of Gretta acknowledges it but miscontrues its source. He responds to his wife's flushed countenance with automatic passion because he believes himself to be the cause of her own. In the traditional rendering of the story, Galatea's blush signifies her sexual compliance ("The lips he kisses / Are real indeed, the ivory girl can feel them, / And blushes and responds"[4]); in Joyce's revision of it, Gretta's signifies her sexual elusiveness—her blush functions as the first visible sign of her secret memories of Michael Furey. Over the course of "The Dead," Gabriel aspires to paint his wife, to read her, and—in a sense—to write her, suggesting that he may be able to construct the transcript of her inner world ("—Gretta dear, what are you thinking about? . . . I think I know what is the matter. Do I know?" [*D* 218]). One of his epiphanies lies in his implicit realization that Gretta is not a symbol of anything, that she is not a text whose form and meaning are to be scripted by the desires of the male imagination. Her story of her past reveals her to him as an autonomous sentient being with an emotional life that not only precedes him, but that also may exclude and elude him.

Another androcentric myth Joyce returns to and revises in "The Dead" is the Judgment of Paris, explicitly invoked in Gabriel's after-dinner speech. Although Gabriel disclaims any identification with the classical arbiter of female desirability, he is a Paris figure of sorts, inwardly condemning two of the three "goddesses" he outwardly flatters with praise ("What did he care that his aunts were only two ignorant old women?" [*D* 192]). But in the larger pattern of the story, Joyce inverts the myth, playing on the syntactical ambiguity of the preposition "of": the Judgment of Paris becomes not Paris's judgment of three women but rather three women's judgment *of* Paris. As if to foreshadow what Gabriel is subjected to over the course of the evening, the inverted myth is played in miniature in Mr. Browne's confrontation with "three young ladies" (*D* 182). Mr. Browne refers to them as his admirers, but they resist playing this role, refusing to humor his boorish wit and forcing him subsequently to beat an embarrassed retreat: "His hot face had leaned forward a little too confidentially and he had assumed a very low Dublin accent so that the young ladies, with one instinct, received his speech in silence. . . . Mr Browne, seeing that he was ignored, turned promptly to the two young men who were more appreciative" (*D* 183). The three "goddesses" Gabriel confronts are Lily, Miss Ivors, and Gretta, all of whom speak and react—like the three young ladies—in violation of male expectations and desires; in the process they unsettle Gabriel's vision of himself in the other's eye, a central preoccupation throughout the story. After Lily surprises him with her cynical remark about opportunistic men who are "only all palaver" (*D* 178), Gabriel nervously arranges his cuffs and tie, as if literally attempting to recompose a ruffled self-image. Does the bombastic Gabriel unconsciously read a personal critique into Lily's generalized comment? When Miss Ivors embarrasses him on the dance floor by calling him a West Briton, he starts to dread her gaze ("He avoided her eyes for he had seen a sour expression on her face") and then defensively reduces it to a pair of "rabbit's eyes" (*D* 190). The thought of her potentially judgmental perspective produces an uneasy anticipation of intense self-consciousness: "It unnerved him to think that she would be at the supper-table, looking up at him while he spoke with her critical quizzing eyes" (*D* 192). The most devastating judgment, of course, comes from Gretta, who condemns him ultimately through her indifference, by figuratively failing to look at him at all. Initially Gabriel longs to "see some ardour in her eyes" (*D* 217), but as she starts to speak of her past, "her eyes made [him] feel awkward" (*D* 219). The awkwardness increases when in the end he is forced to look at her eyes looking fondly into the eyes of another man—"I can see his eyes as well as well!" she exclaims (*D* 221). Both her story and the mirror throw back at Gabriel a painfully flawed self-image, showing forth in an epiphanic flash of involuntary insight an elided vision of the self. They force him to see himself in contradiction to his desires, to look at himself from the "critical quizzing eyes" of a hypothetical judgmental goddess. Joyce uses the peripheral perspectives of the three "goddesses" in "The Dead" to disrupt and disturb androcentric vision, to decenter the focus of the narrative's predominantly male vantage and to deflate the self-serving desires of the protagonist's male ego.

The female I/eye in *Portrait* has much of the same equivocal power that it has in "The Dead": the power to incite sexual desire and confidence, on the one hand, the power to humiliate and shame, on the other. Emma Clery signifies her interest in Stephen through a visual gesture that has a decidedly kinetic impact ("through the circling of the dancers and amid the music and laughter her glance travelled to his corner, flattering, taunting, searching, exciting his heart" [*P* 69]). At the Whitsuntide play,

Stephen performs explicitly for this female gaze and gains self-assurance by envisioning it ("He saw her serious alluring eyes watching him from among the audience and their image at once swept away his scruples, leaving his will compact" [P 85]); the indifference he reads into her failure to meet him after his theatrical act produces a profound sense of mortification. Later Emma's imagined gaze acutely intensifies Stephen's guilty feelings ("The image of Emma appeared before him and, under her eyes, the flood of shame rushed forth anew from his heart" [P 115]); in *Ulysses* this judgmental female I/eye will return as an obsession—and in more omnipotent form—in the imago of the maternal ghost ("Her glazing eyes, staring out of death, to shake and bend my soul. On me alone. . . . Her eyes on me to strike me down" [U 10/9]). In the final chapter of *Portrait*, Stephen's response to the female I/eye that holds the power to unnerve him is to objectify it safely in a poem, to turn it into a text ("*Your eyes have set man's heart ablaze*" [P 223]). The villanelle elides the censorious potential of Emma's eye, reducing it to a signifier of erotic temptation. She is stereotyped as the woman who looks only in order to be looked at sexually ("*And still you hold our longing gaze / With languorous look and lavish limb*" [P 223]). The poem records Stephen's recurrent impulse to sexualize Emma, to re-create her imaginatively as an archetypal temptress, and to texualize her, to subject her to the male artist's will. If "The Dead" closes with a painful recognition of the female I/eye's independent vision, *Portrait* closes with a repressive occlusion of this capacity.

As feminist critics Sandra Gilbert and Susan Gubar have pointed out, "From Eve, Minerva, Sophia, and Galatea onward, . . . patriarchal mythology defines women as created by, from, and for men, the children of male brains, ribs, and ingenuity."[5] The motif of the male creating the female, molding her into art even, can be found in Joyce's fictions as well: in Gabriel's envisioned painting of Gretta; in Stephen's writing of Emma; in Richard's supposed shaping of Bertha ("She is yours, your work" [E 78]); and in HCE's rendering of ALP as highbrow portraiture, the *Mona Lisa*, or lowbrow popular song, "The Jewel of Asia" ("*I am Older northe Rogues among Whisht I Slips and He Calls Me his Dual of Ayessha*" [FW 105]). The male objectification of the female also takes place at the level of the perceptual. If Stephen literally reduces the I/eye of Emma to a poem, Bloom figuratively reduces the I/eyes of various women to texts, transforming them from organs of vision into signs to be read. Bloom assesses actual female eyes as sights, often within an erotic framework, so that a nun's eyes are recalled as the indices of romantic disappointment ("Sister? Sister? I am sure she was crossed in love by her eyes" [U 155/ 127]) and Mrs. Breen's are noted as a remnant physical allurement, as a lingering marker of past sexual charms ("Mrs Breen turned up her two large eyes. Hasn't lost them anyhow" [U 157/129]). In a more straightforward elision of female vision, the faces of the women receiving communion in "Lotus Eaters" are reduced to "blind masks" (*U* 80/66). In moments of self-consciousness, Bloom posits a gaze that is frequently nonexistent, and yet when he confronts real female eyes he almost imagines them as ocelli, partially ignoring their capacity to see.

Joyce shows that these elisions of the female I/eye are ultimately ironic: as is demonstrated in Gabriel's confrontations with Lily, Miss Ivors, and Gretta, men are often most intensely self-conscious in the presence of the female other. Bloom's reduction of Mrs. Breen's eyes to erotic signifiers does not stop him from performing for them, from writing out explicit stage directions in his mind ("Let her speak. Look straight in her eyes. I believe you. Trust me" [*U* 158/129]). Indeed, in male competitions and power struggles throughout Joyce's works, the female I/eye usually plays a central role, but a role sometimes conveniently repressed. When John Henry Menton casually mentions a defeat in a past game of bowls that causes him to treat his competitor disparagingly seventeen years later, he elides the key detail, the real source of his lingering hostility ("—What is [Bloom]? [Menton] asked. What does he do? Wasn't he in the stationery line? I fell foul of him one evening, I remember, at bowls" [*U* 106/88]). The goal, it turns out, is not simply to win the game but to impress the onlooking female I/eye, as the slightly smug recollection of the victor reveals. Thinking about the same contest, Bloom fills in the gap in Menton's account: "Yes, Menton. Got his rag out that evening on the bowlinggreen because I sailed inside him. Pure fluke of mine: the bias. Why he took such a rooted dislike to me. Hate at first sight. Molly and Floey Dillon linked under the lilactree, laughing. Fellow always like that, mortified if women are by" (*U* 115/94–95). The female I/eye is also felt as a presence in Stephen's rivalry with Cranly at the end of *Portrait*—Stephen resents not only Emma's explicit snub of him but also her polite recognition of his friend—and in Farrington's power struggle with his boss in "Counterparts": his rude retort to Mr. Alleyne's question is not simply an instance of oneupmanship in a battle between two men, but rather a ploy to disconcert the demanding employer in front of the admired Miss Delacour (see *D* 91). *Finnegans Wake* often foregrounds the female other at the heart of intersubjective rivalry between men: it reveals her as the envisioned audience ("The litigants . . . were egged on by their supporters in the shape of betterwomen with bowstrung hair of Carrothagenuine ruddiness, waving crimson petties and screaming from Isod's towertop" [*FW* 87]) and hence as the instigator of the desire for mastery in itself, as the cause of the need for the prestige conferred by victory ("dinna forget . . . that the beautiful presence of waiting kates will until life's (!) be more than enough to make any milkmike in the language of sweet tarts punch hell's hate into his twin nicky" [*FW* 116]).

Joyce's representations of the female have been labeled sexist because they often suggest that women are male-defined. Elaine Unkeless, for instance, complains that "like the Wife of Bath or Madame Bovary, Molly Bloom believes . . . she can be fulfilled only by engaging a man's attention."[6] This, however, is a one-sided view of the issue, for Bloom appreciates the attentions of various women as much as his wife enjoys those of various men, both interpreting letters, interested looks, and romantic mementoes as seals of sexual approval. Molly resents what she feels to be sexual apathy on the part of her husband, needing his affection to feel attractive and alive ("its a wonder Im not an old shrivelled hag before my time living with him so cold never embracing me except sometimes when hes asleep" [U 777/639]), but Bloom in turn validates his own appeal through his wife, deciding that he cannot be uncomely because Molly chose him as her spouse ("Pretty girls and ugly men marrying. Beauty and the beast. Besides I can't be so if Molly" [U 369/302]—note the self-serving illogicality of this reflection). On June 16 Molly is thankful for the adulterous liaison that has raised her spirits and made her feel desirable again; Bloom feels correlatively grateful for the mute interest expressed by Gerty MacDowell on Sandymount strand. In fact, before retiring, Bloom pleasurably takes stock of the women who have recently shown any interest in him, regardless of how slight. As he adds the recent letter from Martha to his collection of earlier ones, he has a "pleasant" recollection that "apart from the letter in question, his magnetic face, form and address had been favourably received during the course of the preceding day by a wife (Mrs Josephine Breen, born Josie Powell), a nurse, Miss Callan (Christian name unknown), a maid, Gertrude (Gerty, family name unknown)" (U 722/594). This tallying of female admirers leads to an exotic fantasy of "exercising virile power of fascination" over an elegant courtesan (U 722/594), just as Molly's thoughts of her recent conquest lead to dreams of other possibilities. In Joyce's fictions both men and women *alike* depend on the sexual other to confirm their self-esteem and desirability. As Sheldon Brivic accurately points out, "A cardinal point of Joyce's world from 'The Dead' on is that men derive their being and vitality from the image they project to women, while women . . . gain being through the devotion of men."[7]

The recurrent tendency of Joycean males to elide the female I/eye betrays their desire to deny the extent to which their self-estimation is tied to the sexual other, their desire to imagine themselves as self-contained and self-defined beings. They reflexively aspire to the position of the creating, determining subject, rejecting that of the created, determined object. On the level of the visual, this psychic aspiration translates into a desire to be the seer rather than the seen. As the film theorist Laura Mulvey writes,

In a world ordered by sexual imbalance, pleasure in looking has been split between active/male and passive/female. The determining male gaze projects its fantasy onto the female figure, which is styled accordingly. In their traditional exhibitionist role women are simultaneously looked at and displayed, with their appearance coded for strong visual and erotic impact so that they can be said to connote *to-be-looked-at-ness*.[8]

By examining the conventions of mainstream Hollywood films, Mulvey shows how popular cinema reflects and reinforces this visual power structure: "According to the principles of the ruling ideology and the psychical structures that back it up, the male figure cannot bear the burden of sexual objectification. Man is reluctant to gaze at his exhibitionist like."[9] Joyce's works are interesting to examine from this feminist perspective, because, on the one hand, they reveal—just as popular cinema does—man's resistance to "bear the burden of sexual objectification," his insistent desire to be the active watching subject rather than the passive viewed object. But unlike popular cinema, Joyce's works offer a clear deconstruction of the categories active/male/viewer and passive/female/viewed, particularly in his repeated representations of voyeuristic and exhibitionistic sexual interactions. A close look at "Nausicaa" (often a problem from a feminist point of view) and its follow-up in "Circe" and *Finnegans Wake* enables one to see Joyce's exposé of androcentric visual paradigms. The paradigm that establishes the man as the gaze, while reducing the woman to the signifier of "to-be-looked-at-ness," is revealed as not the natural order of things, but a male perceptual illusion, a deeply rooted psychic defense.

・ ・ ・

The action of "Nausicaa" takes place within an elaborate structure of intersubjective watching and assessment. The young women who appear to be keeping an eye on the three children are in fact keeping an eye on everything else, surveying each other, surveying themselves, and surveying the mysterious gentleman who in turn surveys them, intensifying the self-consciousness of their deportment. The chapter explores, however, not simply the acuity of the eye but also its limitations, its biases and blind spots, as commentators often emphasize, particularly when describing Gerty: her perceptions are filtered through the illusions propagated by nineteenth-century fiction and skewed by the myths of contemporary women's magazines;[10] her viewpoint is "characterized by self-inflated infatuations beyond critical questioning, by hyperbole, self-deception, and a basically timid selectivity."[11] These critical assessments of Gerty as perceiving subject interest me, not because they are at all inaccurate, but because they are partial, incomplete, and in the same way, moreover, that

Bloom's own assessments of her are, eliding the same element of female vision—its compromising, even threatening potential. If the first half of the episode satirizes blatantly a particular feminine point of view, the second critiques most subtly a particular masculine one: Gerty's female I/eye in its riskiest (and risqué-est) capacity is precisely what Bloom's male I/eye never sees.

Having internalized androcentric visual structures, Gerty presents herself as an object, fashioning herself as an attractive sight through her elaborate apparel and her carefully contrived poses. She is appropriately described as "as fair a specimen of winsome Irish girlhood as one could wish to see" (*U* 348/285–86), a *specimen* being etymologically "something to look at."[12] She pretends not to notice the male gaze fixed upon her by staring off at the sunset, feigning romantic reflection and feminine unselfconsciousness, casting a veil, so to speak, over her own watching eye. Even when she later exposes her drawers and "she saw that he saw" (*U* 366/300), she is not looking sideways but upward, ostensibly watching the pyrotechnic show, pretending not to notice the more proximate human fireworks just down the strand. Gerty's duplicity is a direct function of her internalization of androcentric paradigms: she seems to realize that an overt betrayal of her own subjectivity would violate cultural expectations and categories. As a result, she turns herself into an invisible eye—"Gerty could see without looking" (*U* 360/295). She is the fictive descendant of Homer's Nausicaa and also of Joyce's own Emma Clery, whom Stephen suspects of possessing "a trick of seeing things without using her eyes frankly" (*SH* 155).

Gerty's devious concealment of the viewing self masks her actual voyeurism, the covert visual pleasure she derives from watching Bloom watch her. After exchanging casual glances with "the gentleman opposite looking," she slyly ventures a better look at him from "under the brim of her new hat" (*U* 356/292), and after she removes it to show off her pretty "nutbrown tresses," she puts it back on "so that she could see from underneath the brim" (*U* 360/295). In his retrospective reading of this gesture, Bloom notes the narcissistic motive ("Took off her hat to show her hair" [*U* 369/302]) but *not* the voyeuristic one. As soon as her friends have left the scene, Gerty takes a slightly bolder look at the stranger and experiences a distinct visual thrill at the sight of him masturbating: "The eyes that were fastened upon her set her pulses tingling. She looked at him a moment, meeting his glance, and a light broke in upon her. . . . His hands and face were working and a tremour went over her" (*U* 365/299). This counter female voyeurism is anticipated by Bertha Supple's furtive spying on "the gentleman lodger . . . that had pictures cut out of papers of those skirtdancers and highkickers and . . . he used to do something not very nice that you could imagine sometimes in the bed" (*U* 365–66/

299–300). In this shared guilty secret that Gerty recollects as she watches Bloom masturbate, the viewing female subject and the viewed female object are separate; on Sandymount strand the two parties become one, Gerty reenacting the roles of both the spying Bertha and the women in the kinetic pictures, "those skirtdancers and highkickers."

In the musings that follow his masturbation, Bloom meditates randomly on the nature of sexual attraction, speculating intermittently about the sources of female desire and producing a range of alternative possibilities. He decides that the erotic longings of women are activated by biological cycles (oncoming menstruation [*U* 368/301]), intersubjective power struggles (female rivalry [*U* 370/303], male aloofness and inaccessibility [*U* 368/301]), diurnal rhythms ("the evening influence" [*U* 376/ 308]), and olfactory stimulation, a provocative "mansmell" that signifies latent sexual longings as readily as the odors emitted by animals (*U* 375/ 307). But oddly enough, Bloom does not think of women being stimulated visually, through provocative sights, in an elision of the possibility of female scoptophilia that becomes highly ironic within the context of "Nausicaa." The female eye for him is, first and foremost, an aesthetic object for his own pleasure, and only secondarily an organ of sight: "Those girls, those girls, those lovely seaside girls. Fine eyes she had, clear. It's the white of the eye brings that out not so much the pupil. Did she know what I? Course. Like a cat sitting beyond a dog's jump. . . . Eyes all over them. Look under the bed for what's not there. Longing to get the fright of their lives. Sharp as needles they are" (*U* 371/304). Even though Bloom muses here about the optical acuity of women, he does not conceptualize the female I/eye as possibly prurient, sexually intrusive, as the organ of kinetic stimulation, as a compromising I/eye that secretly enjoys taboo visions—although that is exactly what Gerty's is. During the first half of "Nausicaa," Gerty's I/eye is aimed—however obliquely—at sexual stimulation, surveillantly waiting for her friends to exit so that she and Bloom can get on with their mutual seduction, and encouraging them to do so by reminding them that it is getting late. This prurient and finally compromising female I/eye is precisely what Bloom does not see. In watching Gerty, he is tricked by an "optical illusion" (*U* 376/308) in every sense of the phrase: not simply a delusory sight, a deceptive object or vision, but rather a delusory site of sight, a deceptive subject, her vision in itself, the voyeuristic I/eye that Gerty hides.

Bloom's failure to recognize Gerty's unequivocal countervoyeurism in "Nausicaa" is ultimately not surprising: despite his curiosity about the secrets of female desire, his thoughts are dominated by a perceptual paradigm in which the woman is the object of the male I/eye, its instrument of arousal. This perspective of androcentric pleasure can be seen in the ways Bloom conceptualizes Gerty: as a young woman "on show" for him (*U*

368/301); as a pretty sight for men to admire visually ("O sweet little, you don't know how nice you looked" [*U* 376/308]); and as a substitute for Martha's letter, an alternative erotic object, one female text replacing another ("Anyhow I got the best of that. Damned glad I didn't do it in the bath this morning over her silly I will punish you letter" [*U* 368/301]). Variants of this perceptual mode which consistently elides the female as subject reappear in his thoughts about "Mutoscope pictures in Capel street: for men only. Peeping Tom" (*U* 368/301); in his ensuing memory of the passage from *Sweets of Sin*, narrated from the vantage point of the desirous male ("Felt for the curves inside her *deshabille*" [*U* 368/302]); in his assessment of prostitutes as mindless performing toys, manipulated by male patrons ("Parrots. Press the button and the bird will squeak" [*U* 370/303]); in his recollective assumption that a secretary hurrying up a flight of stairs is another exhibitionist "on show" for male viewers ("Typist going up Roger Greene's stairs two at a time to show her understandings" [*U* 372/304]); and even in his yen for a portrait of his wife in her sexual prime ("Wish I had a full length oilpainting of her then" [*U* 376/308]). A commentator on "Nausicaa" repeats the paradigm in summarizing the episode's plot, sustaining the conventional sexual dichotomy (male subject/female object) that "Nausicaa" subtly subverts: "A voyeuristic man and an exhibitionistic girl sight one another; at a considerable distance they go through their charade; and they part."[13]

Tinged by the bitter assumption that Molly has consummated her affair, Bloom's assessments of women in "Nausicaa" become unmistakably jaundiced at points: if Gerty's perceptual bias is romantic, Bloom's at this hour tends toward the cynical. Bloom's thoughts, however, are not simply skewed: his ken contains a blindspot as glaring as any that afflicts the episode's heroine. Although his kinetic response to Gerty's "performance" on Sandymount strand takes place under the double veil of clothing and twilight, his masturbation is fairly overt insofar as he knows she can see what he is doing ("Did she know what I? Course. Like a cat sitting beyond a dog's jump" [*U* 371/304]). In spite of this knowledge, he fails to think of her as a voyeur or recognize the full extent of her own visual pleasure, refusing to see her as the pruriently viewing subject, himself as the exhibitionist object. But after all, since when is fairly overt masturbation *not* an exhibitionist act?

Bloom fully recognizes the scoptophiliac dimension of Gerty's gaze only in the unconscious fantasies of "Circe," where he suddenly sees the young temptress as a voyeur as well as an exhibitionist. In the stage direction adjoined to her appearance, Gerty enters "*leering*" and "*ogling*," her facial expression emphasizing her visual arousal. Bloom pretends not to recognize her, guiltily denying his own voyeurism ("I? When? You're dreaming. I never saw you" [*U* 442/361]), even though her response to it is envisioned as being appropriately split, Gerty's accusations reflecting both indignation and pleasure, a sense of having been violated and of having been honored and aroused.

The three fashionably dressed society ladies who appear later in "Circe" are more unequivocally censorious of Bloom's prurient impulses, excoriating him for an entire series of scandalous sexual advances, including other voyeuristic improprieties. These specters protest not simply his stranger sexual inclinations, but also his appropriation of them as sexual objects, his use of them as instruments for his bizarre fantasized pleasures: although we cannot trace these minatory apparitions back to June 16 as we can Gerty, we can speculate that they are other women whom Bloom has voyeuristically watched in the more distant past and spun some racy daydreams around, their specters perhaps awakened by the more recent recollection of the well-dressed woman he attempted to spy on in "Lotus Eaters" as she mounted her carriage. Undoubtedly assuming that these women he has furtively watched are ignorant of his prying eyes and his lustful imagination, Bloom paranoiacally sees them in "Circe" as possibly watching him secretly in return and—even worse—reading his mind, surmising his guilty desires. The compromising female I/eye, earlier elided, has suddenly become fully visible.

Toward the end of the ongoing parade of specters, Bloom confronts the Nymph, a composite phantasm forged from his earlier thoughts about nuns, the nude statues in the museum, and—preeminently—the picture hanging over his bed. Psychically connected to the accusatory society ladies, she is a literal female object (a picture, a statue) suddenly imbued with subjectivity, Bloom imagining in a moment of paranoia the living woman behind these cultural artifacts he has voyeuristically enjoyed. When her material form appropriately shatters to reveal the human sexual subject behind the cold idealized image, Bloom sees her as compromised and debased (*"her plaster cast cracking, a cloud of stench escaping from the cracks"* [U 553/451]), though this female object-turned-subject is compromising and debasing as well ("What have I not seen in that chamber? What must my eyes look down on?" [U 547/446]). Emerging from a picture entitled *The Bath of the Nymph* (U 65/53), the offended specter is clearly an avatar of Diana, so that Bloom becomes here a sort of Actaeon, the mythical hunter caught in a moment of voyeuristic intrusion by the gaze of the sexual other, the legendary male espied and punished by the female I/eye. One of the society ladies may also be linked to the goddess of hunting, dressed as she is in riding paraphernalia (see U 467/381) and originating in part from Bloom's conscious thoughts about a "weightcarrying huntress" (U 160/131).

In the course of "Circe," Bloom not only sees the female I/eye but actually becomes it. When he switches genders during his confrontation with Bello, being female is psychically associated with being a servant, a text, a prostitute, and of course an animal. In his masochistic visions, his unconscious understanding of femininity is dramatically revealed and brutally turned against him. Plumbing the political possibilities of the Circean topos from Homer, Joyce explores in this extended hallucination what it might *literally* feel like to become the animal: during his fantasized metamorphosis, Bloom experiences the culturally appropriated beast's oppression and pain—the sensation of being sat on and ridden, of being beaten and eaten. After Bello informs his victim that "I shall have you slaughtered and skewered in my stables," the stage direction suggests that Bloom envisions himself (or, more accurately, herself) as the carnivore's breakfast he consumed earlier in the day: "*Bloom squeals, turning turtle*" (*U* 532–33/434)—the gesture clearly recalls the treatment received by the burned pork kidney ("By prodding a prong of the fork under the kidney he detached it and turned it turtle on its back" [*U* 65/53]).

Another detail from the early morning of June 16 that contributes to the Circean transformation here is the book *Ruby: the Pride of the Ring*. In fantasy Bloom assumes the subjectivity of the servant girl and actively experiences the abuse that the disenfranchised are often vulnerable to ("You will make the beds, get my tub ready, empty the pisspots in the different rooms. . . . Hop! You will dance attendance or I'll lecture you on your misdeeds, *Miss Ruby*, and spank your bare bot right well, miss, with the hairbrush" [*U* 539/439, emphasis added]). If in waking reality Bloom textualizes the female, in unconscious hallucination he becomes the female text: his identifications include not only Ruby from the briefly glimpsed book illustration, but also "Martha and Mary," the sisters of Lazarus objectified in a recollected painting, and Marie Kendall ("*A charming soubrette, with dauby cheeks*"), the pantomime star whose image is displayed on mass-produced advertising posters (*U* 535–36/ 437). In his female role, Bloom finally gets *inside* the clothing he has fetishistically admired from the *outside*, to discover that femininity is not so much a seductive physical sight as it is a site of potential physical disfiguration and discomfort: "As [the whores] are now so will you be, wigged, singed, perfumesprayed, ricepowdered, with smoothshaven armpits. . . . You will be laced with cruel force into vicelike corsets of soft dove coutille with whalebone busk to the diamondtrimmed pelvis, the absolute outside edge, while your figure, plumper than when at large, will be restrained in nettight frocks" (*U* 535/437). Bloom's imaginative transformation into servant, text, prostitute, and animal allows him to find out what it might be like to be the "other" of patriarchal culture: in political terms, the abject, in perceptual terms, the object—to literalize the point, he even turns into pieces of furniture ("Footstool! Feel my entire weight" [*U* 531/433]; "I shall sit on your ottoman saddleback every morning" [*U* 532/434]). Bloom's confrontation with Bello is sometimes read as a classic masochistic fantasy that borders on the pornographic in its contours and details. But this perverse psychodrama, I would argue, has clear political import: it forces the male protagonist both to recognize and to assume the oppressed perspectives he reifies or elides.

• • •

Toward the end of "Nausicaa," Bloom wonders if Gerty will return to the scene of their silent seduction. We will never know, of course, if Gerty does come back to the strand in the fictive future of *Ulysses*, but Wakean readers will find her again in the dream, where she returns as one of the determinants of Issy. In *Ulysses* Bloom merely *associates* Gerty with Milly on account of their shared narcissism and youthful appeal; in the *Wake* Gerty, in a sense, *becomes* the daughter, particularly as she manifests herself in 2.1. Just as Gerty has noticed the cooling of Reggy's interest (a sexual rejection Bloom intuits), Issy too has recently suffered a romantic setback ("Her beauman's gone of a cool. Be good enough to symperise"); but neither young woman despairs of her future, both going out at twilight with secret hopes of new prospects ("among the shades that Eve's now wearing she'll meet anew fiancy, tryst and trow" [FW 226]). Like the modern Nausicaa, the Wakean daughter is artfully attired in "catchmire stockings, libertyed garters, shoddyshoes, quicked out with selver" (FW 226). Despite her lameness, Gerty is particularly proud of her petite Cinderella-like feet and successfully displays them as a fetish to catch Bloom's attention ("perhaps he could see the bright steel buckles of her shoes if she swung them like that thoughtfully with the toes down" [U 357–58/293]). The artifice returns in the dream in the behavior of young Issy: "Cinderynelly angled her slipper; it was cho chiny yet braught her a groom" (FW 224).

Like the young women in "Nausicaa," Issy and her spectrum of friends (the Floras or the rainbow girls) speak in a subtle but suggestive language in 2.1: "a darktongues, kunning" that includes mute gestures ("signics of her dipandump helpabit" [FW 223]), provocative visual cues ("Withasly glints in. Andecoy glants out" [FW 222]), and seductive scents ("duskcended airs" [FW 226]). Because androcentric culture often implicitly censures female desire, denigrating the actively lustful woman as the slut or the floozy, the young women in these chapters can speak their longings only in alternative silent discourses—one of which is what Bloom calls the "language of flowers. [Women] like it because no-one can hear" (U 78/ 64). The pantomimic performance in 2.1 contains explicit references to the similarly pantomimic gender acts in "Nausicaa": "Teaseforhim. Toesforhim. Tossforhim. Two. Else there is danger of. Solitude" (FW 246). This sounds like a metonymic description of the ploys "two" of the young women use to attract Bloom's gaze, with the hope of avoiding the stigma of undesirability and the possibility of sexual "solitude": it contains references to Cissy's cute maternal masquerade, her teasing and cajoling of the children ("Teaseforhim"), to Gerty's fetishistic exhibition-ism ("Toesforhim"), and to her flawed athletic display, her throwing of the twins' ball ("Tossforhim"). In "Nausicaa" the playing children and provocative young women are clearly distinguished groups of characters; but in 2.1 the games and the seduction return conflated, producing a bi-furcated narrative characteristic of the dream. The concomitant schism in the vision of Issy and her companions—as innocent, playful girls and tempting, artful sirens—is part of a larger split in the daughter figure that appears throughout the text.

The figurations of the Wakean daughter record the dream return of the threat of a compromising or critical female I/eye, that threat males in the waking worlds of the earlier fictions frequently attempt to repress. One of the key enigmas of Issy centers around what she has seen and knows, a psychic uncertainty reflected in the contradictory imagoes of her and in-scribed as well in her very name: its mirrorlike structure (Is-sy) suggests the self-enthralled narcissist, while its potential homonym (I see) suggests the viewing gaze. At points "her shellback thimblecasket mirror only can show her dearest friendeen" [FW 561]), or in other words reveals to her only her own reflection. She becomes the self-sufficient young girl who uses her double as a plaything to ward off loneliness and desire: "Pussy is never alone, . . . for she can always look at Biddles and talk petnames with her little playfilly" (FW 561–62). Other representations of her, how-ever, foreground not her narcissistic innocence but rather her intrusive curiosity, a curiosity unequivocally visual, sometimes coded as spying:

the magazine wall, where our maggy seen all (FW 7)

Liddell lokker through the leafery (FW 270)

eysolt of binnoculises (FW 394)

meye eyesalt (FW 484)

Netta and Linda, our seeyu tities and they've sin sumtim (FW 527)

suistersees (FW 538)

The uncertain trajectory of the daughter's gaze is betrayed not only in the larger contradictory conceptualization of her, but also in divisions within individual imagoes. Because the dreamer remains unsure about the daughter figure's visual knowledge, in one of the earliest accounts of his sin, her evidence against him is characteristically split—"*visibly diver-gent,* as wapt from wept, on minor points touching the intimate nature of this, a first offense" (FW 34, emphasis added).

Directed alternately toward self and others, Issy's discourse redupli-cates the ambiguous focus of her vision: one moment her voice sounds narcissistically obsessed with cosmetics, clothing, or her personal appear-

ance; the next moment it speaks to or about others with a wicked preco-
ciousness, her self-flattering prattle ("Simply adorable! Could I but pass
my hands some, my hands through, thine hair!") being regularly punctuated with nasty gossip, often about a paternal figure ("dare all grandpas-
sia! He's gone on his bombashaw. Through geesing and so pleasing at
Strip Teasy up the stairs" [FW 527]). At its most satiric, Issy's discourse
sounds like a direct inversion of Gerty's, the latter's flattering and roman-
ticizing gaze turned into a deflationary one, her unquestioning reverence
of all figures paternal (her alcoholic father, her priest, her older admirer
on Sandymount strand) turned into blatant cynicism. While Gerty remains blind to the sexual dimension in her confessions to Father Conroy,
Issy exposes her cleric as a patent philanderer. The jaunty and caustic
lyrics she composes to reveal her profane knowledge are a far cry from the
insipid verses ("*Art thou real, my ideal?*" [U 364/298]) admired by her
sentimental precursor:

> How vain's that hope in cleric's heart
> Who still pursues th'adult'rous art,
> Cocksure that rusty gown of his
> Will make fair Sue forget his phiz!
>
> (FW 146, my transposition)

In the dreamtext Joyce frequently reverses the young virgin's patrio-
latrous voice, exposing a hostility and irreverence that are perhaps the
repressed antithetical underside of blind female devotion to flawed patriarchal authority.

The ambiguous focus of Issy's attention can be accounted for by examining the ambiguity of female narcissism itself. The art critic John Berger
offers a helpful comment when discussing sanctimonious images of female narcissists painted by males:

> The mirror was often used as a symbol of the vanity of woman. The mor-
> alizing, however, was mostly hypocritical. You painted a naked woman be-
> cause you enjoyed looking at her, you put a mirror in her hand and you
> called the painting Vanity, thus morally condemning the woman whose na-
> kedness you had depicted for your own pleasure.
>
> The real function of the mirror was otherwise. It was to make the woman
> connive in treating herself as, first and foremost, a sight.[14]

Joyce's narcissistic females are indeed often presented as working to display themselves as visually pleasing sights, as voyeuristic objects, yet
herein lies the potential paradox of narcissism that he stresses in both
Ulysses and *Finnegans Wake*: in order to present oneself as a voyeuristic
object, one must first be aware of a voyeur, and to be secretly aware of a
voyeur is to be a voyeur oneself, a furtively viewing subject. Mirrors can

help in this process of stealthy gazing, for as any fan of spy movies knows, they often reflect much more than one's own image, although they may give the impression that one is enthralled with it. In Joyce's works the duplicitous female mirror is often more figurative than literal, a stance of self-absorption that may mask a prying voyeuristic eye leveled at the other. In one of the imagined monologues of the daughter in the *Wake*, Issy reminds herself, "Musforget there's an audience" (*FW* 147), as if she realized that she has betrayed her self-consciousness, revealed her awareness that she is being watched by an other.

Alternately self-enthralled and acutely aware of others, Issy is the dream return of the narcissistic and yet highly self-conscious Gerty Mac-Dowell. Because Issy is a dream image, however, the dual focus of her attention—like the other divisions in her personality—cannot be taken as an objective reality: as Shari Benstock has emphasized, "it may not be Issy who is 'split,' but rather the father's image of her which divides itself."[15] The daughter's divided gaze must be examined as part of the psychic dialectic of wishes and fears that constitutes the only real referentiality of HCE's dream. Given the father's prurient (and often voyeuristic) designs on her that emerge in the unconscious fantasies of the *Wake*, Issy's split vision may well reflect a male desire that her ken be narcissistically delimited, countered by an uneasy dread that she sees much more, that her self-enthrallment is a feint, a pose, that she is not simply a pretty sight, but also—like Gerty—a potentially compromising site of sight.

The designation of the dualistic daughter as "the peeress of generals . . . Misses Mirtha and Merry" (*FW* 529) is interesting to trace back and compare to its precedent appearance in Bloom's thoughts in "Lotus Eaters": "Martha, Mary. I saw that picture somewhere I forget now old master or faked for money. He is sitting in their house, talking. Mysterious. . . . She listens with big dark soft eyes. Tell her: more and more: all" (*U* 79/64–65). One portion of the recalled picture represents one of the sisters of Lazarus listening to Jesus. No doubt on account of her "big dark soft eyes," this doubly passive female—entranced by male discourse, reified in a painting—is animated in the *Wake* as the voyeuristic Issy whose perspective threatens to compromise male authority figures ("the peeress of generals"); in the dream those eyes have lost their respectful regard, having been transformed into a possibly mocking gaze, viewing with amusement ("Mirtha and Merry") whatever they have espied.

The temptress in the dream is recurrently symbolized by Manneken-Pis, a fountain of a urinating child in Brussels. This imago may hint that HCE, in part a reincarnation of Bloom, may have shown some voyeuristic interest in a statue; but it also may express a lingering wish to reduce the female to pure object. Several other imagoes of the dualistic daughter similarly label her as the signifier of "to-be-looked-at-ness": as "two stripping baremaids" (FW 526), Issy and her double recall the exhibitionist Miss Douce and Miss Kennedy of "Sirens," and as "dinky pinks deliberatively summersaulting off her bisexycle" (FW 115), they mark the return of the female cyclists Bloom enjoys ogling. Elsewhere the two girls appear as actresses on stage and screen, professional artistic objects: "Rhidarhoda and Daradora . . . playing breeches parts for Bessy Sudlow in fleshcoloured pantos" (FW 434); "the legintimate lady performers of display unquestionable, Elsebett and Marryetta Gunning, H_2O" (FW 495). This guise implies a conscious artistry accompanied by a feigned unawareness of the audience, an imperviousness to the viewer that is totally studied and spurious.

Laura Mulvey has argued that cinematic viewing is essentially a legitimized cultural outlet for voyeuristic desires. The conventions of film screening she describes to support her contention are analogous to those governing theatrical spectacles, which Joyce would have been even more familiar with:

> At first glance, the cinema would seem to be remote from the undercover world of surreptitious observation of an unknowing and unwilling victim. What is seen of the screen is so manifestly shown. But the mass of mainstream film, and the conventions within which it has consciously evolved, portray a hermetically sealed world that unwinds magically, indifferent to the presence of the audience, producing for them a sense of separation and playing on their voyeuristic fantasy. Moreover, the extreme contrast between the darkness in the auditorium (which also isolates the spectators from one another) and the brilliance of the shifting patterns of light and shade on the screen helps to promote the illusion of voyeuristic separation. Although the film is really being shown, is there to be seen, conditions of screening and narrative conventions give the spectator an illusion of looking in on a private world. Among other things, the position of the spectators in the cinema is blatantly one of repression of their exhibitionism and projection of the repressed desire onto the performer.[16]

The connection between voyeurism and the viewing of filmed or staged performances is firmly established in Joyce's fictions. Bloom's juvenile spying on a neighbor, for instance, has all the accouterments of theatrical spectatorship—operaglasses, curtains, and a framed female object ("Lotty Clarke, flaxenhaired, I saw at her night toilette through illclosed curtains with poor papa's operaglasses" [U 549/448]). One of the society ladies in "Circe" claims that Bloom exploits the theater for specific voyeuristic opportunities, exposing its more general—albeit usually veiled—psychic functions ("He said that he had seen from the gods my peerless globes as I sat in a box of the Theatre Royal at a command performance of La Cigale" [U 465/379]). As Mulvey implies, the audience assumes the role of the actively watching male subject, while the staged or screened image becomes the equivalent of the watched female object: the gender categories imposed on the two positions resurface in the *Wake* when HCE becomes the "Turk of the theatre . . . [who] bepiaster[s] the buik-danseuses [bellydancers in Danish] from the opulence of his omnibox" (*FW* 98) or the duke who watches "*The Bo' Girl* and *The Lily* on all horserie show . . . from his viceregal booth" (*FW* 32). These screen memories of the dreamer's sin contain clear residues of those perceptual reifications of the female, seen so clearly in Joyce's waking worlds; they support Mulvey's claim that "man is reluctant to gaze at his exhibitionist like."[17] But in a variation on these theatrical images in the *Wake*, HCE is up on the screen/stage with the dualistic female: he assumes the imago of the American film star Noah Beery (*FW* 64) and "reel[s] the titleroll opposite a *brace of girdles* in Silver on the Screen" (*FW* 134, emphasis added). This version of the sin can be read as the return, in significantly revised form, of Bloom's theatrical conceptualization of his encounter with Gerty: "See her as she is spoil all. Must have the stage setting, the rouge, costume, position, music. The name too. . . . Nell Gwynn, *Mrs Bracegirdle*, Maud Branscombe. Curtain up" (*U* 370/303, emphasis added). In waking reality the male sees the female as the seductive display, the performer; in details of the *Wake*, the Bloom reincarnated within the dreamer recognizes that he too is the actor, the self-conscious object of the female I/eye, contriving, for instance, to present himself from the best possible angle ("Ought to attend to my appearance my age. Didn't let her see me in profile" [*U* 369/302]). The young women in "Nausicaa" are not the only ones capable of stagy self-presentations; in its contrasting representations of this earlier theater of desire, the Wakean dream alternately denies and confirms this truth.

The transgression the dreamer wants both to remember and to forget appears in countless guises, ultimately irreconcilable, reflecting an array of anxieties and wishes. One strand of these proliferative accounts hints that HCE is a male voyeur threatened by the possibility of female voyeurism, by the woman as viewing subject secretly looking at the male as viewed object. The story of Diana and Actaeon, the confrontation between hunter and huntress that provides the mythic substructure for several of the female accusations in "Circe," returns even more explicitly in the Wakean dream as the mythic parallel to this version of HCE's sin. A true lover of venery, the older HCE is imaged as "the icepolled globetopper . . . haunted by the hottest spot under his equator like Ramrod, the meaty hunter, always jaeger for a thrust" (*FW* 435), while the dualistic daughter appears as "a deuce of dianas ridy for the hunt" (*FW* 43) and is often surrounded by seven young girls, like Diana protected by her seven nymphs ("THE FLORAS . . . form with valkyrienne licence the guard for /

IZOD" [FW 220]). By one account, the father has fallen "all because, loosed in her reflexes, she seem she seen Ericoricori coricome huntsome with his three poach dogs aleashing him" (FW 622–23). The daughter with her potentially duplicitous mirror—ostensibly lost in her reflection ("loosed in her reflexes") but perhaps noticing nonetheless her voyeur ("she seem she seen")—corresponds to Diana in her pond with its reflecting surface (referred to in Humphries' translation of Ovid as "the cool crystal"[18]); the spying oedipal sons become the "three poach dogs," the hounds that tear apart their master, Actaeon transformed into a stag; while the father plays the part of the ill-fated hunter ("Ericoricori coricome huntsome") who inadvertently stumbles upon the bathing goddess, just as HCE, by some reports, accidentally stumbles upon the urinating girls. Diana's "pool" provides a conveniently overdetermined associative image, easily linked to both micturition and mirror.

In Ovid's account, Actaeon's role as a voyeur, however unwitting, is as unequivocal as the ensuing wrath of the exposed and outraged Diana; in the Wake this subject/object dichotomy becomes more complicated, as the dreaming psyche explores not only the obvious ambiguity in the myth as to who is hunting whom ("hounded become haunter, hunter become fox" [FW 132]), but also the subtler ambiguity as to who is the real voyeur, and hence who is the genuinely exposed party. The positional uncertainty of the male is economically conveyed in the images that represent him as voyeuristic subject and compromised object simultaneously— holding a telescope, for instance, that is also an erection ("This is big Willingdone mormorial tallowscoop Wounderworker obscides on the flanks of the jinnies" [FW 8]). A similar vision of the son in 1.7 stresses not only this positional instability but also its inherent dangers, as the telescope is suddenly turned on the prying male viewer, albeit in the form of a bulldog revolver—Actaeon's punitive hounds in a more contemporary guise perhaps: "he did take a tompip peepestrella throug a threedraw eighteen hawkspower durdicky telescope . . . [and] got the charm of his optical life when he found himself . . . at pointblank range blinking down the barrel of an irregular revolver of the bulldog with a purpose pattern" (FW 178–79). In his appropriation of this mythic text, the dreamer asks himself the question never considered in standard versions of the story as it has evolved within the androcentric literary tradition: what did the male looker look like as he watched the compromised female? Was he perhaps aroused? We know what Actaeon saw at that crucial moment of confrontation—but what about Diana?

The sons who spy voyeuristically on the father and the daughter in this account of the sin are in their turn threatened by the female gaze. Testifying in 3.3, Shaun concedes that he himself was titillated when he witnessed the ambiguous exhibitionistic/voyeuristic encounter between HCE and the young girls: "—Peequeen ourselves, the prettiest pickles of un-matchemable mute antes [*mutandes*: drawers in Italian] I ever bopeeped at, seesaw shallsee, since the town go went gonning on Pranksome Quaine." The girls are referred to as "white in black arpists at cloever spilling," the sound of their urine spilling in the clover disguised as "chamber music," the tinkling of a piano or harp. When one of the in-quisitors points out that these figurative musicians may have been aware of his presence as a voyeur ("And were they watching you as watcher as well?"), Shaun adamantly denies the possibility, disturbed by its implica-tions: "—Where do you get that wash? This representation does not ac-cord with my experience. They were watching the watched watching. Vechers all" (*FW* 508–9). Shaun aims to circumscribe the scope of the female gaze and situate himself outside its ken, for if the girls have noticed him, he has been duped. Assuming himself to be the watcher, the safely hidden spy, he may in fact have been the watched, the viewed object rather than the viewing subject—like father, like son. The inquisitor's "representation" of the female gaze clashes with Shaun's "experience" as a male voyeur, unsettling the certainty of his delimited point of view.

The daughter Issy takes after her mother, a "mirrorminded curios-itease" (*FW* 576), the dreamer's wife who may also have spied on his guilty activities ("his ambling limfy peepingpartner" [*FW* 580]) and who possesses a gaze with a potentially searing impact ("For lispias harth a burm in eye but whem it bames fire norone screeneth" [*FW* 348]). The female becomes a Medusa figure, though one with a gaze whose threat may lie in its seductiveness, a gaze sometimes surreptitiously hidden be-hind a veil—like Gerty's amorous eyes hidden stealthily beneath the brim of a hat: "Maye faye, she's la gaye this snaky woman! . . . Veil, volantine, valentine eyes" (*FW* 20). In the final dream vision of ALP in Book 4, however, this covering of the female eye is envisioned not as an act of duplicity but as an act of mercy. ALP promises not to look at her husband ("I'll close me eyes. So not to see" [*FW* 621]), a sensitive indulgence given his physical appearance, possibly marred beyond the aid of modern med-icine ("despair of Pandemia's postwartem plastic surgeons" [*FW* 263]), and his psychic dread of the female gaze as an agency of exposure. But here the wife is envisioned as tolerant of her spouse's falls, moral as well as physical, forgiving of whatever she has seen or knows of his foibles, tactfully leaving them unspecified, and offering even a redemptive cleans-ing: "All men has done something. Be the time they've come to the weight of old fletch. We'll lave it. So" (*FW* 621). The dream repeatedly brings to light a repressed truth of androcentric culture: that men are often gyno-centrically defined, created by the female other, desirous of being seen positively in her eye, but fearing the opposite. As Bloom concedes in the telling thought on Sandymount strand that anticipates the unconscious revelations of "Circe" and the dreamworld of the *Wake*, "See ourselves as others see us. So long as women don't mock what matter?" (*U* 376/307).

• • •

The wishful lingering visions in the dreamworld that represent the woman as object and the man as subject are replicated in scenarios in which the female plays the slave to a male master: the correspondence between the two sets of imagoes highlights the political implications of the visual relationship. The temptresses' appearance in the guise of household servants links them both to Mary Driscoll, the Blooms' former scullerymaid who was purportedly the target of her employer's sexual advances, and to "the nextdoor girl," whose "vigorous hips" Bloom eyes in the porkbutcher's shop (*U* 59/48). He later thinks of this young woman as the maid from the well-known nursery rhyme ("Perhaps hanging clothes out to dry. The maid was in the garden" [*U* 68/55]), a representation of female domestic help that returns in the dream with a clear sexual twist ("the mayds was midst the hawthorns shoeing up their hose" [*FW* 135]). Perhaps the tempting daughter is conflated with the female servant in the *Wake* because the two figures can be roughly substitutional, psychologically speaking, as Joyce may have known from "Fragment of an Analysis of a Case of Hysteria": Freud imposes on Dora an identification with two different female domestics who had amorous ties to paternal figures. During one of the trial scenes in "Circe" it is argued that "the young person [Mary Driscoll] was treated by the defendant as if she were his very own daughter" (*U* 464/378)—an exoneration that surely backfires insofar as it may only prove Bloom's displaced incestuous desire for Milly.

The Wakean vision of the temptresses as lower class may indicate Joyce's ongoing awareness of the sexual predation to which female domestics were particularly vulnerable, doubly powerless in patriarchal culture as a woman and a servant. It can also be read psychoanalytically as the representation of a mental defense that plays on class structures and prejudices—as an attempted lowering of the object of desire to the rank of maidservant or prostitute (*"a Pair of Sloppy Sluts plainly Showing all the Unmentionability"* [*FW* 107]; "deuce of damimonds" [*FW* 134]) in an effort to shift guilt, to stigmatize and discredit the female through implied inferior social standing. A similar psychic maneuver appears at the end of the Mary Driscoll scene in "Circe," when Bloom pleads superior social class as implicit proof of his innocence ("I was just chatting this afternoon at the viceregal lodge to my old pals, sir Robert and lady Ball, astronomer royal, at the levee. Sir Bob, I said . . ." [*U* 465/379, Joyce's ellipsis]). The defendant is then ironically assailed by the three society ladies who turn class snobbery to the defendant's disadvantage, implying that his sexual guilt is compounded by his presumptuous violation of social boundaries ("This plebeian Don Juan observed me from behind a hackney car" [*U* 467/381]). Class distinctions are often invoked in the arena of allegations and reproaches in Joyce's fictions, albeit never with any success, hierarchical stratification remaining subject to infinite refinement and expansion.

Although Bloom's assault on Mary Driscoll may be only a psychic reality, a taboo fantasy, his interest in the scullerymaid is visible enough to Molly to prompt her to give the young woman her week's notice. In a Wakean inversion of the earlier fiction, the wife is envisioned not firing the tempting female servants but rather hiring them—and even schooling them in seductive gestures by demonstrating an exhibitionist dance upon a windowsill, in a tableau that foreshadows the young temptresses' appearance elsewhere as skirtkickers or actresses performing upon a stage:

> every shirvant siligirl or wensum farmerette walking the pilend roads, Sawy, Fundally, Daery or Maery, Milucre, Awny or Graw, usedn't she make her a simp or sign to slip inside by the sullyport? . . . Calling them in, one by one . . . and legging a jig or so on the sihl to show them how to shake their benders and the dainty how to bring to mind the gladdest garments out of sight and all the way of a maid with a man and making a sort of a cackling noise like two and a penny or half a crown and holding up a silliver shiner. Lordy, lordy, did she so? Well, of all the ones ever I heard! Throwing all the neiss little whores in the world at him! (*FW* 200)

This bizarre vision of the wife selflessly pandering for her husband should be read, I suspect, as a wishful fantasy that doubly legitimizes the predation of the father, making sexual favors part of the servants' remunerated services and adding to the contract the wife's clear endorsement.

As a repressed desire, Bloom's interest in the family's former female domestic never directly enters his conscious thoughts, although it is obliquely betrayed in his passing advocacy of very young male servants, who would presumably offer temptations to no one: "I often thought it would be better to have boy servants. Up to fifteen or so. After that, of course . . ." (*U* 104/86, Joyce's ellipsis). In "Circe" the defense counsel tries to rationalize the guilty desire by translating the situation to another cultural context, by arguing that Bloom (as Moses) thought momentarily he was in Egypt, where pharaohs had free rein with their female thralls: "My client is an infant, a poor foreign immigrant who started scratch as a stowaway and is now trying to turn an honest penny. The trumped up misdemeanour was due to a momentary aberration of heredity, brought on by hallucination, such familiarities as the alleged guilty occurrence being quite permitted in my client's native place, the land of the Pharaoh"

(*U* 463/377–78). A similar cultural transposition, with an identical psychic motivation, returns in *Finnegans Wake* when the tempting servants become Egyptians (*"the Parlourmaids of Aegypt"* [*FW* 104]) or servile eastern concubines secured to entertain and arouse the master ("a pfurty pscore of ruderic rossies haremhorde for his divelsion" [*FW* 285]). The imagoes of the father as the pharaoh with his "haremhorde" or, analogously, the Mormon Joseph Smith ("Yussive smirte" [*FW* 262]) with his multiple wives bespeak a wish for female devotion in compensatory excess. In less auspicious guise, however, the temptations of the female thralls are marked as a danger: their seductive wiles may make the father feel his age more acutely, proving only his imminent impotence ("He spenth his strenth amok haremscarems. Poppy Narancy, Giallia, Chlora, Marinka, Anileen, Parme" [*FW* 102]). In their most mythic form, their pose of obedient surrender hides even more fatal powers, a capacity to bestow the kiss of death ("Houri of the coast of emerald, arrah of the lacessive poghue, Aslim-all-Muslim, the resigned to her surrender . . . with so valkirry a licence as sent many a poor pucker packing to perdition" [*FW* 68]). The sexual charms of the bevy of women, in short, are charged with contradictory affects, like those of the temptress from "Nausicaa" whose compliant sexual performance leaves Bloom feeling initially rejuvenated—"The strength it gives a man" (*U* 370/303)—but ultimately spent—"Drained all the manhood out of me, little wretch" (*U* 377/308).

The male fantasy of the eastern harem woman is impelled by a fearful fascination with feminine powers and a concurrent wish for feminine servitude, an ambivalent psychic dynamic that emerges in *Ulysses*. Recalling his dream of Molly from the night before, Bloom reads her Turkish attire as a signifier of female dominance ("She had red slippers on. Turkish. Wore the breeches. Suppose she does?" [*U* 381/311–12]), and she is accordingly imperious when this dream specter materializes later in "Circe." But this unconscious image of Molly elaborates the initial fragmented memory, and in doing so exposes the misprision contained in Bloom's conscious interpretation of the partially recalled dreamtext: the fetterchain linking his spouse's ankles in the Circean version is a minor but eloquent detail, betraying the fantasy of female enslavement within the threatening vision. One detail of Molly's Turkish garb—the yashmak—resurfaces in the *Wake* when ALP is envisioned as "my delights, my jealousy, ymashkt, beyashmakt, earswathed, snoutsnooded" (*FW* 547). This vision of the "beyashmakt" woman returns in one of the accounts of ALP's marriage to HCE, a context that clarifies even more markedly the wish for female subjugation that motivates the exotic and erotic imago from popular eastern lore. The account highlights HCE's capture and appropriation of ALP, the fetterchain from Circean fantasy finding its Wakean transformation in the locked chain of a chastity belt: "I pudd a name and wedlock boltoned round her the which to carry till her grave" (FW 548).

In Joyce's works, women often escape these attempted male appropriations of them by reflexively turning inward and backward to their personal pasts. The end of *Ulysses* resembles "The Dead" in its representation of the wife eluding her husband through romantic retrospection; but in the later work the memories are utterly private, presented from a wholly internal narrative vantage. The richness of Molly's closing recollections of her girlhood contributes to the final impression of her female autonomy that emerges even in the face of her continuing desire for countless male admirers. As she thinks back to the day she spent on Howth with Bloom almost sixteen years ago, she recalls, "I gave him all the pleasure I could leading him on till he asked me to say yes and I wouldnt answer first only looked out over the sea and the sky *I was thinking of so many things he didnt know* of Mulvey and Mr Stanhope and Hester and father and old captain Groves" (U 782/643, emphasis added)—what follows is the elaborate vision of Gibraltar in which Bloom starts to merge with Mulvey. Molly's closing reveries interweave two distinct but not mutually exclusive memories: a moment of union and tacit understanding balanced by a concurrent sense of her private female past as uniquely and irrevocably her own.

Joycean males often intuit that their wives escape them through secret recollections, through prior experiences unknown to them; in response, they develop psychic strategies that allow them to attempt to capture what eludes them. Bloom's infamous catalogue of Molly's "lovers" in "Ithaca" is one such compensatory measure, a controlled and controlling intellectual response to his wife's errant desires and ultimately unknowable sexual history. As Robert Boyle has emphasized, the list cannot be taken too literally, made up as it is of men who, in Bloom's experience or speculations, have shown any interest in Molly as a sex object or who would know anything personal about her sex life (hence the inclusion of a doctor and a priest).[19] The roster is significantly missing Lieutenant Stanley G. Gardner and also assumes "Mulvey to be the first term of [the] series" (U 731/601), whereas Molly's memories reveal that Mr. Stanhope has shown a prior muted interest in her, as has an early (unnamed) male voyeur from next door. Bloom thinks he knows his wife's erotic history, yet pieces of it clearly escape his ken.

Bloom's curiosity about Molly's sexual past finds its Wakean counterpart in the ALP chapter (1.8), where the washerwomen attempt to chronicle the female's erotic life and to figure out the details of her fall into sexuality—the who, the where, the when, and the how of her earliest encounter: "Waiwhou was the first thurever burst? ... Then whereabouts in Ow and Ovoca?" (*FW* 202–3). By one account, linked to several versions of the sin in the park, ALP's fall was simply into sexual self-consciousness, one of the women arguing that her first erotic experience was a visual one, an embarrassed excitement felt when the young girl noticed a voyeuristic admirer: "She thought she's sankh neathe the ground with nymphant shame when he gave her the tigris eye! O happy fault!" (*FW* 202). Molly has a similar recollection of an early sexual pleasure, remembering when Mr. Stanhope "was watching me whenever he got an opportunity at the band on the Alameda esplanade . . . our eyes met I felt something go through me like all needles my eyes were dancing I remember after when I looked at myself in the glass hardly recognised myself the change" (*U* 756/622). The assertion of ALP's visual seduction is quickly contradicted, the contentious laundresses being able to agree only that, like Molly, the Wakean female has had encounters with a number of men, starting at a young age ("She must have been a gadabcount in her day, so she must, more than most. Shoal she was, gidgad. She had a flewmen of her owen" [*FW* 202]). In order to get to the first, they try moving toward the Liffey's source near Sally Gap, where one of the gossips decides that her earliest fall was literal, a toddler tripping in the woods—or water spilling out of a mountain rock: "first of all, worst of all, the wiggly livvly, she sideslipped out by a gap in the Devil's glen while Sally her nurse was sound asleep in a sloot and, feefee fiefie, fell over a spillway" (*FW* 204).

The washerwomen's investigative problem, of course, lies in ALP's naturalistic status as an age-old river, her "bed" having been numerously and easily "violated": men walking across her, washing their hands in her, drinking from her stream, sailing their boats up her, bursting her "bar." To further complicate the situation, the first assault on ALP may have been singular or plural, a lone invading vessel or an entire militia of ships: "Someone he was, whuebra they were, in a tactic attack or in single combat" (*FW* 202). ALP's multiple lovers in 1.8 express a psychic fear and desire simultaneously. On one level the dream vision bespeaks an anxiety about rivals from the past that may be lurking in his wife's heart and mind: the countless men in the chronicle of ALP are the Michael Fureys and Harry Mulveys of the dreamworld. But under the dynamics of mediated desire, sexual competitors also work to confirm and compound the desirability of the love object, as *Ulysses* makes clear. Molly and Bloom are each secretly gratified that the other has admirers and unconsciously use their own extramarital liaisons (with Boylan and Martha, for instance) to prove their desirability and to provoke and recapture their spouse's gaze. In the *Wake* HCE similarly celebrates his own erotic tastes in the vision of his wife's countless seducers and affirms his own desirability in the fantasies of multiple "other women."

Joyce's works frequently record a male desire to appropriate the female as well as various strategies for doing so: speculative explorations of her past, intellectual investigations of the "text" of her body, artistic renderings of her image, physical dominations of her will, perceptual occlusions of her independent subjectivity. But equally apparent is Joyce's interest in the way the female potentially threatens the male ego and ultimately eludes the male mind. In the dreamworld she finds her correlative in nature in the mobile and protean river, whose essence can never be captured and controlled. The psychic effort to contain the sexual other is imaged geographically, when the male landscape tries to hold in the fluvial ALP; but her song in 1.8 speaks her need for a "plumper" bankside, for a freedom that tempts her to leap her confines: "*Only for my short Brittas bed made's as snug as it smells it's out I'd lep and off with me to the slobs della Tolka or the plage au Clontarf to feale the gay aire of my salt troublin bay and the race of the saywint up me ambushure*" (FW 201). ALP's singing of her need for release is apt, for it is in discursive gestures of all varieties that the women in the dream attempt to reappropriate their autonomy, by reinscripting themselves and recording their perspectives.

· · ·

In Joyce's waking worlds, the attempts by men to envision women writing betray unmistakable limitations in the male imagination. Bloom, for instance, thinks of female letter writers as a potentially intriguing sight, as a visual lure that would easily promote the sale of commercial goods. He has recommended to Wisdom Hely, his former employer in the stationery business, an advertising gimmick featuring "a transparent showcart with two smart girls sitting inside writing letters, copybooks, envelopes, blottingpaper. . . . Smart girls writing something catch the eye at once. Everyone dying to know what she's writing" (U 154/127). The ad pretends to think female subjectivity, when in fact it only sees it as a convenient mystery to be commercially exploited; instead of thinking female subjectivity the ad actually negates it, insofar as the women have been reduced to provocative visual objects—they are "smart" only in the sense of being stylishly dressed, not mentally acute. Exactly what they are writing does not matter at all—it is clearly only the image, the simulacrum of female writing, that is needed to make the ad work. When Bloom shares this idea with Stephen in "Ithaca," the young artist transforms it into a sexual drama that perfectly reveals the scotoma frequently afflicting his vision of the female:

What suggested scene was then constructed by Stephen?
Solitary hotel in mountain pass. Autumn. Twilight. Fire lit. In dark corner young man seated. Young woman enters. Restless. Solitary. She sits. She

goes to window. She stands. She sits. Twilight. She thinks. On solitary hotel paper she writes. She thinks. She writes. She sighs. Wheels and hoofs. She hurries out. He comes from his dark corner. He seizes solitary paper. He holds it towards fire. Twilight. He reads. Solitary.

What?
In sloping, upright and backhands: Queen's Hotel, Queen's Hotel, Queen's Hotel, Queen's Ho . . . (*U* 684/560, Joyce's ellipsis)

Stephen's constructed scenario here is connected to that moment in "Scylla and Charybdis" when he briefly espies a young woman in the library, logically presumed to be Emma Clery: "Is that . . . ? Blueribboned hat . . . ? Idly writing . . . ? What? . . . . Looked . . . ?" (*U* 215/177, Joyce's ellipses). The man in Stephen's sexual drama shares its author's curiosity here about the female text, a text that creates in the male psyche an intellectual lacuna, signified through proliferative ellipses and question marks. In "Ithaca" Stephen fills that lacuna with the most facile of sexist clichés: forced to think female subjectivity in the form of a letter, he can imagine only bored and mindless scribblings.

The imaginative paucity that plagues male attempts in waking life to think a female text disappears in the Wakean nightworld where the female writer returns in varying guises. The dreamer envisions ALP chronicling his past in a personal biography ("her murmoirs" [*FW* 387]), a newspaper ("our national rooster's rag" [*FW* 220]), or—most consistently—the ominous nightletter ("Her untitled mamafesta memorialising the Mosthighest" [*FW* 104]). ALP is linked to the letter in various capacities—as its commissioner, its discoverer, its hider, its interpreter, and as one of its creators. Gilbert and Gubar have argued that because women in patriarchal societies lack "the pen/penis which would enable them . . . to refute one fiction by another, [they] have historically been reduced to *mere* properties, to characters and images imprisoned in male texts . . . generated solely . . . by male expectations and designs. . . . As a creation 'penned' by man, moreover, woman has been 'penned up' or 'penned in.'"[20] The Wakean female is similarly confined, figuratively the creation of a male dreamer, literally the creation of a male author; but rather then being "pen-less" as well as "penned in," she is imagined writing from her unique vantage point, always perplexing, often subversive. The verbal threat inherent in the female letter is the counterpart to the visual threat inherent in the female gaze. If the female gaze critiques male subjectivity, then the letter affords the space to inscribe this other point of view.

The opening of the letter chapter (1.5) of the *Wake* records a psychic effort to get into the *content* of ALP's text, to penetrate to a site of female writing, to go beyond those limited waking visions of mere sights of female writing. The specific and proliferative titles of ALP's "mamafesta" replace those ellipses marking Stephen's response to Emma's writing, that provocative blank at the center of Bloom's eye-catching ad, or those vacuous doodles in Stephen's elaboration of it. The absence in the waking works returns as superfluous presence in dream, when HCE tries to imagine the female testament that may save or ruin him. Reflecting his deepest hopes and fears, some names for the document augur praise (*"The Best in the West"*) or redemption (*"The Augusta Angustissimost for Old Seabeastius' Salvation"*), while others allude to the threat of filial conspiracy (*"How the Buckling Shut at Rush in January"*) or scandal in the form of a woman's exposé of a man's sexual performance (*"In My Lord's Bed by One Whore Went Through It"*; *"He Perssed Me Here with the Ardour of a Tonnoburkes"*). Some promise a resolution of the issue of sexual responsibility for the dreamer's fall, albeit with predictably contradictory results: through a reference to *Macbeth* (*"Look to the Lady"*), one title suggests a concession of female guilt, pointing to the wife who spurs her husband on to fatal ambitions, though another blames the man himself (*"Siegfield Follies and or a Gentlehomme's Faut Pas"* [FW 104–6]).

Under the transformative logic of the *Wake*, ALP's multiple possible letters become her litter of multiple children (her "superflowvius heirs" [FW 526]) or her multiple gifts, catalogued by the washerwomen in 1.8. ALP's seemingly generous distribution of Christmas parcels takes on unsavory overtones when we remember that on a naturalistic level Anna Livia is the anal Liffey of "dear dirty Dublin": her presents may be the trash people have thrown into her which in flood she vengefully returns to them ("like Santa Claus at the cree of the pale and puny . . . with a Christmas box apiece for aisch and iveryone of her childer, the birthday gifts they dreamt they gabe her, the spoiled she fleetly laid at our door! On the matt, by the pourch and inunder the cellar" [FW 209]). Like the tidings offered in her letter, her tidal offerings are ambiguously valenced, possibly injurious or rehabilitating: the river's effluvia may be the source of illness ("a cough and a rattle and wildrose cheeks for poor Piccolina Petite MacFarlane" [FW 210]), but its benigner properties may offer cures ("spas and speranza and symposium's syrup for decayed and blind and gouty Gough" [FW 211]). The contradictory nature of ALP's "gifts," both physical and textual, betray the dreamer's uneasiness about what sorts of medicine—for body and psyche—she has to offer a dying man.

The *Wake* invites us to read this female bearer of gifts and letters as the return of at least two female figures from Joyce's earlier fictions, the first being Maria from "Clay." In her provocative reinterpretation of the short story, Margot Norris has demonstrated how cruelly Maria is treated by those around her, how vulnerable she is in an androcentric culture that marks aged and unmarried women as insignificant and undesirable;[21] in the Wakean dream this devalued female has her revenge when residues of her character resurface in inverted form in the images of ALP as an elderly domestic. In "Clay," for instance, Maria is treated shoddily in the cake-shops she visits; in dream she retaliates as "Hanah Levy, shrewd shroplifter" (*FW* 273). The forbearing old woman becomes the plundering outlaw, her yashmak and apron—the visible signs of her sexual oppression—turning into a bandit's mask ("with a naperon for her mask" [*FW* 11]). Norris argues that when the children insert the saucer of clay into the Hallow Eve's game, they hope Maria will interpret it as "shit" and recoil with embarrassment, betraying her own dirty mind;[22] in the *Wake* ALP in the guise of Kate pays back in kind, offering to others "*Shite*! will you have a plateful?" (*FW* 142)—this is the anthropomorphic version of the river's gift to the city of its own detritus and sewage. In dream the elderly woman returns with a malicious and rebellious spirit, implicitly protesting her mistreatment in the waking world of androcentric Dublin.

This deliverer of suspect letters and litter can also be conceptualized as a dream vision of Molly, who contemplates writing an exposé of Bloom's anomalous impulses in a moment of exasperation with her quirky spouse ("he wanted to milk me into the tea well hes beyond everything . . . if I only could remember the 1 half of the things and write a book out of it the works of Master Poldy yes" [*U* 754/621]). In *Finnegans Wake* the dreamer envisions what Bloom would fear if he had access to some of his wife's schemes and suspicions, as he pictures ALP actually embarking upon such a slanderous enterprise, recording for posterity in a succinct and frank letter his questionable transactions with "apple harlottes" and "honeys [who] wore camelia paints" (*FW* 113): a dream allusion to a wife who knows that her spouse has been visiting the brothel district. The image of the female writer in the nightworld is frequently not so much a provocative eye-catcher, material for an ad campaign, as it is a paranoiac threat, material for a smear campaign. In her most disturbing guise, ALP appears as "Cowtends Kateclean, the woman with the muckrake" (*FW* 448), who in the course of her scavengings in the midden discovers "the fairest sin the sunsaw" (*FW* 11). The vision makes sense as a dream transmogrification of a wife in the role of domestic detective, searching her husband's belongings for signs of transgression—a role Molly sounds thoroughly familiar with ("first Ill look at his shirt to see or Ill see if he has that French letter still in his pocketbook I suppose he thinks I dont know deceitful men all their 20 pockets arent enough for their lies" [*U* 772/635]). In the consoling dialectical reversal of this vision, the wife is represented burying or erasing any damaging evidence, or—even better—shredding testimony she never even bothered to write: "she, of the jill-daw's nest who tears up lettereens she never apposed a pen upon" (*FW* 276).

The compromising version of the letter that appears in 1.5 may be a written testimonial derived from the fragmented artifact gleaned from the dump, as Shari Benstock has suggested: "like a good critic, [Biddy/ALP] has come up with a 'reading' of the letter (or some bits of it) that bears little—if any—resemblance to the original document."[23] Because the connection between the two texts remains opaque, we are left to wonder if the hen's report records or constructs HCE's "feebles," dutifully transcribes or scandalously exposes them by filling in the gaps of the initial litterish document. Within the dream's dualistic structure, the female letter is at points the byproduct of the male fall, the text constructed from his remains, at others the cause, the text that has reduced him to his shattered state. There are hints that the woman in the act of writing subverts patriarchal origins and critiques patriarchal authority, bringing down the father through her story, forcing him to read his own guilty desires— hence we hear "About that original hen" (FW 110). In 1.5 the dreamer tries to reassure himself that the ominous challenge the female critic/ author offers to the father's word, the androcentric logos, is only an unsubstantiated rumor: "No, assuredly, they are not justified, those gloompourers who grouse that letters have never been quite their old selves again since that weird weekday in bleak Janiveer . . . when to the shock of both, Biddy Doran looked at literature" (FW 112). But elsewhere associated with the noxious contents of Pandora's box (FW 212), the message of ALP's letter threatens the welfare of the dreamer, just as the effluvia of the river's litter threaten the welfare of the city. One of Issy's provocative footnotes tellingly represents female writing as transgression, as a violation of a forbidden textual domain: "Dear and I trust in all frivolity I may be pardoned for trespassing but I think I may add hell" (FW 270).

ALP's final long letter in Book 4 is highly equivocal, oddly schizophrenic. It sounds exculpatory in its attestation that the male has not mistreated the female ("Item, we never were chained to a chair, and, bitem, no widower whother soever followed us about with a fork on Yankskilling Day" [FW 618]) and trusting in its disbelief of HCE's detractors ("What those slimes up the cavern door around you, keenin, (the lies is coming out on them frecklefully) had the shames to suggest can we ever? Never!" [FW 615]). Yet reference to the father's homosexual buggery is compromising, his potential fate inauspicious, and the description of him highly unflattering: "Meaning: one two four. Finckers. Up the hind hose of hizzars. . . . Conan Boyles will pudge the daylives out through him. . . . The big bad old sprowly all uttering foon!" (FW 617). The text also contains a sinister announcement of an impending funeral, clearly the father's own ("His fooneral will sneak pleace by creeps o'clock toosday" [FW 617]). Disturbingly duplicitous, the nightletter is often envisioned as not only a distinctly feminine work of art, but also a byproduct of female artfulness: "The letter! The litter! And the soother the bitther! Of eyebrow pencilled, by lipstipple penned. Borrowing a word and begging the question and stealing tinder and slipping like soap" (FW 93). The missive may be evidence of the female's "stealing tinder," of her creation of the document from her foragings, or of her usurpation of the male verbal prerogative, the father's word—evidence, in short, of her stealing his thunder. The form of this female text is protean, elusive ("slipping like soap"), its message often distrustfully censored, elided ("begging the question"). But it frequently also resembles—in part or in total—a letter copied from a writing manual: chattily banal, properly formulaic, totally unoriginal ("borrowing a word"), questionably sincere.

The tension in the female letter becomes clearest in the practice letter Issy writes during the homework lesson. Shari Benstock has pointed out that "as Issy learns to write letters (following the model set forth by her mother's letters) she retraces her father's sin, remembers an act in which she was a complicit witness; her writing is the return of repressed, it is the 'trace' of desire."[24] The daughter's role as witness and transcriber, I would emphasize, is a threatening uncertainty, a psychic fear rather than a known actuality. But in contrast to the provocative insinuations of Issy's text, both its format and the gestures she makes as she composes it are conventional, contrived, a series of verbal and physical posturings.

Joyce received from Nora a well-known letter that a friend suggested was taken from a letter-writing book. Richard Ellmann speculates that "the notion of her pathetically adopting so much artifice in the face of his own attempt at total sincerity gave Joyce a hint for the amorality of woman, to be invoked later in force."[25] Although this interpretation of Joyce's response may be true, I suspect he also started to see the cultural pressures on women that drive them to such artifice—the pressures to be "proper," to please men in socially endorsed forms. In "Penelope," after all, Joyce represents Molly recalling how during courtship she had to fake a sort of mental virginity, feeling socially compelled to say the correct things in response to Bloom's queries about the level of her sexual knowledge: "he wrote me that letter with all those words in it . . . after when we met asking me have I offended you . . . and if I knew what it meant of course I had to say no for form sake dont understand you I said" (U 747/615). (This female confession of feigned verbal ignorance may call into question the authencity of Martha Clifford's coy request, "Please tell me what is the real meaning of that word?" [U 77/63].) Envisioning the female letter in the dream, HCE often reads the subtext beneath the prescribed formalities—the slurs, the desires, the sinister prophecies, the damaging revelations (one of which has a distinctly Mollyesque ring to it—he "kissists my exits" [FW 280]). Alternately conventional and challenging, respectful and irreverent ("Dear. And we go on to Dirtdump. Reverend. May we add majesty?" [*FW* 615]), the hybrid female night-letter reflects the dreamer's ambivalence toward the writing woman, his uncertainty as to what he would like to hear—polite formalities, potentially duplicitous, or blunt truths, potentially disquieting.

In the final monologue of the dream, HCE imagines ALP as the authoress of two letters, one written on his behalf, the other for herself. The first has been crafted with great care and labor and comes from across the sea, "the site of salvocean" (*FW* 623), with a promise of redemption. This letter is a version of the flattering "murmoirs" HCE dreams his wife will write about him after his death: "The arzurian deeps o'er his humbodumbones sweeps. And his widdy the giddy is wreathing her murmoirs as her gracest triput to the Grocery Trader's Manthly. Mind mand gunfree by Gladeys Rayburn!" (*FW* 387). The second more personal document records ALP's *own* desires and violates androcentric law. She has buried this letter at the sound of the thunder, the signifier of patriarchal interdiction, but thinks that some day the lost transcript of her hopes will return: "When the waves give up yours the soil may for me. Sometime then, somewhere there, I wrote me hopes and buried the page when I heard Thy voice, ruddery dunner" (*FW* 624). This final bifurcation of ALP's letter along gender lines hints that female writing within androcentric structures is inevitably a double document, containing both an official and repressed text: the former speaks the language of male desire, telling the father what he might like to hear, while the latter tells a different story, one that is at odds with patriarchal imperatives and concerns—or perhaps has nothing to do with them at all. This dualistic letter mentioned within the final monologue is a miniature of the monologue as a whole, for ALP's speech, as I will argue in the next chapter, is indeed a double document, uttered in conflicting tongues as it were.

Joyce's waking fictions often record a male resentment of female discourse, an implicit desire to censor it, a preference for the voiceless female visual object, a preference seen most patently in an early portrait of the artist: "Stephen sat down beside one of the daughters and, while admiring the rural comeliness of her features, waited quietly for her first word which, he knew, would destroy his satisfaction" (*SH* 46). When women are permitted to speak, are actively sought out as participants in ostensible dialogues, males often try to control what they say. Martha's missive, for instance, can be viewed as the perverse counterpart of the proper copybook letter, insofar as much of her writing sounds prescribed, artificial. Bloom clearly attempts to control the female voice, manipulating his correspondent into uttering the language of his particular masochistic brand of male desire. Bloom's need to be the "dictator" of female psyche and speech resurfaces in his own recollection of an encounter with a prostitute ("Girl in Meath street that night. All the dirty things I made her say. All wrong of course. My arks she called it" [*U* 370/303]) and in Molly's disgruntled account of a sex game he makes her play, during which she is asked to speak the words that will allow her husband to cuckold himself and to turn her into a whore ("who is in your mind now tell me who are you thinking of who is it tell me his name who tell me who the german Emperor is it yes imagine Im him think of him can you feel him trying to make a whore of me what he never will" [*U* 740/610]). In the *Wake* this urge to control the female word at least partially disappears: in the irrepressible and often subversive footnotes of Issy; in the spontaneous singing, chattering, and laughing of ALP; and in the proliferative and compromising discourse of the ordinarily marginalized washerwomen, who imitate the rhetorical mode of the "gossipaceous" riverwoman (*FW* 195) they describe.

But male subjects in Joyce's waking and night works alike are plagued by a recurrent sense that women have access to an "other" language, often audibly silent, a language comprehensible only to other females and implicitly threatening to the excluded—and effectively deaf—male listener. Bloom feels that Molly and Milly understand and communicate with each other in elusive and perhaps nonverbal ways—through "a preestablished natural comprehension in incomprehension" (*U* 736/606). In the margins of the nightlesson, Issy and her addressee are glossed as "*Procne, Philomela*" (*FW* 307), the sisters who subvert the censoring powers of the male tyrant by inventing an alternative mode of expression—the visual text of weaving. Even the imagined voice of ALP, the vehicle for one of the clearest speeches in the dream, is occasionally marked as the incomprehensible, as a string of mere fragments of sense ("With lipth she lithpeth to him all to time of thuch and thuch and thow on thow. She he she ho she ha to la. Hairfluke, if he could bad twig her!" [*FW* 23]). Joyce adumbrates—almost as a present absence, as it were—a linguistic space beyond male discourse. In his representations of men who try to listen to this alternative female language but still fail to understand totally what they hear, he inscribes the potential limits to his own auditory forays into that terrain.

Chapter 7

"RETURNING NOT THE SAME": ALP'S FINAL MONOLOGUE IN *FINNEGANS WAKE*

I CLOSE this study of *Finnegans Wake* with an examination of ALP's monologue—the finale of the dream and of the Joycean corpus—as a particularly rich site of returns, the end containing numerous shards of stories composed in early and midcareer. In the inconclusive conclusion of the *Wake*, Joyce rewrites psychic crises from the prior fictions as they might have been dreamed, as they might have been reconstructed in the night narratives of three male figures in archetypal familial roles. The unifying theme of these psychic crises from waking reality is emotional sundering; the theme of their dream return precarious reconciliation. Stories from the earlier works can be discerned returning with a difference—"Returning not the same" (*U* 377/308)—as the dreamtext probes rejected possibilities, unexplored perspectives, and alternative endings, endings wishful and yet inseparable from oppositional anxieties. These dream revisions of the waking world are poetically superimposed, creating a palimpsestic fantasy, overdetermined in its suggestiveness and indeterminate in its psychic resolutions. On one level, the end of the *Wake* is the dream of a husband, very much like Bloom, who in sleep envisions not a marital rift, but rather a reaffirmation of the marital bond. On another level, it is the dream of a son, very much like Stephen, who in sleep envisions not defection from a mother, but rather filial rapprochement with her. On yet another level, it is the dream of a father, very much like Mr. Hill in "Eveline," who in sleep sees not a daughter's possible departure from the family but rather her dutiful return. But the complexities of dream language render these wishful visions ambiguous, each containing residually less sanguine endings: a wife thinking of other men, a mother dying, a daughter in despair abandoning an oppressive patriarchal home. ALP's monologue demonstrates beautifully the way earlier stories relentlessly wander and return in the Wakean dream, eschewing conclusion and closure, submitting themselves instead to the revisionary psychic exigencies of perpetual anxiety and desire.

ALP's monologue seems to mitigate the uncompromising otherness of the female principle in the *Wake*: critics suggest that here we finally hear the actual voice of ALP, even those who elsewhere in their analyses take into account the dream's unmistakably male subjectivity. Shari Benstock, for instance, suggests that ALP's monologue is divorced from the rest of the *Wake*, providing "an alternative vision against which Earwicker's dream vision can be measured," and discusses the final pages of the dream as if they were not colored by male wishes and fears, as if their narrative status were comparable to that of Molly's soliloquy at the close of *Ulysses*: "It is left to Anna Livia, who has the final 'word' in the novel, to confirm the future for her daughter. . . . ALP's hints seem to suggest that diverse and flighty Issy will grow into the calm and unified mother/ wife that Anna Livia now is."[1] Clive Hart describes the final pages of the book as "the closest thing to 'interior monologue' in *Finnegans Wake*," as a "stream of almost unmodified Dublin speech."[2] I read the final speech, in contrast, as a continuation of the ex-centric dreamtext, as the fantasized voice of the female other heard once again, discoursing primarily on the dream's favorite subject—the dreamer himself. The *Wake* critics who imply the voice is "real" overlook the fact that the closing monologue contains reversals and contraries which make little sense on the level of realistic or waking narrative, and that it generates rich visual and verbal condensations, often working dialectically, following the logic seen throughout the dreamtext.

I have argued that the male dreamtext betrays a recurrent fear of the female eye—the literal visual organ and the alien perspective it represents—as an unwelcome critical vantage point, an agency of potential exposure. In the final monologue, though, ALP is imagined tactfully censoring her visual field, reassuring her spouse that she will not look at him in his fallen state, that she will think instead of how he looked when young: "Maybe that's why you hold your hodd as if. And people thinks you missed the scaffold. Of fell design. I'll close me eyes. So not to see. Or see only a youth in his florizel, a boy in innocence, peeling a twig, a child beside a weenywhite steed" (*FW* 621). This politely veiled female eye, which blocks out unpleasant sights and replaces them with happier ones, provides an apt figure for the final monologue's dominant discourse: the kindly, optimistic, and circumlocutory speech is the verbal equivalent of ALP's censored gaze. As constituted by her language here, ALP is endowed with many of the trappings of a fantasy woman, a male imago of the perfect wife—adoring, soothing, forgiving, and redemptive (although this is only one extreme of a dialectical image). Her mellifluous voice becomes the agent of renewal in itself, bidding HCE to rise and giving him the encouragement to do so. The close of the dream represents, on one level, an invalid's vision of being revived from a coma by a caring mate, of suddenly waking up from a deathlike state—a sort of plausible version of the "Tim Finnegan's Wake" song. It is surely a wishful vision, but also a fearful one, the dreamer imagining not simply revival, but also how he might be treated and spoken to upon his reentry into the world of the waking. Earlier he is described as a man who "stutters fore he falls and goes mad entirely when he's waked" (FW 139)—the phrase adumbrates the psychic perils inherent in this vision of return.

During the first part of the monologue, ALP is represented performing a series of nurturing and redemptive activities for HCE: laying out clean laundry, boosting his ego, taking him on a rejuvenatory outing, speaking to him with fondness and optimism. Many of the anxieties from earlier in the dream are implicitly assuaged here: the dread of nakedness before the other, for instance, dissipates with the prospect of clothes. The clothes return, moreover, cleansed of their earlier spots and stains, those residual signifiers of taboo desires, and they also apparently fit the dreamer's form, eliminating the prior fears of being the unfittable misfit. The anxious visions of a hanging ("Slip on your ropen collar and draw the noosebag on your head" [FW 377]) are deflated to a mere request to don a shirt collar and a stock, a tightly fitting neckcloth. But ALP's monologue generates a double discourse, the surface statement often contrasting with the insinuation, the sanguine circumlocution with the sad implication. Her inventory of HCE's apparel, for example—"Here is your shirt, the day one, come back. The stock, your collar. Also your double brogues" (FW 619)—may evoke a simple domestic image of a wife picking out her husband's clothes, or a sadder vision of her helping an invalid get dressed, perhaps even trying to reteach him the names of common objects. Indeed, the emphasis on identification, naming, and basic recall at many points in the speech may imply an envisioned assumption (on her part) of a derangement in the mental faculties that control such abilities. ALP is even heard identifying herself, recalling with gentle insistence old verbal endearments, with the probable intent of jogging her spouse's memory ("I am leafy speafing. . . . I am leafy, your goolden, so you called me, may me life, yea your goolden" [FW 619]). In his imagined return, HCE sadly hears himself being addressed as a victim of senility, as a person well into his second childhood. ALP's offer to hold her spouse's "great bearspaw" (FW 621) when they go on their imagined walk is a gesture that can be construed as affectionate, romantic even, or utterly humiliating. It may reveal the dreamer's anticipated unsteadiness and his need of guidance, for at points in this closing dream vision he does not seem to know where he is ("You know where I am bringing you? You remember?" [FW 622]). ALP's remarks on the locales that they pass sound, on one level, like idle and friendly conversation, but betray, on another, HCE's possible disorientation. He envisions himself returning to a world suspiciously unfamiliar to him, awakening from what he feels has been a single night's sleep only to find his environs have drastically altered. If earlier a blunt voice tells the dreamer that such disorientating changes should discourage any wishful thoughts of rising ("take your laysure like a god on pension and don't be walking abroad. Sure you'd only lose yourself in Healiopolis now" [FW 24]), ALP, more disingenuously, dismisses them as psychically meaningless, as differences that signify nothing. She is heard passing off radical changes in the environs as perfectly natural and plausible, pretending that cities can literally spring up over night, presumably in order to circumvent the truth of the dreamer's prolonged slumber: "Why, them's the muchrooms, come up during the night. Look, agres of roofs in parshes. Dom on dam, dim in dym. And a capital part for olympics to ply at" (FW 625). When one inquires into the logical motives behind the imagined speech acts that comprise the final monologue, disturbing possibilities frequently emerge, creating a subtext that bespeaks all too clearly the dreamer's dread of his own potential helplessness and subsequent infantilization.

The final segment of the dream contains returns of several of Bloom's thoughts on Sandymount strand, where he looks out at the giant embedded in Howth and discovers a hypothetical eye: "Howth settled for slumber, tired of long days, of yumyum rhododendrons (he was old) and felt gladly the night breeze lift, ruffle his fell of ferns. He lay but opened a red eye unsleeping, deep and slowly breathing, slumberous but awake. And far on Kish bank the anchored lightship twinkled, winked at Mr Bloom" (U 379/310). This imagined eye returns as a gaze in ALP's speech immediately after she mentions HCE's sins, described in circumlocution as mere "stunts," performed "before the naked universe. And the bailby pleasemarm rincing his eye" (FW 624). The twinkling and winking eyes of Howth Head—the Kish lightship and the Bailey lighthouse ("Howth. Bailey light. Two, four, six, eight, nine. See" [U 376/308])—are transformed in dream into a psychological policeman ("bailby pleasemarm") whose vigilant gaze has been offended: his "rincing" of his eye suggests a simultaneous wincing and rinsing, as if to cleanse the organ of a shocking sight. If a brief detail from the final monologue records the return of a winking eye from "Nausicaa," its central donnée involves the return of a winkle of a man. In his fantasy of a return to an unfamiliar world after years of sleep, the dreamer implicitly identifies with another prolonged slumberer whose part Bloom on Sandymount remembers enacting years ago in a game of charades: "Rip van Winkle we played. Rip: tear in Henny Doyle's overcoat. Van: breadvan delivering. Winkle: cockles and periwinkles. Then I did Rip van Winkle coming back. . . . Twenty years asleep in Sleepy Hollow. All changed. Forgotten. The young are old. His gun rusty from the dew" (U 377/309).

Rip van Winkle returning from his slumber, sailors returning from voyages, soldiers returning from war, treasure maps in bottles returning from the sea, a man returning from an evening stroll along the beach, murderers returning to the scene of a crime, youthful days returning from the past, a half-remembered dream returning from the previous night's sleep: Bloom's thoughts on Sandymount obsessively wander among returns of all varieties, driven by a subconscious preoccupation with his own imminent return, his uneasy homecoming to an adulterous wife. But Bloom briefly considers also a happier return—a return that might restore the marital bond—in the form of a nostalgic outing to Howth, the site where the couple first made love: "Tired I feel now. Will I get up? O wait. Drained all the manhood out of me, little wretch. She kissed me. Never again. My youth. Only once it comes. Or hers. Take the train there tomorrow. No. Returning not the same" (*U* 377/308). Bloom's mental meanderings here set in proximity feelings of inertia, thoughts of physical rising, and a consideration of emotional renewal through a sentimental journey—all elements prominent in the first part of ALP's speech. In order to understand the psychological texture of this discourse, perhaps the reader should once again imagine HCE as a somnolent Bloom, aged and feeling his physical debilitation, recalling a much earlier though similar somatic sensation (following a temptation scene, no less, involving a nubile young woman that reminds him of his daughter and his wife when young), a somatic sensation that calls forth from the timeless resources of the unconscious his associative thoughts at that earlier moment in time. The final monologue can be read as the return of the contemplated return, as an envisioning of that possibility that Bloom considers momentarily ("Take the train there tomorrow") but rejects as a futility ("No. Returning not the same"): in the wishful world of dream, the unromantic conclusion of waking life is reversed, replaced with a vision of a trip to Howth Head as the very remedy for rejuvenation, both personal and marital.

"Les go dutc to Danegreven" (*FW* 622), ALP suggests, alluding to Duncriffan, a promontory on Howth, and the Dublin United Tramways Company (the D.U.T.C.) that ran the tram to Howth summit. Bloom's thoughts about Howth in "Nausicaa" ("Where we. The rhododendrons. I am a fool perhaps. He gets the plums, and I the plumstones. Where I come in. All that old hill has seen. Names change: that's all. Lovers: yum yum" [*U* 377/308]) are echoed in ALP's description of the locale's eternally romantic and floral appeal, a description that contains, however, no allusions to adultery and no residual cynicism, as if the earlier meditations return to the dying dreamer in purged form: "You'll know our way from there surely. Flura's way. Where once we led so many car couples have follied since" (*FW* 623). Bloom's recollection of Howth takes him backward in time to Luke Doyle's party, where he courted Molly and pretended he was van Winkle, that rough nineteenth-century incarnation of Odysseus whom on June 16 he subliminally identifies with. The movement of ALP's speech reduplicates the retrospective trajectory of these thoughts, the dream wife pointing out for her mate the site of one of their earliest trysts: "Here, weir, reach, island, bridge. Where you meet I. The day. Remember! Why there that moment and us two only? I was but teen, a tiler's dot" (*FW* 626). If at the end of *Ulysses* Molly privately affirms her bond to her husband through sexual reminiscence, at the end of the *Wake* ALP is imagined doing so openly, using romantic recollection selflessly to revive her fallen mate, reminding him of his gentler moments as a lover as well as his fiercer ones ("One time you'd stand fornenst me, fairly laughing, in your bark and tan billows of branches for to fan me coolly. And I'd lie as quiet as a moss. And one time you'd rush upon me, darkly roaring, like a great black shadow with a sheeny stare to perce me rawly" [*FW* 626]). The ensuing fond remembrance of their marriage vows, however, turns suddenly sad as ALP realizes that the death described then as the remote and hypothetical condition of separation has become a not-so-distant reality ("How you said how you'd give me the keys of me heart. And we'd be married till delth to uspart. And though dev do espart. O mine! . . . And can it be it's nnow fforvell?" [*FW* 626]). The nostalgic return to the past in the *Wake* has a very different associative and affective end point than in *Ulysses*, the return evoking the projected moment of absolute parting.

The scrap of paper in "Nausicaa" that Bloom alternately identifies as a letter, a page of a copybook, and a treasure map in bottle delivered to the shoreline "parcels post" (*U* 381/312) also returns in ALP's monologue, assuming in its overdetermined form all three of these guises:

> We can sit us down on the heathery benn, me on you, in quolm unconsciounce. To scand the arising. . . . At the site of salvocean. And watch would the letter you're wanting be coming may be. And cast ashore. That I prays for be mains of me draims. Scratching it and patching at with a prompt from a primer. And what scrips of nutsnolleges I pecked up me meself. Every letter is a hard but yours sure is the hardest crux ever. Hack an axe, hook an oxe, hath an an, heth hith ences. But once done, dealt and delivered, tattat, you're on the map. Rased on traumscrapt from Maston, Boss. After rounding his world of ancient days. Carried in a caddy or screwed and corked. On his mugisstosst surface. With a bob, bob, bottledby. (*FW* 623–24)

The scrap of paper that ALP claims will put the dreamer "on the map" seems to offer a lasting geographical memorial of the self. Bloom has entertained similar fantasies of being put "on the map" for public commemoration, when a Circean official proclaims that "the thoroughfare hitherto known as Cow Parlour off Cork street [shall] be henceforth designated Boulevard Bloom" (*U* 479/391). But in addition to being a map, a letter, and a copybook exercise, ALP's textual artifact also assumes human contours, taking shape as a fantasy lover written in her imagination, the man of her dreams (the "mains of me drains") whose return from the sea she patiently awaits. This vision of a woman longing for both a letter and a man is the dream correlative of Molly in her Gibraltan girlhood, awaiting the return of her first Odysseus: "Molly darling he called me what was his name Jack Joe Harry Mulvey was it yes . . . *he said hed come back* Lord its just like yesterday to me . . . he went to India *he was to write* the voyages those men have to make to the ends of the world and back . . . I was thinking of him on the sea all the time after" (*U* 761–62/626–27, emphasis added). The Wakean conflation of letter and lover suggests that for ALP arriving males and arriving mail are to some degree substitutional. Waiting for a text that she herself scripted, she is the dream avatar of Molly, who in moments of emotional deprivation and boredom sends missives to the self, freely interchanging textual and sexual companionship ("the days like years not a letter from a living soul except the odd few I posted to myself with bits of paper in them so bored sometimes" [*U* 757/623]).

If the outing to Howth at the end of the dream records the return of the return contemplated in "Nausicaa," then its implicit purpose is marital renewal, a reaffirmation of earlier vows. But the reconciliatory gestures of the dream woman are qualified, the visions of excessive devotion calling to mind their opposite—visions of Mollyesque infidelity—if only in subtle peripheral details. In her final retrospective wanderings, ALP not only alludes to the man of her dreams, a sailor lover reminiscent of the naval lieutenant Mulvey, but also hints at another emotional attachment, a soldier lover reminiscent of the army lieutenant Gardner, whose death from enteric fever during the Boer War Molly recalls on the morning of June 17. If Bloom is the husband reincarnated within HCE, in the final dream speech he envisions the occupation of the suitor that eluded his Ithacan catalogue. The dream woman's general lament for dead warriors sounds like it may be motivated by a more personal loss: "If I lose my breath for a minute or two don't speak, remember! Once it happened, so it may again. Why I'm all these years within years in soffran, allbeleaved. To hide away the tear, the parted. It's thinking of all. The brave that gave their. The fair that wore. All them that's gunne" (*FW* 625). ALP's breathlessness here recalls another well-known recollection of Molly's—"yes 16 years ago my God after that long kiss I near lost my breath yes" (*U* 782/643)—but its precise source remains ambiguous: is it induced by her romantic recollection of Howth itself, by her emotional return to her shared past with her husband? Or by the memory of the other men she elliptically mentions? ALP's loss of breath is also simply a prosaic symptom of aging—and the first harbinger of the extreme physical tolls the envisioned journey will ultimately take on the older wife of the dream.

The journey has a disturbing finality to it, ALP mentioning that "we will take our walk before in the timpul they ring the earthly bells. In the church by the hearseyard" (*FW* 621). An ambiguity about the true purpose of the outing emerges from the way it is described, ALP referring to it as a "journee saintomichael" (*FW* 621)—a journey sentimental or a journey to Saint Michael, whom Adaline Glasheen identifies as the "receiver of the souls of the dead."[3] The thought of being escorted to the spot of a romantic tryst becomes confused with the thought of being escorted to the grave, as in a funeral ritual, erotic "death" perhaps being associated with actual death, the first sexual fall with the final physical fall into mortality. The implied psychological linking of different types of falls here has precedent in "Circe": when the nannygoat present at the Blooms' initial lovemaking on Howth enters the parade of phantasms, a vision immediately ensues of Bloom falling "*from the Lion's Head cliff into the purple waiting waters*" (*U* 550/449). In *Finnegans Wake* the association is synchronic rather than diachronic, the journey emerging as a dual-layered image, like a picture produced from two negatives. The dreamer imagines his wife leading him to the tip of Howth Head or to the outermost bourne, the afterlife, to the house of the Earl of Howth or to the house of God:

> We might call on the Old Lord, what do you say? There's something tells me. He is a fine sport. Like the score and a moighty went before him. And a proper old promnentory. His door always open. For a newera's day. Much as your own is. You invoiced him last Eatster so he ought to give us hockockles and everything. Remember to take off your white hat, ech? When we come in the presence. And say hoothoothoo, ithmuthisthy! His is house of laws. (*FW* 623)

Previously in the dream, HCE has had explicit visions of his wife not only interring him, loaming him from head to foot, but also actually weaving his grim fate, like an implacable goddess of destiny: "Now she's borrid his head under Hatesbury's Hatch and loamed his fate to old Love Lane" (*FW* 578). In the final monologue the image of the woman burying the dead male is more strongly repressed, carefully hidden beneath an antithetical screen vision, an image of her trying to rejuvenate him.

Although the dominant roles of ALP's addressee are husband and father, she also speaks at points to a son. Hinting at the variable and overdetermined relationship between herself and her audience, she calls him "toddy" (*FW* 619, tot/daddy), "padder avilky" (*FW* 621, *pater*: father in Latin/*a mhic*: son in Irish), and finally "sonhusband" (*FW* 627). Old age and infancy again converging, HCE at the dream's close is at once a child and an adult invalid being treated *like* a child. ALP's allusions to the habits and pleasures of early youth—drooling, nursery rhymes, the chil-

reconciliation: a critical female voice interrupts the dominant strand of the discourse with incremental recurrence. One of the first hints of dissatisfaction is heard in ALP's letter, which reports that "first he was a skulksman at one time and then Cloon's fired him through guff" (*FW* 616): this sounds like one of Molly's complaints about her husband's inability to hold down a job, with its allusion to Joe Cuffe who fired Bloom for giving lip.[6] In the speech that follows, ALP reduces the earlier visions of HCE's knighthood to wishful thinking, conceding the vanity of her high hopes for her husband's future: "He might knight you an Armor elsor daub you the first cheap magyerstrape. . . . And I'll be your aural eyeness. But we vain. Plain fancies. It's in the castles air" (*FW* 623). Her alternative fantasy of HCE as "the first cheap magyerstrape" interweaves allusions to Bloom's frugality and Hungarian origins, and to Stephen's envious admiration of paternal magistrates in *Portrait*. ALP's disappointment here is expressed in mild and even self-reproachful terms, but shortly afterward she closes her remembrance of HCE's architectural ambitions to "scale the summit" with the more straightforward accusation, "All your graundplotting and the little it brought!" (*FW* 624)—a rough echo of Molly's skepticism about Bloom's ability to carry through on his various schemes ("he ought to get a leather medal with a putty rim for all the plans he invents" [*U* 765/630]). At the end of her speech, the dream wife acknowledges even more frankly the discrepancy between her wishful estimation of her husband and the reality of his achievements ("I thought you were all glittering with the noblest of carriage. You're only a bumpkin. I thought you the great in all things, in guilt and in glory. You're but a puny" [*FW* 627]). The female voice grows more and more overtly dissatisfied, ALP ending her speech with both a verbal and physical rejection of her spouse. As the fantasy of the adoring and forgiving helpmate gives way to the more mundane and disturbing vision of the malcontent housewife, the image of the male self that this female other creates and defines crumbles simultaneously.

This subversive discourse can be traced to the monologue's very outset, in what sounds on the surface like unequivocal flattery: "You make me think of a wonderdecker I once. Or somebalt thet sailder, the man megallant, with the bangled ears. Or an earl was he, at Lucan? Or, no, it's the Iren duke's I mean" (*FW* 620). ALP's comparison of HCE to various heroes and adventurers, both mythic and real, appears to be a blatantly gratifying and egotistical fantasy, a patent example of the language of desire, until one remembers that elsewhere in the dream HCE *is* Van der Decken, he *is* Sinbad, he *is* Magellan, he *is* Wellington, the Iron Duke. ALP's "compliment" reduces metaphor to mere simile. The ultimately deflationary intent of the comparison is hinted at in the word "wonderdecker," which combines Van der Decken, the wandering captain of *The*

Flying Dutchman, with *wonderdoktor*, the Dutch word for a quack. This ironic conflation and the emphasis on mere similitude both make it clear that the dreamer's prior heroic guises are simply quixotic masks. His majestic roles are likewise reduced to theatrical trumpery: when ALP recalls "the beardwig I found in your Clarksome bag" and adds, "Pharaops you'll play you're the King of Aeships" (*FW* 625), the earlier grandiose imago of the father as "first pharoah, Humpheres Cheops Exarchas" (*FW* 62) becomes, quite literally, mere costuming.

•   •   •

Prior to the close of the final monologue, the dreamer's preeminent concerns have been his own guilty desires and fears as well as his own human mortality. The unsettling image of the wife's departure or demise may seem to indicate a sudden male sensitivity to the frustrations felt by the female, a lapse in that egocentricity which, Freud argues, constitutes the essence of the dreamworld.[7] But as Joyce shows through the figure of Simon Dedalus in *Ulysses*, the thought of a spouse's death can occasion a sadness that is in part selfish, rooted not only in sorrow for the absent mate but also maudlin self-pity. Simon laments not only his wife's death but also the more personal repercussions of it, the imagined effect it has had on his own familial position: "You're like the rest of them, are you?" Mr. Dedalus grumbles to Dilly with only partial irony, "An insolent pack of little bitches since your poor mother died. . . . Wouldn't care if I was stretched out stiff. He's dead. The man upstairs is dead" (*U* 238/195). The fallen patriarch of the *Wake* betrays very similar fears about how he will be treated by his female offspring, but protects himself from the fate of Simon Dedalus through sanguine fantasy: he hears the departing ALP reassuring him that the daughter will be "sweet for you as I was sweet when I came down out of me mother" (*FW* 627). The anxiety occasioned by the wife's possible flight is negated by wishful thoughts of union with her younger incarnation—a clear example of psychological compensation betraying the dreamer's concern with how marital disaffection and defection would personally affect him.

In *Structure and Motif in "Finnegans Wake,"* Hart has demonstrated that ALP's monologue contains numerous verbal echoes of phrases from "Eveline," its ending in particular.[8] Indeed, the close of the *Wake* and the disturbing story from *Dubliners* share not only specific resonances but also a larger situational similarity. Just as the *Wake* suggests that ALP's flight is motivated by maternal fatigue, by "a hundred cares, a tithe of troubles," "Eveline" similarly hints that Mrs. Hill's death is precipitated by the day-to-day demands placed on her as mother and wife: she has led "that life of commonplace sacrifices closing in final craziness" (*D* 40), a final craziness that ALP shares, conceding that she has grown "loonely in ated self-image is anticipated when ALP is envisioned remembering her father ambivalently ("I'm sure he squirted juice in his eyes to make them flash for flightening me. Still and all he was awful fond to me" [*FW* 626]), like Eveline recalling both her father's violence and his kindness. The double resonance of the phrase "Far calls. Coming, far!" (*FW* 628) re-introjects into the dreamtext the uncertainty of ALP's imagined response to the patriarch, the ambiguity of her nature—either fond, submissive, and childlike, or fearful, mistrusting, and defiant: she may be responding dutifully to the voice of the father (*far*: father in Danish) or rebelliously to the voice of the "far," the distant unknown Eveline is tempted by but ultimately rejects. In his mapping of the verbal correspondences between the end of "Eveline" and that of the *Wake*, Hart juxtaposes one of Frank's last words to Eveline—"Come!" (*D* 41)—with this "Coming, far!" spoken by ALP.[9] The two cries make sense, though, not as verbal analogies or parallelisms but as an entreaty and a response, as a plea and an answer. What is heard here on the final page of the dream, in short, are the words Eveline is unable to speak. In this ambiguous rerendering of the close of the earlier short story, the daughter is imagined acquiescing obediently to the demands of the father *or* responding fervently to the cry of the lover, depending upon what one chooses to hear in that final equivocal "far."

The two visions of the daughter that emerge through the rapidly shifting images and the various verbal ambiguities are incompatible within the framework of a realistic narrative—the daughter cannot return to the father and abandon him simultaneously—but they do make sense as a dialectical narrative of dream. In fact I would argue that the logic of the *Wake*'s seemingly contradictory ending can be best understood if one imagines the father within the dreamer here as Mr. Hill and then speculates about what he might have dreamed about after reading Eveline's letter on the night she attempts to leave her family. The possibility of the daughter's departure, made clear by the letter, would logically produce an intensified unconscious desire for her loyalty, that desire expressed in such clear and overdetermined form at the close of the dream. Mr. Hill's probable conscious response to the attempted escape is anger and violence, a response apparently recalled in the image of the "cold mad feary father" authoritatively brandishing his trident or blackthorn stick: the missing pieces of the earlier story in the dreamtext may provide us with a disquieting hint of what Eveline hypothetically encountered upon her return to the home. But the very threat of the daughter's departure would probably awaken in the father not only feelings of outrage, but also ones of vulnerability and weakness, a sense of uncertain control over the daughter he needs: hence the opposite and fearful dream vision of her opting for the lover over the father, defiantly breaking the familial bond.

me loneness" (*FW* 627)—not only lonely but also loony. In both works the departing mother expects that the dutiful daughter will take her place. Young Eveline must raise "the two young children who had been left to her charge" (*D* 38), having given her ailing mother "her promise to keep the home together as long as she could" (*D* 40). ALP also expresses a hope that her family will stay together—"Try not to part! Be happy, dear ones!"—and leaves in her wake "a daughterwife from the hills again" (*FW* 627—note the allusion to Eveline's last name). The father's desire for the daughter, blatant in the dreamworld, finds a more devious and sinister outlet in the waking reality of *Dubliners*. Eveline lives in fear of her father's violence, afraid that he might "go for her," even though she is nineteen, well beyond the age when children are reprimanded through physical punishments: "she knew that it was that that had given her the palpitations" (*D* 38). The aggressive father of the *Wake* has a similar effect on the daughter, or so he imagines, Issy glossing "the backslapping gladhander" in her footnotes with the remark, "He gives me pulpititions" (*FW* 276).

The palpitations of the young woman signify fear and loathing but also their opposite—unacknowledged desire. A repressed Electra complex lies at the heart of Eveline's story, a complex unwittingly encouraged by the defeated mother, reinforced by the bullying father, and unconsciously acceded to by the passive and paralyzed daughter, who implicitly opts for the stultifying bond to Mr. Hill over a union with someone her own age, a new life with Frank, however ambiguous and uncertain that new life may be. In *Finnegans Wake*, of course, this incestuous drama is played out not within a waking narrative of the daughter's thoughts, but rather in a dream narrative of the father's: the end of the dream in particular records an implicit return to "Eveline" but a return chronicled from a previously unexplored vantage point, that of Mr. Hill. In accordance with the perspectival shift from conscious to unconscious psychic life, Joyce foregrounds the taboo desire only hinted at in "Eveline," bringing it to the surface. Shifting from the daughter's to the father's point of view, Joyce also represents a very different dialectic of anxiety and desire, significantly revising the outcome of the earlier short story. Although the dreaming father in HCE hopes that the daughter will dutifully replace his spouse, he suspects and fears simultaneously that she will not stay with him, that like the mother, she will abandon him. He imagines the fleeing ALP offering her pity, gently hinting that he will have to compete with a younger generation of men for the daughter's loyalties and affections: "I pity your oldself I was used to. Now a younger's there" (*FW* 627). Running counter to the father's incestuous desire for the daughter throughout the dream is the grim epiphany of normal generational cycles, children ineluctably replacing parents rather than bonding with them.

The mother's disillusioned leavetaking at the end of the dream is fore-shadowed much earlier, in the daughter's devious commentary on the grammar book in the homework lesson. Appended to the instruction that counsels Issy to "mind your genderous towards his reflexives such that I was to your grappa . . . when him was me hedon" is an exclamatory footnote that reads, "Frech devil in red hairing! So that's why you ran away to sea, Mrs Lappy. Leap me, Locklaun, for you have sensed!" (FW 268). The apparent incongruity between the text counseling female deference to the male and the marginal comment recording female dis-loyalty and abandonment can be resolved by stressing the latter's inter-pretive status. The daughter is imagined here reading between the lines of "gramma's grammar" (FW 268) and finding in the conventional wis-dom of the distaff text—in its ostensible endorsement of stereotypical sex roles—an epiphanic explanation for ALP's flight. The subversive nota-tion assumes that the older woman has in fact grown tired of acting "gen-derous" toward male "reflexives," weary of playing the wife who caters selflessly to her husband's whims. Although her ensuing departure may be a sin, it may also reflect her good sense ("Mrs Lappy. . . . you have sensed!"). Issy is envisioned as understanding a silent discourse of the female text, detecting the dissatisfaction inherent in its advice, hearing in it not a complacent admission of male superiority but rather a veiled com-plaint against male egotism.

This footnote is interesting to consider in the context of "Eveline," for Eveline too reads and understands an alternative discourse of the mother. Mrs. Hill's implied request to the daughter to assume her role and respon-sibilities is subverted by her final mad and incoherent exclamations, the specific plea qualified by the larger behavioral statement. The daughter perceives a sad logic behind the mother's retreat into lunacy and death, just as Issy intuits the logic behind ALP's analogous departure in the Wake: Eveline's thought of her mother's "life of commonplace sacrifices closing in final craziness" puts selfless maternal duty and ultimate insan-ity into a disturbing cause-and-effect progression, an alarming sequence of inevitability. She decides to break the promise to the mother because she interprets her crazed demise as a counterstatement to the request, as an admonition of what that elicited promise may lead to. Her "sudden impulse of terror" (D 40) can be best accounted for if one assumes that Eveline recognizes unconsciously in her mother's death a premonition of her own possible fate, the memory ultimately fortifying not her sense of duty but her resolve to leave. The daughter vows an active physical escape from her oppressed position—a contrast to the mother's passive psycho-logical escape into madness—though she is pathetically unable to carry through her resolve, apparently forgetting the warning embedded in the earlier recollection. That closing scene of "Eveline" in which the young

woman stands suspended between flight and duty returns at the very end of the Wake, albeit in a much altered and complicated guise.

The final vision of the dream is a highly ambiguous one, one that ex-presses both a desire and a fear through a rapid alternation of images. ALP's union with her "cold mad feary father" (FW 628) reduplicates the previously envisioned union of HCE and his "daughterwife" Issy, provid-ing an overdetermined expression of the desire for father-daughter incest and of the implicit attendant wish for recaptured youth, for eternal re-newal through a bonding with the female child who is reminiscent of the wife when young. In this protean vision of human roles so typical of the dream, Issy is not only wishfully imagined as spouse, but ALP is also seen as daughter, and it is in this capacity that her final gestures—both physi-cal and verbal—become most equivocal. One moment ALP is the obedi-ent daughter dutifully returning to the father, but in the next she is the rebellious daughter, turning away from the father toward the younger lover, the lover whom she sees as a means of escape from patriarchal oppression: "it's sad and weary I go back to you, my cold father, my cold mad father, my cold mad feary father, till the near sight of the mere size of him, the moyles and moyles of it, moananoaning, makes me seasilt saltsick and I rush, my only, into your arms. I see them rising! Save me from those therrble prongs!" (FW 627–28, emphasis added). The intensi-fying vision of the father's wrath ("my cold father, my cold mad father, my cold mad feary father") and the interesting pronominal shift that fol-lows can be logically connected. At first ALP addresses the father himself (as a "you"), but then after envisioning his increasingly threatening mien, she suddenly refers to him more distantly, in the third person ("the mere size of him"), so that she is now imagined talking about the father to someone else. This second addressee is the lover to whom she ultimately turns for a saving embrace ("I rush, my only, into your arms. . . . Save me from those therrble prongs"), like Eveline fantasizing about Frank before she leaves home ("Frank would take her in his arms, fold her in his arms. He would save her" [D 40]). At the end of the earlier short story, the lover is associated with the sea, envisioned as the element that will drown the self ("All the seas of the world tumbled about her heart. He was drawing her into them: he would drown her" [D 41]); at the end of the Wake the father himself plays this annihilating role, cast as he is as "Old Father Ocean" (U 50/42), as both the Irish and Greek sea gods, Mananaan ("moananoaning") and Poseidon, the latter's threatening trident provid-ing a rough imagistic variant of Mr. Hill's threatening blackthorn stick.

The frightening image of the violent father reverses itself in the subse-quent image of the protective father gently carrying the daughter along as he did when she was a child ("Carry me along, taddy, like you done through the toy fair!" [FW 628]). The dialectical structure of this medi-

Indeed, in that final vision of the daughter turning away from him—both verbally and physically—at the sight of his "therrble prongs," the father recognizes his violence not as the means of controlling the daughter, but as the very thing that frightens her away: she is not simply lured away by another but also driven away by his aggression.[10] If earlier in the *Wake* the daughter is envisioned as understanding a silent and subversive discourse of the mother, here she is imagined (on one level of the dialectic) as acting upon that wisdom of the malcontent, seeing the sense and not the sin in running away to sea, realizing the danger inherent in staying with the father and the attraction of that mysterious "far."

At the end of the monologue ALP embraces the sexual, imagining her own erotic surrender: "If I seen him bearing down on me now under whitespread wings like he'd come from Arkangels, I sink I'd die down over his feet, humbly dumbly, only to washup" (*FW* 628). The image stands in opposition to one of Eveline's closing visions at the station, her "glimpse of the black mass of the boat" (*D* 40), inverting color (black/white), religious association (Black Mass/Annunciation, demonic/angelic), and implicit emotional affect (fright/acceptance), while maintaining the linking impression of massiveness. The "black mass of the boat" may embody a vague sexual threat and contribute to Eveline's distress and hesitation (in the *Wake* boats often become explicitly phallic—"with his runagate bowmpriss he roade and borst her bar" [*FW* 197]); at the end of the dream, however, the daughter is represented overcoming all sexual fears, envisioning not only her sexual surrender but also her survival, seeing erotic "death" leading inevitably to self-renewal, resurrection ("I sink I'd die down over his feet, humbly dumbly, only to washup"). The man ALP gives herself to remains characteristically ambiguous, the resonances of the Annunciation suggesting the father-lover, but the allusion to "Arkangels" suggesting the younger lover as well: as B. J. Tysdahl points out, the conclusion to the *Wake* enfolds a reference to Ibsen's *Lady from the Sea*, the lover from Archangel being the Stranger in the play, the young sailor-lover who, as in "Eveline," serves as the father-lover's rival.[11]

In "Eveline" the death of the mother/wife and the possible flight of the daughter are separate narrative events; in the dreamworld they are conflated, intermingled, recognized as analogous departures with similar causalities—weariness over female roles within the patriarchal family. ALP's overdetermined status as dying mother/wife and fleeing daughter leaves the ultimate vision of female journeying and bequeathal of keys ambiguously suspended. Although there is a logical critical tendency to interpret ALP's keys symbolically, their more literal and mundane significance should not be forgotten—they may simply be house keys, like those in anyone's pocket or purse. On one level these keys left behind at the final decision to depart ("Lps. The keys to. Given!" [*FW* 628]) are perhaps passed from ALP-as-mother to Issy-as-daughter, in a wishful vision of dutiful female succession; but in her capacity as daughter, ALP may be returning those keys of the house back to the master himself—they are the keys that may have logically accompanied Eveline's farewell letter, keys perhaps associated with domestic responsibility.

What happens after the female return in "Eveline" can be imagined and is indeed explored from a new perspective in the final dream vision of the *Wake*; what happens after the female wandering projected within this dream vision on the other level of the dialectic cannot, in contrast, be so easily conjectured. In an ending that resonates unmistakably of Ibsen's *Doll House*, the departing female relinquishes the keys of her safe but oppressive domestic position to embrace an unknown that defies conception, resists articulation, arrests the flow of the dream language in midstream. When Joyce returns to "Eveline" in the last pages of the *Wake* and revises it from its inherent male point of view, he adumbrates its abyss, that region beyond envisioning: that region is surely death itself, but also the female other who eludes the dreamer both physically and psychically, perhaps coursing fatalistically toward "that other world," perhaps ecstatically toward freedom.

•   •   •

When I read the end of the *Wake*, I cannot help but think of two contrasting anecdotes from Ellmann's biography of Joyce. Writing about the demands that the artist made on Nora during the early years of their relationship, Ellmann reports that one was total and unqualified acceptance of him, another total honesty and openness on her part. "Joyce made a final trial of her: she must recognize all his impulses, even the strangest, and match his candor by confiding in him every thought she found in herself, especially the most embarrassing. She must allow him to know her inmost life, to learn with odd exactitude what it is to be a woman. This test, the last, Nora passed successfully later in 1909."[12] Writing about the artist's life in 1929, twenty years after this final "test," Ellmann recounts that Joyce once proudly showed his friends a letter from Jung in which the psychoanalyst praised the artist's penetrating representation of the female psyche in "Penelope." In response Nora reputedly remarked of her husband, "'He knows nothing at all about women.'"[13] Like their creator, Joycean males are often curious about what women think and feel—although they often want to know simply what women think and feel about them. The end of the *Wake*, I think, records the difficulty inherent in this venture of wanting "to learn with odd exactitude what it is to be a women," in its insistence on the other's ultimate otherness, her final inaccessibility. If *Ulysses* closes with Molly's memory of her union with

Bloom, with a relived and reaffirmed moment of tacit understanding, the *Wake* closes with a vision of the limits to such mutual comprehension.

Although Joyce implicitly encourages us to connect the end of the *Wake* to the beginning (*Letters* 1:246), his sudden relinquishment of ALP's voice—and the female elusiveness the relinquishment implies—cannot be elided or ignored. Some feminist critics might object to this closing representation of the elusive feminine, by arguing that it merely perpetuates a sexist stereotype: woman as the unknown, the mysterious, as that which defies comprehension. For Joyce, however, female elusiveness is equated with autonomy and independence, with a resistance to those attempted appropriations he repeatedly documents. But as his own earlier pride in having captured the female psyche in "Penelope" strongly suggests, Joyce was not above such proprietorial gestures himself. In order to avoid in his ultimate figuration of the female the very paradigm he criticizes, Joyce may have found it necessary to let ALP escape, to acknowledge the limits of his own understanding of the sexual other. The closing vision of the Wakean female coursing out to sea, embracing an unknown that transports her beyond the delimiting structures of language, escaping the male dreamer's imagination *and* the male artist's pen—such a vision may be Joyce's belated concession to the potential truth of Nora's claim.

NOTES

PREFACE

1. Freud, "The 'Uncanny,'" 370.
2. Gallop, *Reading Lacan*, 114.

CHAPTER 1
INTRODUCTION

1. Quoted in MacCabe, *James Joyce and the Revolution of the Word*, 117.
2. Brivic, *Joyce between Freud and Jung*, 201.
3. In "Lestrygonians," though, Bloom posits a connection between physical diet and the texture of ideational life, speculating that the food an individual eats may determine what sort of literature he would want to create or read (*U* 166/136). See Tucker's comments on this passage in *Stephen and Bloom at Life's Feast*, 62.
4. For further discussion of Joyce's use of textual detritus in his fictions, see Norris's comments in *The Decentered Universe of "Finnegans Wake,"* 130–31 and 137–40, and Levine's article on "Originality and Repetition in *Finnegans Wake* and *Ulysses*."
5. Brivic well summarizes the Freud-Joyce connection and its central problem: Joyce often treated Freud's work disparagingly or ironically both in his art and in many supposed comments recorded by Richard Ellmann. Yet Joyce was inclined to psychoanalytic insight himself before he could have read Freud's work and was clearly later influenced by the psychoanalyst's discoveries (see *Joyce between Freud and Jung*, 9–10). Bishop attributes Joyce's ambivalence toward Freudian thought to his distrust of authoritative theories and generalities and his concomitant preference for "living, concrete immersion in the material under his scrutiny" (*Joyce's Book of the Dark*, 17). For further evidence of and comment on Joyce's knowledge of Freud, see Hoffman's "Infroyce" (particularly 403), Armstrong's "Shem the Penman as Glugg as the Wolf-Man," and Ferrer's "The Freudful Couchmare of ∧d."
6. Freud, *The Interpretation of Dreams*, 574.
7. Lacan, *The Four Fundamental Concepts of Psycho-Analysis*, 24.
8. Kenner, *Flaubert, Joyce and Beckett*, 36.
9. Brivic, *Joyce between Freud and Jung*, 138.
10. Brivic offers an alternative reading of this encounter: he argues that the "Prevention of Cruelty to Animals" is the watchmen's accusation against Bloom, that his humanitarian attitude is his "crime" (see "Social significances of Bloom's psychology in 'Circe,'" 22). Given Bloom's defensive response to the watchmen's words ("A noble work! I scolded that tramdriver . . . for illusing the poor horse"

[*U* 454/371]), I think Bloom is clearly afraid that he is being charged with cruelty, that his treatment of the dog is being misconstrued as abuse.

11. Freud, *The Interpretation of Dreams*, 505.

12. Quoted in Tindall, *A Reader's Guide to "Finnegans Wake,"* 11.

13. Cope, *Joyce's Cities*, 109; see also Bishop, *Joyce's Book of the Dark*, 134–35.

14. See McHugh, *The "Finnegans Wake" Experience*, 9–13.

15. Freud, *The Interpretation of Dreams*, 171.

16. Norris, *The Decentered Universe of "Finnegans Wake,"* 104.

17. Tindall, *A Reader's Guide to "Finnegans Wake,"* 157.

18. Norris, *The Decentered Universe of "Finnegans Wake,"* 17.

19. Bishop, *Joyce's Book of the Dark*, 217 and 225.

20. See Freud, *The Interpretation of Dreams*, 668. The picture of the "French Nurse's Dream" is reproduced as a general example of dream representation in Rose and O'Hanlon's *Understanding Finnegans Wake* (xix), although they fail to mention its particular relevance to the *Wake* itself.

21. Begnal, *Dreamscheme*, 16.

22. Ibid., 51.

23. Bishop, *Joyce's Book of the Dark*, 27.

24. Begnal, *Dreamscheme*, 28. Begnal likens the technique of *Finnegans Wake* to that of "Circe," as do I, but our comparisons are fundamentally different. He implies that the *Wake* has a "basic plot" that is analogous to the "literal narrative," the realistic thread, that emerges from Bloom's experiences in Nighttown (*Dreamscheme*, 51–53); I find structuring principles in the *Wake* that are similar to those which govern the logic of the *hallucinations* in "Circe" (not the episode's overall narrative organization). The "basic plot" of the *Wake* that Begnal delineates is, I think, an arbitrary and artificial critical construct. Phillip Herring's description of Wakean narrative implicitly supports my position: "Plot is unstable in that there is no one plot from beginning to end, but rather many recognizable stories and plot types with familiar and unfamiliar twists, told from varying perspectives" (*Joyce's Uncertainty Principle*, 190).

25. Bishop, *Joyce's Book of the Dark*, 41.

26. Begnal, *Dreamscheme*, 109 and 111.

27. Bishop, *Joyce's Book of the Dark*, 10.

28. Hart, *Structure and Motif in "Finnegans Wake,"* 153.

29. Raleigh, *The Chronicle of Leopold and Molly Bloom*, 245.

30. Begnal, *Dreamscheme*, 47–49.

31. Bowen, *Musical Allusions in the Works of James Joyce*, 59 and 62.

32. Parts of earlier books and articles were extremely important in initially suggesting to me the potentially elaborate and specific connections between the *Wake* and Joyce's prior works. These include Hart's early charting in 1962 of numerous returns of "Eveline" in ALP's final monologue (see *Structure and Motif in "Finnegans Wake,"* 53–55); B. Benstock's discussion of "L. Boom as Dreamer in *Finnegans Wake*" in 1967; Norris's section on "bricolage" in *The Decentered Universe of "Finnegans Wake,"* published in 1974 (see 131–37 in particular); Kopper's "'but where he is eaten'" and his "Limning the Palimpsest," appearing

respectively in 1974 and 1978–79; and Levine's 1979 article, "Originality and Repetition in *Finnegans Wake* and *Ulysses*."

33. McHugh, *Annotations to "Finnegans Wake,"* 338.

34. Norris, "'Mixing Memory and Desire,'" 133.

35. See Bédier, *The Romance of Tristan and Iseult*, 97.

CHAPTER 2

TEXTUAL DESIRE

1. Freud, "Obsessive Acts and Religious Practices," 24.

2. Naremore, "Consciousness and Society in *A Portrait of the Artist*," 125.

3. Hannay, "Confessions of Love in Joyce's *Portrait*," 77.

4. Freud, *Totem and Taboo*, 30.

5. Barthes, *A Lover's Discourse*, 56 and 68.

6. Kenner, *Ulysses*, 143.

7. S. Benstock, "The Letter of the Law," 169.

8. B. Benstock, "Concerning Lost Historeve," 34.

9. B. Benstock, "Every Telling Has a Taling," 18.

10. Although he does not mention Joyce, René Girard discusses literary examples of mimetic desire—desire mediated by fictional models or actual rivals—at length in *Deceit, Desire, and the Novel*.

11. Gifford, *Joyce Annotated*, 208.

12. Naremore, "Consciousness and Society in *A Portrait of the Artist*," 121.

13. For a more elaborate discussion of the ironic contrast Joyce sets up between Gerty MacDowell and Gertrude Flint, the conventional romance heroine, see Devlin, "The Romance Heroine Exposed."

14. Cummins, *The Lamplighter*, 491–92.

15. In *The Lamplighter*, for example, Philip is Emily's stepbrother; as *The Count of Monte Cristo* closes, Edmond Dantès plans to marry Haydée, his ward, the exotic slave girl whom he has unofficially adopted as his daughter.

16. Barthes, *The Pleasure of the Text*, 9–10.

17. Noakes, "The Double Misreading of Paolo and Francesca," 226.

18. Milton, *Paradise Lost*, 185.

19. Power recently located the nineteenth-century reform novel upon which *Ruby: the Pride of the Ring* may have been based ("The Discovery of *Ruby*"); but Gryta has since demonstrated that Joyce's *Ruby* is probably a composite of sources ("Who is Signor Maffei? and Has *Ruby: The Pride of the Ring* Really Been Located?").

20. S. Benstock, "At the Margin of Discourse," 211.

21. McHugh, *Annotations to "Finnegans Wake,"* 293.

22. Reynolds, *Joyce and Dante*, 212.

23. Freud, "On Sexual Theories of Children," 31–33.

24. Ibid., 37.

25. Freud, "Analysis of a Phobia in a Five-Year-Old Boy," 120.

26. Freud, "The 'Uncanny,'" 398–99.

27. Norris, *The Decentered Universe of "Finnegans Wake,"* 46–47.

28. Bédier, *The Romance of Tristan and Iseult*, 35.

29. Begnal, "Love That Dares to Speak Its Name," 141.

30. Reynolds, *Joyce and Dante*, 108.

31. Cheng, "'The bawk of bats' in Joyce's Belfry," passim.

32. Herr, *Joyce's Anatomy of Culture*, 154.

33. Gifford with Seidman provide the lyrics to "Waiting": "Come for my arms are empty! / Come for the day was long! / Turn the darkness into glory, / The sorrow into song. / I hear his footfall's music, / I feel his presence near. / All my soul responsive answers / And tells me he is here" (*Notes for Joyce*, 248).

Chapter 3
"My Multiple Mes"

1. R. Ellmann, *James Joyce*, 544.

2. Glasheen writes that "Joyce told Dr Dan O'Brien that FW was 'about' Finn, lying dying beside the Liffey . . . while history cycles through his mind. Well, maybe. What is sure: Finn is impossible to tell from Finnegan and Phoenix" (*A Third Census of "Finnegans Wake,"* 92). She suggests, in other words, that the unnamed friend is Dr. O'Brien, but her source of information (like Ellmann's) remains undocumented. She sounds as if she may share my skepticism about this statement attributed to Joyce in her hesitating response to it ("Well, maybe").

3. Brivic, "Joyce in Progress," 307.

4. Bishop, *Joyce's Book of the Dark*, 147 and 153.

5. Gifford with Seidman, *Notes for Joyce*, 54.

6. Kenner, "Circe," 354.

7. Senn, "Book of Many Turns," 35.

8. M. Ellmann, "Polytropic Man," 80.

9. Ibid., 79.

10. Ibid., 85.

11. Norris, *The Decentered Universe of "Finnegans Wake,"* 9. For further comments on indeterminate identity in the *Wake*, see Norris on Joyce's use of the Oedipus myth in the same volume, 58–61, and Bishop, *Joyce's Book of the Dark*, 130–33 and 140–42.

12. Freud, *The Interpretation of Dreams*, 630.

13. McCarthy, "The Structures and Meanings of *Finnegans Wake*," 616.

14. Lacan, *The Four Fundamental Concepts of Psycho-Analysis*, 25.

15. Barker, *The Flying Dutchman: A Guide to the Opera*, 41.

16. Norris, "Anna Livia Plurabelle," 205.

17. Kenner, *Ulysses*, 10.

18. Freud, "Family Romances," 45.

19. Gordon, *Finnegans Wake: A Plot Summary*, 67.

20. Freud, "Family Romances," 44.

21. Norris, "Narration under a Blindfold," 213.

22. This fantasy vision of the good legitimate son as *"a fairy boy of eleven, a changeling, kidnapped"* (U 609/497) suggests that Joyce uses the term "change-ling" in its broadest sense, not simply to designate the fraudulent substitute, but rather either child in the swap.

23. See Norris, "The Last Chapter of 'Finnegans Wake,'" 17.

24. O'Dwyer, "Ireland's 'long vicefreegal existence,'" 178.

25. Campbell and Robinson, *A Skeleton Key to "Finnegans Wake,"* 266n.73.

26. Norris, *The Decentered Universe of "Finnegans Wake,"* 83.

27. Herring, *Joyce's Uncertainty Principle*, 11. Herring has convincingly argued that "incertitude may be the dominant theme of the *Wake*" (182), but that Joyce's use of "the uncertainty principle" in his final dreambook is clearly anticipated in the many mysteries and obscurities in the earlier fictions, beginning—most obviously— with the first story of *Dubliners*. Joyce's uncertainty principle can be conceptualized, in a sense, as the structural return of "The Sisters" in the Wakean dream, where it is taken to its utmost limit.

28. Norris, *The Decentered Universe of "Finnegans Wake,"* 82.

29. Freud, *The Interpretation of Dreams*, 564.

CHAPTER 4
"THAT OTHER WORLD"

1. Shakespeare, *Measure for Measure*, 565.

2. Bishop, *Joyce's Book of the Dark*, 371–72.

3. Compare Freud's comment in "The 'Uncanny'": "To many people the idea of being buried alive while appearing to be dead is the most uncanny thing of all. And yet psycho-analysis has taught us that this terrifying phantasy is only a transformation of another phantasy which had originally nothing terrifying about it at all, but was filled with certain lustful pleasure—the phantasy, I mean, of intra-uterine existence" (397).

4. Rose and O'Hanlon, *Understanding Finnegans Wake*, 57.

5. Bishop, *Joyce's Book of the Dark*, 125.

6. Freud, *Totem and Taboo*, 140.

7. Ibid., 150.

8. McCarthy, *The Riddles of "Finnegans Wake,"* 23.

9. Brivic, *Joyce between Freud and Jung*, 210.

10. Norris, *The Decentered Universe of "Finnegans Wake,"* 93.

11. Freud, "The 'Uncanny,'" 395.

12. Norris, "Kafka's Josefine," 381.

13. Freud, "The 'Uncanny,'" 387.

14. Herring, *Joyce's Uncertainty Principle*, 13.

CHAPTER 5
"SEE OURSELVES AS OTHERS SEE US"

1. J. Maddox, *Joyce's "Ulysses" and the Assault on Character*, 24.

2. From "To a Louse; on Seeing One on a Lady's Bonnet at Church"; quoted in Gifford with Seidman, *Notes for Joyce*, 142.

3. Lacan, *The Four Fundamental Concepts of Psycho-Analysis*, 96–97.

4. Ferrer, "The Freudful Couchmare of ∧d," passim.

5. Lacan, *The Four Fundamental Concepts of Psycho-Analysis*, 75.

6. Freud, *The Interpretation of Dreams*, 572–73.

7. For further comments on theatrical frameworks in Joyce, see Herr's discussion of "Circe" (*Joyce's Anatomy of Culture*, 145–49) and Cheng's discussion of *Finnegans Wake* (*Shakespeare and Joyce*, 32–53).

8. It is fruitful to examine the Wolf Man's dream in the context of Freud's remarks made in his later essay "The 'Uncanny.'" In discussing the psychological significance of "doubles," he describes the process in ego-development whereby the gaze of the other evolves in the subject's mind, the process whereby the watching wolves are created: "A special faculty is formed there, able to oppose the rest of the ego, with a function of observing and criticizing the self and exercising a censorship within the mind, and this we become aware of as our 'conscience.' . . . The fact that a faculty of this kind exists, which is able to treat the rest of the ego like an object—the fact, that is, that man is capable of self-observation—renders it possible to invest the old idea of a 'double' with a new meaning" (388). Conscience, in Freud's terms, is not only the father's law or word internalized but also the father's eye internalized.

9. Lacan, *The Four Fundamental Concepts of Psycho-Analysis*, 84 and 77.

10. Parallactic vision has been accessibly defined as "an instance of sending the observant mind in two, or more, different positions [*sic*] and having it compare notes" (Senn, *Joyce's Dislocutions*, 79).

11. Freud, "From the History of an Infantile Neurosis," 220.

12. Glasheen, *A Third Census of "Finnegans Wake*," liv.

13. Norris, *The Decentered Universe of "Finnegans Wake*," 37–39.

14. Glasheen, *A Third Census of "Finnegans Wake*," 289.

15. Bédier, *The Romance of Tristan and Iseult*, 48–51.

16. Ibid., 100–101.

17. McHugh, *Annotations to "Finnegans Wake*," 389.

18. Joyce's use of an overhead perspective to signify voyeurism may be another borrowing from the case history of the Wolf Man. Freud writes, "a high tree is a symbol of observing, of scoptophilia. A person sitting on a tree can see everything that is going on below him and cannot himself be seen. Compare Boccaccio's well-known story, and similar *facetiae*" ("From the History of an Infantile Neurosis," 229n.).

19. Norris, *The Decentered Universe of "Finnegans Wake*," 61.

20. Begnal and Eckley, *Narrator and Character in "Finnegans Wake*," 20. In his more recent study, *Dreamscheme*, Begnal remains "fairly convinced" that there is not a single dreamer in the *Wake* (xv).

21. Norris, "Anna Livia Plurabelle," 199.

22. Zimmerman, "Leopold Paula Bloom," 176–77.

23. Herr, *Joyce's Anatomy of Culture*, 171.

24. Norris, "Modernism, Myth, and Desire in Joyce's 'Nausicaa,'" 48–49.

Chapter 6
The Return of the Repressed

1. For a broader discussion of Joyce's attitude toward women, as reflected in his letters, his personal and professional relationships, and his fictions, see Scott's excellent study, *Joyce and Feminism*.

2. Munich, "'Dear Dead Women,' or Why Gabriel Conroy Reviews Robert Browning," 132.

3. Ovid, *Metamorphoses*, 243.

4. Ibid., 243.

5. Gilbert and Gubar, *The Madwoman in the Attic*, 12.

6. Unkeless, "The Conventional Molly Bloom," 153.

7. Brivic, "Joyce in Progress," 325.

8. Mulvey, "Visual Pleasure and Narrative Cinema," 418.

9. Ibid., 419–20.

10. Henke, "Gerty MacDowell: Joyce's Sentimental Heroine," 133 and 136.

11. Senn, "Nausicaa," 301–2.

12. Ibid., 210.

13. J. Maddox, *Joyce's "Ulysses" and the Assault on Character*, 81.

14. Berger, *Ways of Seeing*, 51.

15. S. Benstock, "The Genuine Christine," 172.

16. Mulvey, "Visual Pleasure and Narrative Cinema," 416.

17. Ibid., 420.

18. Ovid, *Metamorphoses*, 62.

19. Boyle, "Penelope," 314.

20. Gilbert and Gubar, *The Madwoman in the Attic*, 12–13.

21. Norris, "Narration under a Blindfold," passim.

22. Ibid., 212.

23. S. Benstock, "The Genuine Christine," 185.

24. S. Benstock, "The Letter of the Law," 176.

25. R. Ellmann, *James Joyce*, 168.

CHAPTER 7
"RETURNING NOT THE SAME"

1. S. Benstock, "The Genuine Christine," 177 and 190–91.

2. Hart, *Structure and Motif in "Finnegans Wake,"* 55.

3. Glasheen, *A Third Census of "Finnegans Wake,"* 193.

4. Norris, "The Last Chapter of 'Finnegans Wake,'" passim.

5. B. Maddox writes, "Once May Joyce considered leaving her husband; she told her priest, who was furious and sent her back" (*Nora*, 33). For an account of Nora's threatened departures, see R. Ellmann, *James Joyce*, 687–88.

6. McHugh, *Annotations to "Finnegans Wake,"* 616.

7. Freud, *The Interpretation of Dreams*, 301.

8. Hart, *Structure and Motif in "Finnegans Wake,"* 53–55.

9. Ibid., 54.

10. Compare Nora's flight from Galway after she is beaten by her uncle "with a big walkingstick" because she has been walking out with a young man (*Letters* 2:72–73; quoted in Scott, *Joyce and Feminism*, 66–67).

11. Tysdahl, *Joyce and Ibsen*, 178 and 210.

12. R. Ellmann, *James Joyce*, 294.

13. Ibid., 629.

BIBLIOGRAPHY

Armstrong, Alison. "Shem the Penman as Glugg as the Wolf-Man." *A Wake Newslitter* 10 (1973): 51–59.

Barker, Frank Granville. *The Flying Dutchman: A Guide to the Opera*. London: Barrie and Jenkins, 1979.

Barthes, Roland. *A Lover's Discourse: Fragments*. Translated by Richard Howard. New York: Hill and Wang, 1978.

————. *The Pleasure of the Text*. Translated by Richard Miller. New York: Hill and Wang, 1975.

Bédier, Joseph. *The Romance of Tristan and Iseult*. Translated by Hilaire Belloc and Paul Rosenfeld. New York: Vintage, 1945.

Begnal, Michael H. *Dreamscheme: Narrative and Voice in "Finnegans Wake."* Syracuse: Syracuse University Press, 1989.

————. "Love That Dares to Speak Its Name." In *A Conceptual Guide to "Finnegans Wake,"* edited by Michael H. Begnal and Fritz Senn, 139–48. University Park: Pennsylvania State University Press, 1974.

Begnal, Michael H., and Grace Eckley. *Narrator and Character in "Finnegans Wake."* Lewisburg: Bucknell University Press, 1975.

Benstock, Bernard. "Concerning Lost Historeve." *A Conceptual Guide to "Finnegans Wake,"* edited by Michael H. Begnal and Fritz Senn, 33–55. University Park: Pennsylvania State University Press, 1974.

————. "Every Telling Has a Taling: A Reading of the Narrative of *Finnegans Wake*." *Modern Fiction Studies* 14 (1969): 3–26.

————. "L. Boom as Dreamer in *Finnegans Wake*." *PMLA* 82 (1967): 91–97.

Benstock, Shari. "At the Margin of Discourse: Footnotes in the Fictional Text." *PMLA* 98 (1983): 204–25.

————. "The Genuine Christine: Psychodynamics of Issy." In *Women in Joyce*, edited by Suzette Henke and Elaine Unkeless, 169–96. Urbana: University of Illinois Press, 1982.

————. "The Letter of the Law: *La Carte Postale* in *Finnegans Wake*." *Philological Quarterly* 63 (1984): 163–85.

Berger, John. *Ways of Seeing*. London: BBC and Penguin, 1972.

Bishop, John. *Joyce's Book of the Dark: "Finnegans Wake."* Madison: University of Wisconsin Press, 1986.

Bowen, Zack. *Musical Allusions in the Works of James Joyce*. Albany: State University of New York Press, 1974.

Boyle, Fr. Robert, S.J. "Penelope." In *James Joyce's "Ulysses": Critical Essays*, edited by Clive Hart and David Hayman, 407–33. Berkeley: University of California Press, 1974.

Brivic, Sheldon. *Joyce between Freud and Jung*. Port Washington: Kennikat, 1980.

————. "Joyce in Progress: A Freudian View." *James Joyce Quarterly* 13 (1976): 306–27.

————. "Social significances of Bloom's psychology in 'Circe.'" In *Joyce & Paris: Papers from the Fifth International James Joyce Symposium*, edited by J. Aubert and M. Jolas, 20–22. Paris: Publications de l'Université de Lille, 1979.

Campbell, Joseph, and Henry Morton Robinson. *A Skeleton Key to "Finnegans Wake."* New York: Penguin, 1980.

Cheng, Vincent. "'The bawk of bats' in Joyce's Belfry: The Flitter-mouse in the Feminine." In *Joycean Occasions: Selected Essays from the 1987 James Joyce Milwaukee Conference*, edited by Michael Gillespie, Mel Friedman, and Janet Dunleavy. Newark: University of Delaware Press, forthcoming.

————. *Shakespeare and Joyce: A Study of "Finnegans Wake."* University Park: Pennsylvania State University Press, 1984.

Cope, Jackson I. *Joyce's Cities: Archaeologies of the Soul.* Baltimore: Johns Hopkins University Press, 1981.

Cummins, Maria. *The Lamplighter.* Boston: John P. Jewett, 1854.

Devlin, Kimberly. "The Romance Heroine Exposed: 'Nausicaa' and *The Lamplighter.*" *James Joyce Quarterly* 22 (1985): 383–96.

Ellmann, Maud. "Polytropic Man: Paternity, Identity and Naming in *The Odyssey* and *A Portrait of the Artist as a Young Man.*" In *James Joyce: New Perspectives*, edited by Colin MacCabe, 73–104. Bloomington: Indiana University Press, 1982.

Ellmann, Richard. *James Joyce.* Oxford: Oxford University Press, 1982.

Ferrer, Daniel. "The Freudful Couchmare of ∧d: Joyce's Notes on Freud and the Composition of Chapter XVI." *James Joyce Quarterly* 22 (1985): 367–82.

Freud, Sigmund. "Analysis of a Phobia in a Five-Year-Old Boy." In *The Sexual Enlightenment of Children*, edited by Philip Rieff, 47–183. New York: Collier, 1963.

————. "Family Romances." In *The Sexual Enlightenment of Children*, edited by Phillip Rieff, 41–45. New York: Collier, 1963.

————. "Fragment of an Analysis of a Case of Hysteria." In *Dora: An Analysis of a Case of Hysteria*, edited by Philip Rieff, 21–144. New York: Collier, 1963.

————. "From the History of an Infantile Neurosis." In *Three Case Histories*, edited by Philip Rieff, 187–316. New York: Collier, 1963.

————. *The Interpretation of Dreams.* Translated by James Strachey. New York: Avon, 1965.

————. "Obsessive Acts and Religious Practices." In *Character and Culture*, edited by Philip Rieff, 17–26. New York: Collier, 1963.

————. "On Sexual Theories of Children." In *The Sexual Enlightenment of Children*, edited by Philip Rieff, 25–40. New York: Collier, 1963.

————. *Totem and Taboo.* Translated by James Strachey. New York: Norton, 1950.

————. "The 'Uncanny.'" In *Collected Papers*, translated by Joan Riviere. 5 vols. New York: Basic Books, 1959. 4:368–407.

Gallop, Jane. *Reading Lacan.* Ithaca: Cornell University Press, 1985.

Gifford, Don. *Joyce Annotated: Notes for "Dubliners" and "A Portrait of the Artist as a Young Man."* Berkeley: University of California Press, 1982.

Gifford, Don, with Robert J. Seidman. *Notes for Joyce: An Annotation of James Joyce's "Ulysses."* New York: Dutton, 1974.

Gilbert, Sandra M., and Susan Gubar. *The Madwoman in the Attic: The Woman Writer and the Nineteenth Century Literary Imagination.* New Haven: Yale University Press, 1979.

Girard, René. *Deceit, Desire, and the Novel: Self and Other in Literary Structure.* Translated by Yvonne Freccero. Baltimore: Johns Hopkins University Press, 1965.

Glasheen, Adaline. *A Third Census of "Finnegans Wake."* Berkeley: University of California Press, 1977.

Gordon, John. *Finnegans Wake: A Plot Summary.* Dublin: Gill and Macmillan, 1986.

Gryta, Caroline Nobile. "Who Is Signor Maffei? and Has *Ruby: The Pride of the Ring* Really Been Located?" *James Joyce Quarterly* 21 (1984): 321–28.

Hannay, John. "Confessions of Love in Joyce's *Portrait.*" *University of Dayton Review* 17 (1985–86): 77–81.

Hart, Clive. *Structure and Motif in "Finnegans Wake."* London: Faber & Faber, 1962.

Henke, Suzette. "Gerty MacDowell: Joyce's Sentimental Heroine." In *Women in Joyce,* edited by Suzette Henke and Elaine Unkeless, 132–49. Urbana: University of Illinois Press, 1982.

Herr, Cheryl. *Joyce's Anatomy of Culture.* Urbana: University of Illinois Press, 1986.

Herring, Phillip F. *Joyce's Uncertainty Principle.* Princeton: Princeton University Press, 1987.

Hoffmann, Frederick J. "Infroyce." In *James Joyce: Two Decades of Criticism,* edited by Seon Givens, 390–435. New York: Vanguard, 1948.

Kenner, Hugh. "Circe." In *James Joyce's "Ulysses": Critical Essays,* edited by Clive Hart and David Hayman, 341–62. Berkeley: University of California Press, 1974.

―――. *Flaubert, Joyce and Beckett: The Stoic Comedians.* Boston: Beacon, 1962.

―――. *Ulysses.* London: George Allen & Unwin, 1980.

Kopper, Edward A. "'but where he is eaten': Earwicker's Tavern Feast / Book II, chapter iii." In *A Conceptual Guide to "Finnegans Wake,"* edited by Michael H. Begnal and Fritz Senn, 116–38. University Park: Pennsylvania State University Press, 1974.

―――. "Limning the Palimpsest: Joyce's Other Works at the *Wake.*" *Modern Language Studies* 9 (Winter 1978–79): 42–46.

Lacan, Jacques. *The Four Fundamental Concepts of Psycho-Analysis.* Edited by Jacques-Alain Miller. Translated by Alan Sheridan. New York: Norton, 1978.

Levine, Jennifer Schiffer. "Originality and Repetition in *Finnegans Wake* and *Ulysses.*" *PMLA* 94 (1979): 106–20.

MacCabe, Colin. *James Joyce and the Revolution of the Word.* London: Macmillan, 1979.

Maddox, Brenda. *Nora: The Real Life of Molly Bloom.* Boston: Houghton Mifflin, 1988.

Maddox, James H., Jr. *Joyce's "Ulysses" and the Assault on Character.* New Brunswick: Rutgers University Press, 1978.

McCarthy, Patrick. *The Riddles of "Finnegans Wake."* Cranbury, N.J.: Associated University Presses, 1980.

———. "The Structures and Meanings of *Finnegans Wake.*" In *A Companion to Joyce Studies*, edited by Zack Bowen and James F. Carens, 559-632. Westport, Conn.: Greenwood, 1984.

McHugh, Roland. *Annotations to "Finnegans Wake."* Baltimore: Johns Hopkins University Press, 1980.

———. *The "Finnegans Wake" Experience.* Berkeley: University of California Press, 1981.

Milton, John. *Paradise Lost.* Edited by Merritt Y. Hughes. Indianapolis: Odyssey, 1962.

Mulvey, Laura. "Visual Pleasure and Narrative Cinema." In *Women and the Cinema*, edited by Karyn Kay and Gerald Peary, 412–28. New York: Dutton, 1977.

Munich, Adrienne Auslander. "'Dear Dead Women,' or Why Gabriel Conroy Reviews Robert Browning." In *New Alliances in Joyce Studies*, edited by Bonnie Kime Scott, 126–34. Newark: University of Delaware Press, 1988.

Naremore, James. "Consciousness and Society in *A Portrait of the Artist.*" In *Approaches to Joyce's "Portrait,"* edited by Thomas F. Staley and Bernard Benstock, 113–34. Pittsburgh: University of Pittsburgh Press, 1976.

Noakes, Susan. "The Double Misreading of Paolo and Francesca." *Philological Quarterly* 63 (1983): 221–39.

Norris, Margot. "Anna Livia Plurabelle: The Dream Woman." In *Women in Joyce*, edited by Suzette Henke and Elaine Unkeless, 197–213. Urbana: University of Illinois Press, 1982.

———. *The Decentered Universe of "Finnegans Wake."* Baltimore: Johns Hopkins University Press, 1974.

———. "Kafka's Josefine: The Animal as the Negative Site of Narration." *Modern Language Notes* 98 (1983): 366–83.

———. "The Last Chapter of 'Finnegans Wake': Stephen Finds His Mother." *James Joyce Quarterly* 25 (1987): 11–30.

———. "'Mixing Memory and Desire': The 'Tristan and Iseult' Chapter in *Finnegans Wake.*" In *James Joyce: The Centennial Symposium*, edited by Morris Beja et al., 132–36. Urbana: University of Illinois Press, 1986.

———. "Modernism, Myth, and Desire in Joyce's 'Nausicaa.'" *James Joyce Quarterly* 26 (1988): 37–50.

———. "Narration under a Blindfold: Reading Joyce's 'Clay.'" *PMLA* 102 (1987): 206–15.

O'Dwyer, Riana. "Ireland's 'long vicefreegal existence': A Context for *Finnegans Wake* 34–36." In *The Seventh of Joyce*, edited by Bernard Benstock, 178–81. Bloomington: Indiana University Press, 1982.

Ovid. *Metamorphoses.* Translated by Rolfe Humphries. Bloomington: Indiana University Press, 1955.

Power, Mary. "The Discovery of *Ruby.*" *James Joyce Quarterly* 18 (1981): 115–21.

Raleigh, John Henry. *The Chronicle of Leopold and Molly Bloom: "Ulysses" as Narrative.* Berkeley: University of California Press, 1977.

Reynolds, Mary T. *Joyce and Dante: The Shaping Imagination.* Princeton: Princeton University Press, 1981.

Rose, Danis, and John O'Hanlon. *Understanding Finnegans Wake: A Guide to the Narrative of Joyce's Masterpiece.* New York: Garland, 1982.

Scott, Bonnie Kime. *Joyce and Feminism.* Bloomington: Indiana University Press, 1984.

Senn, Fritz. "Book of Many Turns." In *"Ulysses": Fifty Years,* edited by Thomas F. Staley, 29–46. Bloomington: Indiana University Press, 1974.

———. "Nausicaa." In *James Joyce's "Ulysses": Critical Essays,* edited by Clive Hart and David Hayman, 277–311. Berkeley: University of California Press, 1974.

———. *Joyce's Dislocutions.* Edited by John Paul Riquelme. Baltimore: Johns Hopkins University Press, 1984.

Shakespeare, William. *Measure for Measure.* In *The Riverside Shakespeare,* edited by G. Blackmore Evans, 550–86. Boston: Houghton Mifflin, 1974.

Tindall, William York. *A Reader's Guide to "Finnegans Wake."* New York: Farrar, Straus and Giroux, 1969.

Tucker, Lindsey. *Stephen and Bloom at Life's Feast: Alimentary Symbolism and the Creative Process in James Joyce's "Ulysses."* Columbus: Ohio State University Press, 1984.

Tysdahl, B. J. *Joyce and Ibsen: A Study in Literary Influence.* New York: Humanities Press, 1968.

Unkeless, Elaine. "The Conventional Molly Bloom." In *Women in Joyce,* edited by Suzette Henke and Elaine Unkeless, 150–68. Urbana: University of Illinois Press, 1982.

Zimmerman, Michael. "Leopold Paula Bloom: The New Womanly Man." *Literature and Psychology* 29 (1979): 176–84.

INDEX